EVERYWOMAN: Studies in History,
Literature, and Culture

Susan Gubar and Joan Hoff-Wilson
General Editors

On her honeymoon in Venice, Italy, July 7, 1905. —*Franklin D. Roosevelt Library*

WITHOUT PRECEDENT

The Life and Career of
ELEANOR ROOSEVELT

EDITED BY

Joan Hoff-Wilson and
Marjorie Lightman

Indiana University Press

BLOOMINGTON

Library of Congress Cataloging in Publication Data
Main entry under title:

Without precedent.

(Everywoman: studies in history, literature, and
culture)
Includes index.
1. Roosevelt, Eleanor, 1884–1962—Addresses, essays,
lectures.   2. Presidents—United States—Wives—Biography
—Addresses, essays, lectures.   I. Hoff-Wilson, Joan.
II. Lightman, Marjorie.   III. Series: Everywoman.
E807.1.R48W48   1984   973.917'092'4 [B]   83-49062
ISBN 0-253-19100-9
ISBN 0-253-20327-9 (pbk.)
1 2 3 4 5 88 87 86 85 84

Contents

PART 3 POLITICAL FRIENDSHIPS

PART 4 PARADOXES

FOREWORD *by Joseph P. Lash*

Much has been written about the Age of Roosevelt. Most of it centers on Franklin D. Roosevelt. One of the virtues of this Eleanor Roosevelt centenary book is that it undertakes to fill gaps in our knowledge of her role in this historic period. The difficulties of the task are not to be underestimated. Eleanor Roosevelt was a person of enormous vitality. Her presence during the Roosevelt years was everywhere. But her real influence was spiritual, not one of laws, appointments, the management of great government bureaus. She was like a warming gulf stream during those years, but the evidence of how she worked, especially during the White House period, is often difficult to elucidate. She went to great lengths to deny and conceal her influence because she knew that in a man's world, which government and politics were at the time, the charge of "petticoat rule" could be fatal to the cause or person she was promoting. Moreover, FDR, a great leader, was not the most accommodating of men when it came to acknowledging his wife's role in his life.

The scholars represented in this volume have performed a major task of archival excavation and reconstruction and the result is a vivid portrayal of a rare American personality—a deeply political woman who eschewed the normal rewards of politics such as office, pomp, and power in the interests of spreading the Golden Rule.

Beyond Eleanor Roosevelt's presence in the events of the times is her influence on America. An English social critic has written, "in her personal struggle for self-awareness she was the greatest of the Roosevelts." The luminous personality that resulted from that struggle is hard to recapture in words—the way a room came alive when she entered; the way others needed large offices and ceremony to inform the world of their importance while she exalted the meanest of occasions and the dingiest of rooms simply by her presence. Right after Pearl Harbor she flew out to a West Coast that expected Japanese bombers at any moment. "If we have trouble anywhere," she wrote, "I must go because it does seem to calm people down."

One might say of her as she once said of her great-grandmother Ludlow, "she was character." This volume and the celebration of the centennial of Eleanor Roosevelt's birth serve to remind us that her approach to problems such as racism, poverty, and war can still help us, but beyond that she has moved into the pantheon of great Americans whose appeal is timeless.

PREFACE

This collection of essays about the unprecedented public career of Eleanor Roosevelt is the product of an equally unprecedented collaboration between two historical organizations located in different parts of the country: The Organization of American Historians, whose national headquarters is at Indiana University in Bloomington, and The Institute for Research in History, located in New York. Funded in part by the Rockefeller Foundation, the book represents one facet of a project designed by the two organizations to celebrate throughout 1984 the centennial of the birth of Eleanor Roosevelt.

The book is a first in another sense as well. With its publication, Indiana University Press launches a new series that will explore women's role in human culture through a number of historical, literary, and social science studies. The purpose of this series, under the editorial supervision of Susan Gubar and Joan Hoff-Wilson is to demonstate the importance of women's contributions over time and to dispel remaining misconceptions and stereotypes. To fulfill these goals, the editors will seek out and publish original monographs, as well as theoretical studies—books accessible to the academic, the student, and the general reader. Since the series is aimed at breaking new ground, in addition to synthesizing existing material, manuscripts will be accepted about the Third World in addition to western cultures. Indiana University Press initiates its new series, EVERYWOMAN: STUDIES IN HISTORY, LITERATURE, AND CULTURE, with these essays about Eleanor Roosevelt's extraordinary life and career.

The OAH and the Institute want to thank the following individuals who helped produce this book in record time. Working out of New York preparing the manuscript for production were: Dr. Esther Katz, assistant director of the Institute for Research in History and Dr. William Zeisel, director of Editors & Scholars, a division of the Institute. In Bloomington Donna Littrell, OAH administrative assistant, coordinated the establishment and work of the National Advisory Board for the Eleanor Roosevelt Centennial Project and kept all the authors apprised of each others' projects and progress.

Finally our thanks go to the authors themselves who produced their essays under considerable pressure and to the following members of the advisory board for their ideas and early support of this segment of the 1984 Eleanor Roosevelt Centennial Project cosponsored by the Organization of American Historians and

The Institute for Research in History: Susan Becker, William H. Chafe, Blanche Wiesen Cook, Tamara K. Hareven, Susan Hartmann, David M. Kennedy, Richard S. Kirkendall, Joseph P. Lash, William E. Leuchtenburg, Richard Lowitt, Abigail Q. McCarthy, Pauli Murray, James Paterson, Elisabeth Israels Perry, Lois Scharf, Arthur M. Schlesinger, jr., Ingrid Winther Scobie, Barbara Sicherman, Martha H. Swain, Winifred D. Wandersee, Susan Ware, Nancy J. Weiss, and Robert L. Zangrando.

INTRODUCTION

Eleanor Roosevelt (1884–1962) is justly placed among the great women of American history. She affected the course of events during her life and left a legacy of values that continues to influence public policy. An examination of her contribution to her own times, and the values she espoused that resonate in our times, forms the basis for this collection of essays on the centennial of her birth. The essays pay respect to a public career without precedent. They also seek to understand the conditions of restraint and advantage that were at one and the same time particular to the personal circumstances of her life and general to the position of women in American society.

This book is divided into four parts. The first section on the political education of Eleanor Roosevelt includes three essays: a biographical sketch by William H. Chafe that provides the reader with a frame of reference for the major events in ER's private and public life; a review of ER's career in Democratic politics from the 1920s until her death, by Susan Ware; and a case study about Eleanor Roosevelt and the Women's City Club of New York in the 1920s, by Elisabeth Israels Perry. Her longstanding involvement with the issues of civil rights and peace, and with young people form the second group of essays. Joanna Schneider Zangrando and Robert L. Zangrando explore the changing attitudes of the times toward blacks and ER's role in that process. Winifred D. Wandersee concentrates on the youth movements of the 1930s, and Blanche Wiesen Cook traces ER's position on peace over the course of two world wars and the early years of the Cold War. The third group of essays examines three of Roosevelt's political friendships and her influence on Democratic party

politics. Martha H. Swain details the partnership between Ellen Woodward and ER in addressing the needs of women during the Great Depression; Ingrid Winther Scobie traces her impact on the political career of
Helen Gahagan Douglas; and Richard S. Kirkendall relates the role of ER
in Democratic politics and the vice-presidential nomination of Henry
Wallace. In the last section of essays, Abigail Q. McCarthy suggests the
paradox inherent in the "office" of the first lady, while Tamara K. Hareven and Lois Scharf theorize about Eleanor Roosevelt's place in the
American reform and feminist traditions.

In the late nineteenth and early twentieth centuries, many middle- and
upper-class women began to apply and expand their private, domestic
experiences to national and international affairs. These women initially
worked as Progressives in the social justice wings of both the Republican
and Democratic parties, and later, many of them became active in the
reforms of the New Deal. Whether married or single, they saw the world
around them as a seamless web of housekeeping. "Women are house
keepers," Jeannette Rankin once said. "Government is house keeping for
the nation." Between 1930 and 1960, Eleanor Roosevelt's national and
international reputation far surpassed that of all other American women
activists. As this book indicates, her life and her work remain a source of
inspiration as well as controversy.

All too often her life has been portrayed as a melodrama. Born into one
of the politically and socially elite American families, Roosevelt had a
loveless childhood and, once married, shared her husband with a
domineering mother-in-law, another woman, and finally with a country
rent by depression and war. According to the standard litany, perseverance, if not love, triumphed, and ER gradually emerged as an independent personality. The transformation is said to have begun after her
husband's bout with polio in 1921 and to have been completed after his
death in 1945. Little wonder that sober, historical examination of her
political contributions has paled beside these soap opera elements of her
life.

This collection of essays, published in the centennial year of her birth,
reflects the latest scholarship about the public career of Eleanor Roosevelt.
As such, they reveal the contradictions in her long and eventful life, that
in part derive from a series of interlocking paradoxes. Most notable was
the enduring tension between her traditional view of women as devoted
wives and mothers and her own painful, but nonetheless successful break

with domesticity. Furthermore, she inherited from turn-of-the-century women reformers the belief that political change was achieved through nonpartisan efforts of education. Her behavior, however, became that of a skillful professional politician within the inner circles of the Democratic party. The position of first lady constituted yet another contradiction— neither elected nor empowered by official sanction, but nonetheless encumbered with public responsibilities. Finally, like most women professionals and political activists in the first half of the twentieth century, Eleanor Roosevelt had to face unequal constraints in her private and public life. Such women had a good deal of freedom in their private lives, but in their public lives they adopted traditional female propriety in order to be effective when operating in male political circles. Thus, ER's public actions gained a heightened respectability when pursued in the name of her disabled husband.

In examining these various paradoxes, the authors disagree over whether to call Eleanor Roosevelt a radical feminist or a liberal reformer. While Susan Ware portrays her as a "liberal feminist," Lois Scharf distinguishes between feminists and reform-minded women and then places ER firmly in the camp of reformers, not feminists. The authors also disagree over why Roosevelt was so slow to support such major female reform issues as suffrage, peace, child-labor laws, and the Equal Rights Amendment. Perry explains the delay as part of the natural progression of ER's political education in the 1920s; others like Ware, Cook, and Hareven attribute it to the influence of particular individuals, while Scharf claims her "gradualism" on such issues reflects her lack of sympathy with radical feminism. Many of the authors—Joanna and Robert Zangrando, Cook, Kirkendall, Ware, Swain, and Wandersee—also differ on the degree to which ER influenced FDR and the Democratic party, as well as on the reasons why she turned her attention to international reform following World War II.

The essays in this book are organized to guide the reader through Eleanor Roosevelt's long public career. They trace the acquisition of political skills, which moved her from the periphery of power in the years she worked with nonpartisan women's groups, to the heart of Democratic party politics. Compromise was the price of this transition. Perry and Ware discuss her adaptation of single-issue educational politics, to the more general political programs of the Democratic party. The Zangrandos describe the nature of ER's pragmatic compromises with respect to rights for blacks. Cook, Scharf, and Hareven document her increasingly global view after 1945 that led her outside the realm of domestic reform almost entirely to become ombudswoman for the world.

Several recurring themes emerge in the essays. Again and again they stress ER's conviction that political freedom was best assured by democratic institutions of government and that the responsibility of society was to allow for the fullest expression of individual human dignity through an equality of opportunity in the political and educational processes. ER's was both a moral and practical conviction: it was only just and right that discrimination against blacks end. The Zangrandos detail how her moral position assumed practical application as she used her political skill and her access to power in order to move toward a less discriminatory society. The tension between what was possible in the complex weave of Democratic party politics and what was the moral end sought forms the basis of their analysis of ER and civil rights from the 1930s through the 1950s. They point out that the circumstances during and after World War II increased Roosevelt's cautiousness about civil rights. As early as 1943 she feared that blacks were beginning to "do too much demanding" to the detriment of the American image abroad. Thus, in 1947 she refused to bring an NAACP indictment of American race relations before the United Nations, and in 1956 ER was instrumental in preventing the Democratic party from adopting a strong civil-rights plank. Rights won by individuals, not demanded by groups, guided her attitude toward reform throughout her life.

Eleanor Roosevelt's commitment to the sanctity of individual rights is further underscored by Wandersee's study of the American Youth Congress and the American Student Union during the late 1930s and early 1940s. Wandersee explores the pressure placed on ER to disassociate from such student groups in light of alleged Communist infiltration. Roosevelt's conviction that it was essential for young people to be involved in politics, even if their position were disagreeable, led her to give their demands special attention even though she exposed herself to accusations of Communist sympathy. When she finally ended her support for the youth movement on the eve of U.S. entrance into the Second World War, she never doubted that the students would come to see the democratic process as the only effective means to achieve their ideals.

Roosevelt's belief in the democratic process gave purpose to her garnering of political skills. The biographical essay written by Chafe, and Ware's study of ER and Democratic politics in the postsuffrage era, form a complementary examination of her accrual of political know-how in the service of reform. Perry maintains a similar theme in her detailed vignette of Roosevelt during her years of work in the Women's City Club of New York before she became a national figure and after her marriage and childbearing years. ER led the committees at the City Club that articulated nonpartisan positions on issues such as municipal and state reform, low-cost housing, and the dissemination of birth control information. Ware views this work in the tradition of women's political activities that were issue-oriented and extended the concerns of hearth and kin to the public sphere.

As both Perry and Ware note, however, the City Club's nonpartisan position also kept it outside the horse-trading of New York politics. The women at the City Club were respected by virtue of their individual positions in society and the integrity they brought to public education on particular social issues and the general workings of government. During these same years, Roosevelt also became active in the New York Democratic party. As Ware and Chafe note, she revealed her talent for grassroots organizing when she built the women's division of the state party. If from her club work she learned the value of education for reform politics, then it was from the county-by-county canvassing among Democratic women in New York that she learned to build a political organization.

Ware opens her essay with the image of Eleanor Roosevelt waiting outside closed doors, behind which party men were shaping the 1924 Democratic platform. Vainly she sought an audience to present the carefully researched position papers which came of her work at the Women's City Club. Wandersee describes a different scene that occurred sixteen years later. After the signing of the Nazi-Soviet Pact of 1939, the American Student Union and the American Youth Congress abruptly stopped supporting the New Deal's mildly interventionist foreign policy position based on collective security considerations. In 1940, after leaders of the American Student Union booed and hissed her husband's remarks at an official White House reception, ER spoke to the students. This time she did not present carefully studied, nonpartisan arguments. Point for point, she defended the administration's policies. Now she spoke from a powerful position, within the same party whose locked committee doors had excluded her a decade and a half earlier.

In the years between these two incidents, Roosevelt had traveled a path set much earlier. Her friends had long included the leading women activists of her era. Her friendships with women were, according to Chafe, a reasonable evolution from her educational experience at Allenswood in London where the headmistress, Marie Souvestre, was herself a strong-minded woman, radical both in her personal life and her politics. In the New York Women's City Club, Perry points out, ER found a "who's who" of New York women of achievement and social activism. It was with these women, who had cut their political teeth in the suffrage fight, or who had fought for social justice as Progressives, that ER initially learned her politics.

The experience of the 1924 Democratic Platform Committee, however, illuminated for Eleanor Roosevelt the difference in the power of men within the party and the power of her circle of women friends who either studied issues or who sought political change outside the established parties. She became convinced that only from a traditional political base could women effect change. Perhaps, as Ware suggests, Eleanor Roosevelt never wavered in making her choice to bring women reformers into the ranks of the Democratic party, rather than to pursue social justice through political action more reminiscent of the single-issue approach of the suffragists. Regardless of how consciously she made this choice, it marked her, Scharf argues, as a reformer and placed her on a collision course with members of the National Woman's Party (NWP) who continued to practice a very gender specific brand of politics throughout the 1920s and 1930s.

When she moved into the White House in 1933, Roosevelt brought with her a small group of women—part of New York's social and educational elite. In Washington she found more women of such status and achievement. Swain details the relationship between ER and Ellen Woodward, a Mississippi woman who had compiled a remarkable record in state administration. She came to Washington in 1933 to head the Women's Division of the Federal Emergency Relief Administration (FERA), and pursued the usually forgotten interests of women in the federal work programs. In addition to a circle of like-minded women, the first lady brought the tradition of attention to individuals inherited from the suffragists and used by Roosevelt herself to organize the Women's Division of the New York State Democratic Committee. ER's travels were legendary, as were her responses to the personal pleas addressed to her in countless letters. Swain recounts how personal letters from women unable to find satisfaction from the local authorities were moved by ER through the bureaucracy, often with surprising rapidity. The Zangrandos and Hareven essays demonstrate that she bestowed the same attention on the problems of individual blacks; Cook notes ER's concern for refugees; Wandersee for young people. She was accessible to all those who wanted their voice to be heard.

Even historian Mary Ritter Beard, who suspected there was too much *noblesse oblige* in the Roosevelts' style, perceived how quickly ER's caring attitude transformed the image of the White House among the depression-stricken public. On November 5, 1933, in the New York *Herald Tribune*, Beard wrote:

> To an amazing degree the White House has become a popular tribunal. Behind its portico the First Lady of the Land hears indulgently every case that comes before her. Whereas the undistinguished masses in preceding generations could only turn to a Dorothea Dix or a Beatrice Fairfax and a daily paper for sympathetic guidance, this suffering generation may bring its more complex problems to the very center of the nation. The First Lady's mountainous correspondence receives her personal attention and she replies with an air of intimacy to each and every writer, her comments reflecting her own large experience in household and public affairs.

This mode of personal attention, sensed by many and experienced by a surprisingly large number, became Eleanor Roosevelt's hallmark. It was, however, a reactive approach to domestic reform. She used the political process to ameliorate blatant inequalities around those issues where she personally witnesed suffering and discrimination. She also reacted personally to foreign policy situations. Cook's account of ER's visit with concentration camp victims immediately after World War II provides a case in point. Only when a woman fell before her crying "Israel" did Roosevelt come to understand the meaning of an independent state of Israel to millions of Jews, who, like this one woman, had suffered at the hands of the Nazis. From that moment, she steadfastly supported the establishment of the state of Israel.

Cook's essay, however, is not limited to a discussion of ER's post-World War II policies. It traces her evolution from an unqualified supporter of the Allies during the First World War to a qualified supporter of the internationalist wing of the peace movement in the 1920s and 1930s. As a "realistic pacifist" she supported both military preparedness and conscription between the wars. Cook also describes her antifascist stance, from the defense of the Lincoln Brigade during the Spanish Civil War through the

Second World War. Roosevelt's foreign policy career climaxed with her position on the UN Human Rights Commission in the early years of the Cold War. At no time did ER pursue peace at any price; peace without political freedom ensured by institutions of democratic government was meaningless. In the twentieth century, the pursuit of such peace all too often meant that she supported war.

Eleanor Roosevelt's views on peace were not those of the National Woman's Party led by the militant feminist Alice Paul. As the author of the first equal rights amendment submitted to Congress in 1923, Paul and her followers insisted that this issue be on the agenda at all international conferences. Until the late 1930s they successfully argued for equal rights at Pan-American Conferences. According to Scharf, ER believed that working women had special needs recognized in existing legislation protecting them in the work place. Thus, Roosevelt opposed the activities of the National Woman's Party at home and abroad between the wars, out of the conviction that endorsement of a blanket equal rights amendment would endanger working women around the world. However, in 1948 she finally accepted a compromise with NWP and Third World women representatives in the wording of the UN Declaration of Human Rights—accepting the term "all people" in place of "all men." Nonetheless, the divisiveness that the debate over equal rights created among American women activists continued at home long after it had been settled at the UN. That debate, Scharf argues, is the key to understanding the split between reformers and feminists in ER's lifetime and beyond.

These collected essays portray Eleanor Roosevelt as a woman who had already embarked upon an independent career before FDR became governor of New York in 1928. From the time she went to school in London at age fourteen until her death sixty-four years later, many of those experiences occurred as ER functioned, publicly and privately, in a shifting network of women friends with whom she shared intense personal relationships based on a passion for political reform. These kinds of relationships gave women like Roosevelt the confidence and support necessary to participate in professions dominated by men and in the nation's public life. Consequently, when ER moved to the White House she was, by virtue of her previous educational, social, and political experiences, the best-prepared wife of a president since Abigail Adams.

What emerges perhaps most forcefully from the essays is a sense of the individual citizen's ability to effect change. Women who, like ER, lived their adults lives in the first half of the twentieth century, assumed that equality of opportunity would produce a more equal society. During the 1960s it became evident that equal opportunity without compensatory action for disadvantaged groups was not enough, and this realization brought forth a new stage in the American dialectic of equality. Roosevelt could not move from her lifelong belief in individual equality of opportunity to endorse remedial action that would dramatically alter group relationships, whether based on sex or race. Such equality of results remains unrealized.

While Eleanor Roosevelt belonged to an older Progressive tradition, she and her circle of friends captured the hearts of Americans to a degree unmatched by later generations of women activists. While they focused their energies primarily on the issues of social welfare and international peace, they shared a conviction about the potential for human, individual contributions in all walks of life. Their hope, optimism, and unabashed patriotism may seem naive in our more cynical times. Nonetheless, the fact remains that Victorian America produced several generations of the most influential women reformers in our history. In retrospect, their humanitarian goals certainly far exceeded their means for achieving them. Yet in 1984 we might well envy a time when women activists actually believed most foreign and domestic problems could be solved by well-intentioned individuals acting for the common good.

We would be well served if women today with similar backgrounds would similarly persevere in the cause of reform. Among women of our times and hers, Eleanor Roosevelt stands out for her belief that the individual matters to the well-being of the country and the world. In 1958, four years before her death, she observed in a speech at the UN:

> Where, after all, do universal human rights begin? In small places, close to home—so close and so small that they cannot be seen on any maps of the world. Yet they are the world of the individual persons; the neighborhood he lives in; the school or college he attends; the factory, farm, office where he works. Such are the places where every man, woman, and child seeks equal justice, equal opportunity, equal dignity without discrimination. Unless these rights have meaning there they have little meaning anywhere. Without concerned citizen action to uphold them close to home, we shall look in vain for progress in the larger world.

Joan Hoff-Wilson
Executive Secretary
Organization of American Historians

Marjorie Lightman
Executive Director
The Institute for Research in History

WITHOUT PRECEDENT

PART
I

THE POLITICAL
EDUCATION OF
ELEANOR ROOSEVELT

William H. Chafe

Biographical Sketch

B OTH BY FATE *and personal will, Eleanor Roosevelt became the most important public woman of the twentieth century. As much as anyone, she represented that generation of women born in the late nineteenth century who moved from a Victorian role of dependency to a new assertion of self. Although committed to the traditional ideal of women as supporters of husbands and family, she also personified the strength of the independent woman and became famous throughout the world for her advocacy of the poor, the disenfranchised, and the oppressed. Yet behind her public image lay a private personality tormented by the quest for emotional support, warmth, and intimacy. The interaction of her private and public roles offers a dramatic story, compelling in its richness, and in its testimony to one person's struggle to find individual fulfillment in the process of making the world a better place in which to live.*[1]

Anna Eleanor Roosevelt[2] was born in New York City on October 11, 1884, the first child and only daughter of Elliott Roosevelt and Anna (Hall) Roosevelt. Descended on both sides from distinguished colonial families active in commerce, banking, and politics, she seemed destined to enjoy all the benefits of class and privilege. Yet by the time she was ten,

[1] Portions of this essay are derived from the author's biographical sketch of ER published in *Notable American Women*, vol. 4 (Cambridge, Massachusetts, 1981).
[2] Throughout the book Anna Eleanor Roosevelt is referred to as Eleanor when others are also identified by their first names. This usuage occurs primarily when her childhood or close relationships are discussed. Otherwise, she is referred to as Eleanor Roosevelt, and Roosevelt, or ER, when it is necessary to distinguish her from FDR. Mrs. Roosevelt is not used unless it appears in direct quotations from the period [Editors' note].

[3]

both her parents had died, as had a younger brother Elliott, leaving her and her second brother Hall as the only survivors.

As a youngster, Eleanor experienced emotional rejection almost from the time she could remember. "I was a solemn child," she recalled, "without beauty. I seemed like a little old woman entirely lacking in the spontaneous joy and mirth of youth." Her mother called her "Granny" and, at least in Eleanor's memory, treated her daughter differently than her son, warmly embracing the boy while being only "kindly and indifferent" to her little girl. From most of her family, young Eleanor received the message that she was "very plain," almost ugly, and certainly "old fashioned." When her parents died, she went to live with her grandmother, who was equally without warmth. As Eleanor's cousin Corinne later remarked, "it was the grimmest childhood I had ever known. Who did she have? Nobody."

In fact, Eleanor had one person—her father. "He was the one great love of my life as a child," she later wrote, "and . . . like many children, I have lived a dream life with him." Described by his friends as "charming, impetuous, high-spirited, big-hearted, generous, [and] friendly," Elliott exhibited ease and grace in his social interactions. With Eleanor, he developed an intimacy that seemed almost magical. "As soon as I could talk," she recalled, "I went into his dressing room every morning and chattered to him . . . I even danced with him, intoxicated by the pure joy of motion. . . . until he would pick me up and throw me into the air." She dreamed of the time when they would go off together—"always he and I . . . and someday [we] would have a life of our own together."

But Elliott's capacity for ebullient play and love also contained the seeds of self-destruction—alcoholism, irresponsibility, cruelty. He never found an anchor, either in public life or business, to provide stability for himself and his family. Elliott's emotional imbalance quickly produced problems in his marriage and banishment from the household. The last four years of his life were like a roller coaster. Elliott nourished the emotional relationship with Eleanor through letters to "father's own little Nell," writing of "the wonderful long rides . . . through the grand snow-clad forests, over the white hills" that he wanted them to enjoy together. But when his long-awaited visits occurred, they often ended in disaster, as when Elliott left Eleanor with the doorman at New York's Knickerbocker Club, promising to return but going off on a drunken spree instead. The pain of betrayal was exceeded only by Eleanor's depth of love for the man she believed was "the only person who really cared." Looking back later in life for an explanation of her inability to express emotions spontaneously, she concluded that the trauma of her childhood was the main cause. "Something locked me up," she wrote.

After her father's death, an emotional void pervaded Eleanor's life until, at age fourteen, she enrolled in Allenswood, a girls' school outside London presided over by Marie Souvestre, daughter of a well-known French philosopher and radical. At Allenswood, the girl found a circle of warmth and support. "She was beloved by everybody," her cousin remarked. "Saturdays we were allowed a sortie in Putney which has stores where you could buy books, [and] flowers. Young girls had crushes and you left [gifts] in the room with the girl you were idolizing. Eleanor's room every Saturday would be full of flowers because she was so admired." Allenswood also provided educational inspiration. Souvestre passionately embraced unpopular causes, staunchly defending Dreyfus in France and the cause of the Boers in South Africa. "I consider the three years which I spent with her as the beginning of an entirely new outlook on life," Eleanor wrote. Marie Souvestre toured the continent with the girl, confiding in her and expressing the affection that made it possible for Eleanor to flower. Describing her stay at Allenswood as "the happiest years of my life," Eleanor noted that "whatever I have become since had its seeds in those three years of contact with a liberal mind and strong personality." The love and admiration were mutual. "I miss you every day of my life," Souvestre wrote her in 1902.

The imprint of Marie Souvestre was not lost when Eleanor returned to the United States at age seventeen to "come out" in New York society. Even in the rush of parties and dances, she kept her eye on the more serious world of ideas and social service. Souvestre had written her in 1901: "Even when success comes, as I'm sure it will, bear in mind that there are more quiet and enviable joys than to be among the most sought-after women at a ball." Heeding the injunction, Eleanor plunged into settlement-house work and social activism.

Much of Eleanor Roosevelt's subsequent political life can be traced to this early involvement with social reform. At age eighteen she joined the National Consumers' League, headed by Florence Kelley. The league was committed to securing health and safety for workers—especially women—in clothing factories and sweatshops. On visits to these workplaces, Eleanor learned firsthand the misery of the working poor and developed a lifelong commitment to their needs. At the same time, she joined the Junior League and commenced work at the Rivington Street Settlement House, where she taught calisthenics and dancing and witnessed both the deprivation of the poor and the courage of slum dwellers who sought to improve their lot. Eleanor discovered that she preferred social work to debutante parties. More and more, she came to be recognized as a key member of a network of social reformers in New York City.

At the same time, however, Eleanor was secretly planning to marry her cousin Franklin Roosevelt, an event that would be followed by a fifteen-year hiatus in her public activities. Like his godfather (Eleanor's father), Franklin was "a gay cavalier," spontaneous, warm, and gregarious. But unlike Elliott, Franklin also possessed good sense and singleness of purpose. Eleanor saw in him the spark of life that she remembered from her father. After their engagement, she even sent to Franklin a letter signed "little Nell," her father's favorite name for her. Franklin, in turn, saw in Eleanor the discipline that would curb his own instincts toward excess.

After their marriage on March 17, 1905, the young Roosevelts settled in New York City while Franklin finished his law studies at Columbia. Franklin's mother Sara had warned Eleanor that she should not continue her work at the settlement house because she might bring home the diseases of the slum, but soon Eleanor was preoccupied with other concerns. Within a year, Anna was born (1906), then the next year James (1907), and two years later Franklin. Although Eleanor cherished her children, it was not a happy time. Sara dominated the household and imposed her will on almost all issues, including the raising of the children. As Eleanor later recalled, her mother-in-law "wanted . . . to hold onto Franklin and his children; she wanted them to grow up as she wished. As it turned out, Franklin's children were more my mother-in-law's children than they were mine." Nor was Sara's possessiveness limited to the children. At the family estate at Hyde Park, she was in total control. At dinner, Franklin sat at one end of the table, his mother at the other, and Eleanor in the middle. Before the fireplace there were two wing chairs, one for the mother, the other for the son. Eleanor was like an uninvited guest.

Fearing that she would hurt Franklin and lose his affection, Eleanor did not rebel. But she did experience a profound sense of inadequacy about her abilities as a wife and mother. Daughter Anna described her mother as unpredictable and inconsistent with the children, sweet one moment, critical and demanding the next. "Mother was always stiff, never relaxed enough to romp . . . Mother loved all mankind, but she did not know how to let her children love her." Eleanor herself recognized the problem. "It did not come naturally to me to understand little children or to enjoy them," she later said. "Playing with children was difficult for me because play had not been an important part of my own childhood." Instead of comforting the children when they experienced pain, she urged upon them an attitude of stoicism and endurance, as if to say that expressing emotion was a sign of bad character. The death of her third child, Franklin, a few months after his birth only reinforced Eleanor's unhappiness and feeling of inadequacy. Three additional children were born in the next six years—Elliott in 1910, Franklin in 1914, and John in 1916. Eleanor was devoted to each, yet motherhood could not be fulfilling in a household ruled by a grandmother who referred to the children as "my children . . . your mother only bore you."

In the years between 1910 and the beginning of World War I, Eleanor Roosevelt's activities revolved more and more around Franklin's growing political career. Elected as the Democratic assemblyman from Dutchess County in 1910, he rapidly became a leader of insurgent anti-Tammany forces in Albany. In 1913 Franklin was appointed assistant secretary of the Navy, and Eleanor, in addition to managing a large household, became expert at hosting the multiple social events required of a subcabinet member, as well as moving the entire household at least twice each year—to Campobello in New Brunswick during the summer, then to Hyde Park and back to Washington. During these years, she fulfilled the many traditionally female social activities expected of her.

America's entry into World War I in 1917 provided the occasion for Eleanor to reassert the public side of her personality. As her biographer Joseph Lash has noted, "the war gave her a reason acceptable to her conscience to free herself of the social duties that she hated, to concentrate less on her household, and to plunge into work that fitted her aptitude." She rose at 5 a.m. to coordinate activities at the Union Station canteen for soldiers on their way to training camps, took charge of Red Cross activities, supervised the knitting rooms at the Navy department, and spoke at patriotic rallies. Her interest in social welfare led to her drive to improve conditions at St. Elizabeth's mental hospital, while her sensitivity to suffering came forth in the visits she paid to wounded soldiers. "[My son] always loved to see you come in," one mother wrote. "You always brought a ray of sunshine."

The war served as a transition for Eleanor's reemergence as a public personality during the 1920s. After Franklin's unsuccessful campaign for the vice-presidency on James Cox's ticket in 1920, the Roosevelts returned to New York where Eleanor became active in the League of Women Voters. At the time of her marriage, she had opposed suffrage, thinking it inconsistent with women's proper role; now, as coordinator of the league's legislative program, she kept track of bills that came before the Albany legislature, drafted laws providing for equal representation for men and women, and worked with Esther Lape and Elizabeth Read on the league's lobbying activities. In 1921 she also joined the Women's Trade Union League—then viewed as "left-leaning"—and found friends there as well as political allies. In addition to working for programs such as the regulation of maximum hours and minimum wages for women, Eleanor helped raise funds for the WTUL headquarters in New York City. Her warm ties to first- and second-generation immigrants like Rose Schneiderman and Maud Swartz highlighted how far Eleanor had moved from the upper-class provincialism of her early years.

When Franklin was paralyzed by polio in 1922, Eleanor's public life expanded still further: she now became her husband's personal representative in the political arena. With the aid of Louis Howe, Franklin's political mentor and her own close friend, Eleanor first mobilized Dutchess County women, then moved on to the state Democratic party, organizing all but five counties by 1924. "Organization," she noted, "is something to which [the men] are always ready to take off their hats." No one did the job better. Leading a delegation to the Democratic convention in 1924, she fought (unsuccessfully) for equal pay legislation, the child labor amendment, and other planks endorsed by women reformers.

By 1928, Eleanor Roosevelt had clearly become a political leader in her own right. Once just a "political wife," she gradually extended that role and used it as a vehicle for asserting her own personality and agenda. In 1928, as head of the national women's campaign for the Democratic party, she made sure that the party appealed to independent voters, to minorities, and to women. She was also instrumental in securing the appointment of Frances Perkins as comissioner of industrial relations in New York after Franklin had been elected governor there. Dictating as many as one hundred letters a day, speaking to countless groups, acting as an advocate of social reform and women's issues, she had become a political personality of the first rank.

Eleanor Roosevelt's talent for combining partisan political activity with devotion to social welfare causes made her the center of an ever-growing female reform network. Her associates included Marion Dickerman and Nancy Cook, former suffragists and Democratic party loyalists; Molly Dewson, a longtime research secretary of the National Consumers League; and Mary Dreier of the Women's Trade Union League. She walked on picket lines with Rose Schneiderman, edited the *Women's Democratic News*, and advised the League of Women Voters on political tactics. Her political sophistication grew. "To many women, and I am one of them," she noted, "it is difficult to care enough [about an issue] to cause disagreement or unpleasant feelings, but I have come to the conclusion that this must be done for a time so we can prove our strength and demand respect for our wishes." By standing up for women in politics, ER provided a model for others to follow. In the process, she also earned the admiring, if grudging, respect of men who recognized a superb organizer when they saw one.

During the 1932 campaign, which led to Franklin's election to the presidency, Eleanor coordinated the activities of the Women's Division of the Democratic National Committee. Working with Mary (Molly) W. Dewson, she mobilized thousands of women precinct workers to carry the party's program to local voters; for example, the women distributed hundreds of thousands of "rainbow fliers," colorful sheets containing facts on the party's approach to various issues. After the election, Mary (Molly) W. Dewson took charge of the Women's Division, corresponding daily with Eleanor both about appointing women to office and securing action on issues that would appeal to minorities, women, and such professional groups as educators and social workers. The two friends were instrumental in bringing to Washington an unprecedented number of dynamic women activists. Ellen Woodward, Hilda Worthington Smith, and Florence Kerr all held executive offices in the Works Progress Administration, while Lorena Hickok acted as eyes and ears for WPA director Harry Hopkins as she traveled across the country to observe the impact of the New Deal's relief program. Mary Anderson, director of the Women's Bureau, recalled that women government officials had formerly dined together in a small university club. "Now," she said, "there are so many of them that we need a hall."

Eleanor Roosevelt not only provided the impetus for appointing these women but also offered a forum for transmitting their views and concerns across the country. Soon after she entered the White House, she began a series of regular press conferences to which *only* women reporters were admitted, and where the first lady insisted on making "hard" news as well as providing social tidbits for the "women's page." She introduced such women as Mary McLeod Bethune and Hilda Worthington Smith to talk about their work with the New Deal. These sessions provided new status and prestige for the female press corps and they also underlined the importance of women's issues to the first lady. Her efforts helped create a community of women reporters and government workers. When the all-male Gridiron Club held its annual dinner to spoof the president and his male colleagues, the first lady initiated a Gridiron Widows' Club where the women in Washington could engage in their own satire.

Largely as a result of ER's activities, women achieved a strong voice in the New Deal. The proportion of women appointed as postmasters shot up from 17.6 percent in 1930 to 26 percent between 1932 and 1938. More important, the social welfare policies of the administration reflected a reform perspective that women like Ellen Woodward and Florence Kerr shared with men like Harry Hopkins and Aubrey Williams. When a particularly difficult issue involving women came up, the first lady would invite Molly Dewson to the White House and seat her next to the president, where she could persuade him of her point of view. ER's own political role appears most clearly in her work on the reelection drive of 1936, when she coordinated the efforts of both men and women and used the "educational" approach developed by the Women's Division in 1932 as a major campaign weapon. More than sixty thousand women precinct workers canvassed the electorate, handing out "rainbow fliers" as the party's principal literature. For the first time women received equal representation on the Democratic Platform Committee, an event described by the *New York Times* as "the biggest coup for women in years."

Eleanor Roosevelt's fear that she would have no active role as a presidential wife had been unfounded. She toured the country repeatedly, surveying conditions in the coal mines, visiting relief projects, and speaking out for the human rights of the disadvantaged. Through her newspaper column "My Day," she entered the homes of millions. Her radio programs, her lectures, and her writings communicated to the country her deep compassion for those who suffered. At the White House, in turn, she acted as advocate of the poor and disenfranchised. "No one who ever saw Eleanor Roosevelt sit down facing her husband," Rexford Tugwell wrote, "and holding his eyes firmly, [and saying] to him 'Franklin, I think you should' . . . or, 'Franklin surely you will not' . . . will ever forget the experience. . . . It would be impossible to say how often and to what extent American governmental processes have been turned in a new direction because of her determination." She had become, in the words of columnist Raymond Clapper, a "Cabinet Minister without portfolio—the most influential woman of our times."

But if Eleanor had achieved an unparalleled measure of political influence, it was in place of, rather than because of, an intimate personal relationship with Franklin. In 1932 Eleanor described a perfect couple as one where two people did not even need to tell each other how they felt, but cared so much that a look and the sound of a voice would tell all. Probably at no time after their first few years together did Franklin and Eleanor achieve that degree of intimacy. Not only was Sara still a dominant presence, but Franklin had embarked on his own interests and enthusiasms, often different from Eleanor's. The differences in their temperaments became a permanent barrier that tormented their relationship. He loved to party; she held back and frowned on his willingness to "let go." In a letter to her daughter Anna from Warm Springs in 1934, Eleanor declared that she "always felt like a spoil-sport and policeman here. . . . I'm an idiotic puritan and I wish I had the right kind of sense of humor and could enjoy certain things. At least, thank God, none of you children have inherited that streak in me."

During the years he was assistant secretary of the Navy, Franklin acted more frequently on his fun-loving instincts. "He deserved a good time," Eleanor's cousin Alice Roosevelt acidly noted, "he was married to Eleanor." A frequent companion on Franklin's pleasurable excursions was Lucy Mercer, Eleanor's social secretary. Over time, the relationship between Lucy and Franklin became intimate, particularly during the summers when Eleanor was absent at Campobello. After Franklin was stricken with pneumonia in the fall of 1918, Eleanor discovered the letters between Franklin and Lucy describing their affair. Although Franklin refused Eleanor's offer of divorce, and Sara engineered an agreement for them to stay together if Franklin stopped seeing Lucy, their marriage would never again achieve the magical possibility of being "for life, for death," one where a word or look would communicate everything. In the wake of the Mercer affair, James Roosevelt later wrote, his parents "agreed to go on for the sake of appearances, the children and the future, but as business partners, not as husband and wife. . . . After that, father and mother had an armed truce that endured until the day he died."

In the eyes of some, Eleanor Roosevelt's emergence as a public figure seemed a direct consequence of profound anger at her husband's betrayal. Yet Eleanor's activism predated her discovery of the Mercer affair. World War I provided the occasion for expressing long-suppressed talents and energies that could be traced back to her early involvement with the National Consumers' League and the settlement house and were rooted, ultimately, in her relationship with Marie Souvestre. The Lucy Mercer affair, like Franklin's polio, reinforced the move toward public self-assertion, but did not itself cause a transformation.

What the Mercer affair did cause was a gradual reallocation of emotional energy away from Franklin and toward others. Through the polio episode and afterward, Eleanor remained devoted to Franklin's care and career. During the 1920s a warmth of tone and feeling continued in her letters to and about him. Yet gradually their lives became separate. Franklin went off on his houseboat in Florida or to Warm Springs, Georgia, with his secretary Missy LeHand. Eleanor stayed away, as if intentionally ceding to others any emotional involvement with her husband. She might have been jealous of Missy (some have said Franklin had "an affair" with her) or even her daughter Anna for easily giving him the fun and enjoyment that was beyond her ability. But a part of her recognized that others must provide what she could not give.

Increasingly, Eleanor appeared to draw on her own family experience when offering advice to others. When a woman wrote her in 1930 about a marital problem, Eleanor replied: "All men who make successes of their work go through exactly the same kind of thing which you describe, and their wives,one way or another, have to adjust themselves. If it is possible to enter into his work in some way, that is the ideal solution. If not, they must develop something of their own and if possible make it such a success they will have something to interest their husbands." In a poignant piece entitled "On Being Forty-five," which she wrote for *Vogue* in 1930, Eleanor elaborated

> Life is a school in which we live all our days, and by middle-age, we should know that happiness . . . is never ours by right, but we earn it through giving of ourselves. You must have learned self-control. No matter how much you care, how much you may feel that if you knew certain things you could help, you must not ask questions or offer help, you must wait until the confidence

is freely given, and you must learn to love without criticism. . . . If you have learned these things by forty-five, if you have ceased to consider yourself as in anyway important, but understand well the place that must be filled in the family, the role will be easy.

Above all, Eleanor concluded, the forty-five-year-old woman must

keep an open and speculative mind . . . and [then] she will be ready to go out and try new adventures, create new work for others as well as herself, and strike deep roots in some community where her presence will make a difference in the lives of others. . . . One can no longer be interested in one's self, but one is thereby freed for greater interest in others and the lives of others become as engrossing as a fairy story of our childhood days.

Taking her own advice, Eleanor increasingly transferred the emotional focus of her life away from Franklin. The political network of women reformers of which she was the center provided intimate friendship as well as political camaraderie. During the 1920s she spent one night a week with Esther Lape and Elizabeth Read, reading books together and talking about common interests. She also became close friends with Women's Trade Union League women like Rose Schneiderman, inviting them to Hyde Park for picnics. Molly Dewson became an especially close friend, and Eleanor wrote in 1932 that "the nicest thing about politics is lunching with you on Mondays." In a revealing comment made in 1927, Eleanor observed that "more than anything else, politics may serve to guard against the emptiness and loneliness that enter some women's lives after their children have grown."

Many of Eleanor's friendships during the 1920s and 1930s were with women who lived with other women. She had become particularly close to Nancy Cook and Marion Dickerman, who lived together in New York City. In 1926 she moved with them into Val-Kill, a newly constructed cottage at Hyde Park, an event that accurately symbolized her growing detachment from Franklin and his mother. Although she returned to the "Big House" at Hyde Park when Franklin was present, it was never without resentment and regret. She and Dickerman purchased Todhundter, a private school in New York, where Eleanor taught three days a week even after Franklin was elected governor of New York. The three women also jointly managed a furniture crafts factory at Val-Kill. The linen and towels at Val-Kill were monogrammed "EMN," and the three women together constituted as much a "family" for Eleanor during those years as Franklin and her children.

There were always "special" relationships, however, and during the 1930s these acquired an intensity and depth that were new to Eleanor's life. One of these was with her daughter Anna and Anna's new love, John Boettiger, a reporter whom Anna had met during the 1932 presidential campaign. Eleanor shared a special bond with her daughter, different from the one she had with her sons. Although the two women had had a difficult relationship during Anna's adolescence and early adulthood, caused partly by Anna's resentment of her mother's "distance" and preference for other, competing personalities like Louis Howe, the two women rekindled their affection during Anna's romance with John. Eleanor seemed to be re-living her early days with Franklin by investing enormous energy and love in Anna and wanting her daughter to find the kind of happiness she felt she had lost forever with her own husband. "I love Anna so dearly," Eleanor wrote John in 1935, "that I don't need to tell you that my willingness to let her go to you speaks much for my *trust and love* of you" (italics mine). Eleanor became a ready accomplice in the young couple's effort to find time alone together before their respective divorces and wrote constantly of her hopes for their happiness. One poignant letter to Anna on Christmas Eve 1935 speaks with particular power to the emotional ties that had developed between mother and daughter. "The dogs and I have felt sad every time we passed your door," she wrote. "It was hard to decorate the tree or get things distributed without you . . . and if anyone says much I shall weep for I have had a queer feeling in my throat when I thought of you. Anyway I am happy that you and John are together for I know you will be happy, so please give him a hug for me and tell him I am grateful for him and what he means to you for every day of my life."

Perhaps Eleanor's most carefree relationship during these years occurred with Earl Miller, a former state trooper who had been Governor Al Smith's bodyguard and who subsequently provided the same service to the Roosevelt family. He encouraged Eleanor to drive her own car, take up horseback riding again, and develop confidence in her own personality. He was strikingly different from her other friends—tall, handsome, a "man's man." Although they talked about ideas and politics, the relationship was more that of "boon companions." With Earl Miller, Eleanor found a way to escape the pressures of her political and social status. She went frequently to his home for visits, had him stay at Val-Kill or her New York apartment, and accompanied him whenever possible for long walks and late-evening suppers. Although some of her friends disliked his tendency to "manhandle" Eleanor, all understood the importance of the relationship, and Marion Dickerman even said that "Eleanor played with the idea of marriage with Earl." Miller himself denied that the subject had ever been raised. "You don't sleep with someone you call Mrs. Roosevelt," he said. But without question, the two had an extraordinarily close relationship, and James Roosevelt later observed that his mother's tie to Miller "may have been the one real romance in [her] life outside of marriage. . . . She seemed to draw strength from him when he was by her side, and she came to rely on him. . . . Above all, he made her feel like she was a woman."

It was Eleanor Roosevelt's relationship with Lorena Hickok, however, that proved most intense during the 1930s and that subsequently has caused the most controversy. The two women became close during the 1932 campaign, when Hickok was covering the prospective first lady in her role as a reporter for the Associated Press. "That woman is unhappy about something," Hickok noted. Eleanor had not wanted Franklin to become president and feared that life in the White House would destroy her independence and cast her in an empty role as hostess and figurehead. As the two women talked about their respective lives, they developed an intimacy and affection so close that Hickok felt compelled to resign her position as a reporter because she no longer could write "objectively" about the Roosevelts.

Within a short time, the two women were exchanging daily letters and phone calls, the contents of which suggested that each woman was deeply infatuated with the other. "Hick darling," Eleanor wrote on March 6, "how good it was to hear your voice. It was so inadequate to try to tell you what it meant. Jimmy was near and I could not say, je t'aime et je t'adore as I long to do but always remember I am saying it and I go to sleep thinking of you and repeating our little saying." The next night, Eleanor was writing again. "All day," she said, "I thought of you, and another birthday I *will* be with you and yet tonight you sounded so far away and formal. Oh! I want to put my arms around you. I ache to hold you close. Your ring is a great comfort. I look at it and think she does love me, or I wouldn't be wearing it!" The two women plotted ways to be together, to steal a few days in the country, to bridge the gap of physical separation that so often stood between them.

> Only eight more days [Hickok wrote]. Twenty-four hours from now it will be only seven more—just a week! I've been trying today to bring back your face—to remember just *how* you looked. . . . Most clearly I remember your eyes, with the kind of teasing smile in them, and the feeling of that soft spot just northeast of the corner of your mouth against my lips. I wonder what we will do when we meet—what we will say when we meet. Well—I'm rather proud of us, aren't you? I think we have done rather well.

Over time, the relationship cooled somewhat under the pressure of Hickok's demands on Eleanor's time and Eleanor's reluctance to give herself totally to her new friend. Hickok was jealous of Eleanor's other friends, even her children. "Darling," Eleanor wrote, "the love one has for one's children is different, and not even Anna could be to me what you are." From Eleanor's point of view, the two were like a married couple whose relationship had to "flower." "Dearest," she wrote, "strong relationships have to grow deep roots. We are growing them now, partly because we are separated. The foliage and the flowers will come somehow, I'm sure of it. . . ." But an impatient Hickok was jealous of Eleanor's other friends and unable to limit the ardor of her affection.

In time, the situation became too much for Eleanor. In an attempt to explain herself to Hickok, she wrote: "I know you often have a feeling for me which for one reason or another I may not return in kind, but I feel I love you just the same and so often we entirely satisfy each other that I feel there is a fundamental basis on which our relationship stands." "Hick" had to understand, Eleanor wrote, "that I love other people the same way or differently, but each one has their place and one cannot compare them." But in the end, Eleanor could not explain herself sufficiently to satisfy Hickok and concluded that she had failed her friend. "Of course dear," she wrote, "I never meant to hurt you in any way but that is no excuse for having done it. It won't help you any but I'll never do to anyone else what I did to you." However much she might try, Eleanor could not let herself go emotionally. As a result, she said, "I am pulling myself back in all my contacts now. I have always done it with the children, and why I didn't know I couldn't give you (or anyone else who wanted or needed what you did) any real food, I can't now understand. Such cruelty and stupidity is unpardonable when you reach my age. Heaven knows I hope in some small and unimportant ways I have made life a little easier for you, but that doesn't compensate." Although the two women remained close during the 1930s and 1940s and continued to share the "special Christmases" that Eleanor reserved for her most intimate friends like Earl Miller, Nan Cook, and Hickok, the two women never resumed the intensity and ardor of their early relationship.

Many observers have speculated on the sexual significance of Roosevelt's relationship with Hickok. Hickok herself appears to have had numerous lesbian involvements, and the intimacy of her correspondence with Roosevelt has suggested to some that the love the two women shared must, inevitably, have had a sexual component as well. Many of Eleanor's other women friends lived together in what were called, at the time, "Boston marriages," and some of these associates undoubtedly found fulfillment through sexual relationships with other women. In all likelihood, Marie Souvestre was one of these. Nor has speculation about Eleanor's sexual life been limited to women. Her son James believed that she had an affair with Earl Miller, and later in her life some believed that she had sexual relationships with other men.

Although the accuracy of such speculation may ultimately be irrelevant, the preponderance of evidence suggests that Eleanor Roosevelt was unable to express her deep emotional needs in a sexual manner. Her friend Esther Lape has recalled the distaste and repugnance with which Eleanor responded to the issue of homosexuality when they discussed a French novel dealing with the topic in the 1920s. Eleanor herself told her daughter that sex was something to be "borne," not enjoyed. Eleanor's own reference to Hickok having "a feeling for me which for one reason or another I may not return in kind" may be an allusion to a sexual component of Hickok's desire that Roosevelt could not reciprocate. Earl Miller, and other men with whom Eleanor was rumored to have had a sexual relationship, have all denied—persuasively—the truth of such conjecture. Moreover, we must never forget that Eleanor was raised in a Victorian culture that attempted to repress the sexual drive. She tied her daughter's hands to the top bars of her crib in order to prevent her from masturbating. "The indication was clearly," Anna recalled, "that I had had a bad habit which had to be cured and about which one didn't talk!"

All of this conforms to Eleanor's own repeated declarations that she could never "let herself go" or express freely and spontaneously her full emotions. A person who had been raised to believe that self-control was all-important was unlikely to consider sexual expression of love—especially outside of marriage—a real option. She might sublimate her sexual drives and seek fulfillment of them through a series of deeply committed, even passionate, ties to a variety of people. But it is unlikely that she was ever able to fulfill these drives through actual sexual intimacy with those she cared most about. She was imprisoned in the cage of her culture, and her own bitter experiences through childhood and marriage reinforced her impulse toward self-control and repression. Within her world, she used verbal and emotional lovemaking to achieve whatever satisfaction she could. But ultimately, she could not liberate herself from that world. She would give to others as much as she could within the confines of her life, but she could not take from others—or give—in a manner that her culture defined as forbidden.

In this context, it is not surprising that Eleanor Roosevelt derived some of her emotional gratification from public life and by giving herself emotionally even to distant correspondents who somehow sensed her willingness to listen to their needs. Such expression of concern constituted the intersection of her public and private lives. Over and over again she answered pleas for help with either a sensitive letter, an admonition to a federal agency to take action, or even a personal check. When a policeman she knew suffered a paralyzing injury, she helped pay for his treatment, visited him repeatedly and, to encourage his rehabilitation, even asked him to help type a book she was composing about her father. The indigent wrote to her because they knew she cared, and in caring she found an outlet for her own powerful emotional needs.

The same compassion was manifested in Eleanor Roosevelt's advocacy of the oppressed. It was almost as though she could fully express her feelings only through externalizing them on political issues. Visiting the poverty-stricken countryside of West Virginia and hearing about the struggle of Appalachian farmers to reclaim land, she became a champion of the Arthurdale Resettlement Administration Project, devoting her lecture fees as well as influence to help the community regain autonomy. Poor textile workers in the South and garment union members in the North found her equally willing to embrace their cause. She invited their representatives to the White House and seated them next to the president at dinner so that he might hear of their plight. She and Franklin had worked out a tacit understanding that permitted her to bring the cause of the oppressed to his attention and allowed him, in turn, to use her activism as a means of building alliances with groups to his left. The game had clear rules: Franklin was the politician, Eleanor the agitator, and frequently he refused to act as she wished. But at least the dispossessed had someone advocating their interests.

Largely because of Eleanor Roosevelt, the issue of civil rights for black Americans received a hearing at the White House. Although Roosevelt, like most white Americans, grew up in an environment suffused with racist and nativist attitudes, by the time she reached the White House she was one of the few voices in the administration insisting that racial discrimination had no place in American life. As always, she led by example. At a 1939 Birmingham meeting inaugurating the Southern Conference on Human Welfare, she insisted on placing her chair so that it straddled both the black and white sides of the aisle, thereby confounding local authorities who insisted that segregation must prevail. Her civil-rights sympathies became most famous when in 1939 she resigned from the Daughters of the American Revolution after the organization denied Marian Anderson permission to perform at Constitution Hall. Instead, the great black artist sang to seventy-five thousand people from the Lincoln Memorial—an idea moved toward reality owing to support from the first lady.

Roosevelt also acted as behind-the-scenes lobbyist for civil rights legislation. She had an extensive correspondence with Walter White, executive secretary of the NAACP, who wished to secure her support for legislation defining lynching as a federal crime. She immediately accepted the role of intermediary and argued that the president should make such a bill an urgent national priority. She served as the primary advocate for the anti-lynching bill within the White House, and she and White became fast friends as they worked toward a common objective. When the NAACP sponsored a New York City exhibit of paintings and drawings dealing with lynching, Roosevelt agreed to be a patron and attended the showing along with her secretary. After White House Press Secretary Steve Early protested about White, she responded: "If I were colored, I think I should have about the same obsession [with lynching] that he has." To the president ER communicated her anger that "one could get nothing done." "I'm deeply troubled," she wrote, "by the whole situation, as it seems to me a terrible thing to stand by and let it continue and feel that one cannot speak out as to his feelings."

Although Eleanor lost out in her campaign for Franklin's strong endorsement of an antilynching bill, she continued to speak forthrightly for the cause of civil rights. In June 1939, in an address before the NAACP's annual meeting, she presented the organization's Spingarn Medal to Marian Anderson. A few weeks later, she formally joined the black protest organization.

As the threat of war increased, Roosevelt joined her black friends in arguing that America could not fight racism abroad yet tolerate it at home. Together with Walter White, Aubrey Williams, and others, she pressed the administration to act vigorously to eliminate discrimination in the Armed Forces and defense employment. Although civil-rights forces were not satisfied with the administration's actions, especially the enforcement proceedings of the Fair Employment Practices Commission created to forestall A. Philip Randolph's 1941 march on Washington, the positive changes that did occur arose from the alliance of the first lady and civil-rights forces. She would not give up the battle, nor would they, despite the national administration's evident reluctance to act.

Roosevelt brought the same fervor to her identification with young people. Fearing that democracy might lose a whole generation because of the depression, she reached out to make contact with the young. Despite warnings from White House aides that her young friends could not be trusted, between 1936 and 1940 she became deeply involved in the activities of the American Student Union and the American Youth Congress, groups committed to a democratic socialist program of massively expanded social-welfare programs. She advanced their point of view in White House circles and invited them to meet the president so that they might have the opportunity to persuade him of their point of view. To those who criticized her naiveté, she responded: "I wonder if it does us much harm. There is nothing as harmful as the knowledge in our hearts that we are afraid to face any group of young people." She was later betrayed by some of her young allies, who insisted on following the Communist party line and denouncing the European war as imperialistic after the Nazi-Soviet Non-Aggression Pact in 1940. Nonetheless, Roosevelt continued to believe in the importance of remaining open to dissent. "I have never said anywhere that I would rather see young people sympathetic with communism," she wrote. "But I have said that I would rather see the young people actively at work, even if I considered they were doing things that were a mistake." It was through her contact with the American Student Union that she first met Joseph Lash, a vigorous leader of the anticommunist faction of the student movement, who would later become as close to her as any one in her life.

With the onset of World War II, the first lady persisted in her efforts for the disadvantaged. When it appeared that women would be left out of the planning and staffing of wartime operations, she insisted that administration officials consult women activists and incorporate roles for women as a major part of their planning. Over and over again, she intervened with war-production agencies as well as the military to advocate fairer treatment for black Americans. After it seemed that many New Deal social-welfare programs would be threatened by war, she acted to protect and preserve measures directed at the young, tenant farmers, and blacks. Increasingly, she devoted herself to the dream of international cooperation, perceiving, more than most, the revolution rising in Africa and Asia, and the dangers posed by the threat of postwar conflict.

When Jewish refugees seeking a haven from Nazi persecution received less than an enthusiastic response from the State Department, it was Eleanor Roosevelt who intervened repeatedly, trying to improve the situation. Parents, wives, or children separated from loved ones always found an ally when they sought help from the first lady. Nowhere was Roosevelt's concern more poignantly expressed than in her visits to wounded veterans in army hospitals overseas. When the world of hot dogs and baseball seemed millions of miles away, suddenly Eleanor Roosevelt would appear, spending time at each bedside, taking names and addresses to write letters to home, bringing the cherished message that someone cared.

Perhaps inevitably, given the stresses of the times, the worlds of Franklin and Eleanor became ever more separate in these years. As early as the 1936 reelection campaign, she confessed to feeling "indifferent" about Franklin's chances. "I realize more and more," she wrote Hickok, "that FDR's a great man, and he is nice, but as a person, I'm a stranger, and I don't want to be anything else!" As the war proceeded, Eleanor and Franklin more often became adversaries. He was less able to tolerate Eleanor's advocacy of unpopular causes, or her insistence on calling attention to areas of conflict within the administration. "She was invariably frank in her criticism of him," one of his speechwriters recalled, "[and] sometimes I thought she picked inappropriate times . . . perhaps a social and entertaining dinner." In search of release from the unbearable pressures of the war, Franklin came more and more to rely on the gaiety and laughter of his daughter Anna and other women companions. One of these was Lucy Mercer Rutherfurd, who began to come to White House dinners when Eleanor was away (with Anna's complicity) and who, unbeknownst to Eleanor, was with the president in Warm Springs when he was stricken by a cerebral hemorrhage and died in April 1945.

With great discipline and dignity, Eleanor bore both the pain of Franklin's death and the circumstances surrounding it. Her first concern was to carry forward the policies that she and Franklin had believed in and worked for despite their disagreements. Writing later about her relationship with Franklin, she said: "He might have been happier with a wife who had been completely uncritical. That I was never able to be and he had to find it in some other people. Nevertheless, I think that I sometimes acted as a spur, even though the spurring was not always wanted nor welcome. I was one of those who served his purposes." What she did not say was that Franklin had served her purposes as well. Though the two never retrieved the intimacy of their early relationship, they had created an unparalleled partnership to respond to the needs of a nation in crisis.

Not long after her husband's death, she told an inquiring reporter, "The story is over." But no one who cared so much for so many causes, and was so effective as a leader, could long remain on the sidelines. Twenty years earlier, ER had told her students at Todhunter: "Don't dry up by inaction, but go out and do new things. Learn new things and see new things with your own eyes." Her own instincts, as well as the demands of others, reaffirmed that advice. Over the next decade and a half, Roosevelt remained the most effective woman in American politics. She felt a responsibility not only to carry forward the politics of the New Deal, but also to further causes that frequently had gone beyond New Deal liberalism. In long letters to President Truman, she implored the administration to push forward with civil rights, maintain the Fair Employment Practices Committee, develop a foreign policy able to cope with the needs of other nations, and work toward a world system where atom bombs would cease to be negotiating chips in international relations.

Appropriately, President Truman nominated the former first lady to be one of America's delegates to the United Nations. At the UN, her name became synonymous with the effort to compose a declaration of human rights embodying standards that civilized humankind would accept as sacred and inalienable. For three years, she argued, debated, lobbied, and compromised until finally on December 10, 1948, the document she had fundamentally shaped passed the General Assembly. Delegates rose in a standing ovation to the woman who more than anyone else had come to symbolize the cause of human rights throughout the world. Even those in the United States who had most opposed her nomination to the delegation applauded her efforts. "I want to say that I take back everything I ever said about her," Senator Arthur Vandenberg of Michigan commented, "and believe me, it's been plenty." At times a figure of scorn and ridicule during the New Deal, Roosevelt was now fast becoming a national heroine, even to former enemies.

The cause of world peace quickly became as central to Roosevelt's efforts as anything in which she had engaged before. With the same emotional fervor that had earlier characterized her response to the dispossessed, Roosevelt reached out to the victims of war. "The weight of human misery here in Europe," she said after a visit to Germany and its concentration camps, "is something one can't get out of one's heart." In moving speeches that vividly portrayed the suffering wrought by war, she sought to educate America to its responsibilities in the postwar world. She had driven through England in 1928, she told her audience, noting the names of all the young men who had died during World War I. Now, she had completed the same kind of journey through Germany. "There is a feeling that spreads over the land," she said, "the feel of [a] civilization that of itself might have a hard time coming back." If America wished to avoid such a world, it must avoid isolationism and wake up to the necessity of helping those who had suffered.

Although Roosevelt disagreed profoundly with some of the military aspects of U.S. foreign policy, she supported the broad outlines of America's response to Russia in the developing Cold War. In debates at the UN, she learned quickly that Soviet delegates could be hypocritical, and on more than one occasion she responded to Russian charges of injustice in America by proposing that each country submit to investigation of its social conditions—a suggestion the Soviets refused. When Henry Wallace and other liberal Americans formed the Progressive party in 1947 with a platform of accommodation toward the Soviet Union, Roosevelt demurred. Instead, she spearheaded the drive by other liberals to build Americans for Democratic Action, a group that espoused social reform at home and support of Truman's stance toward Russia.

Through public speeches and her newspaper column, as well as her position at the UN, Roosevelt remained a singular public figure, able to galvanize the attention of millions by her statements. She became one of the staunchest advocates of a Jewish nation in Israel, argued vigorously for civil rights, and spoke forcefully against the witch-hunts of McCarthyism, attacking General Dwight Eisenhower when he failed to defend his friend George Marshall from Senator McCarthy's smears. Although Eisenhower did not reappoint her to the United Nations when he became president in 1953, she continued to work tirelessly through the American Association for the United Nations to mobilize public support for international cooperation. She also gave unstintingly of her time to the election campaigns in 1952 and 1956 of her dear friend Adlai Stevenson, a man who brought to politics a wit and sophistication Roosevelt always admired.

It was the private sphere, though, that remained most precious. "The people I love," ER wrote her friend and physician David Gurewitsch, "mean more to me than all the public things. . . . I only do the public things because there are a few close people whom I love dearly and who matter to me above everything else. There are not so many of them and you are now one of them." Gurewitsch was a constant companion after she met him in 1947. She traveled with him to Europe, mothered him, and depended upon him for devotion and nurturance. Some even thought he was her lover.

The same kind of relationship—perhaps even deeper—existed with Joe Lash, the young man from the American Student Union whom she had met in the late 1930s. Lash, too, became an intimate companion, spending evenings with her in her New York apartment and weeks at a time at Hyde Park. "I love to be with you dear boy," Eleanor wrote. "I never want to be alone when I'm with people I love." She brought him presents, corresponded with him almost daily, and looked forward eagerly to times when they could be together. "Do come up whenever you are free," she wrote Lash. "I'll be at the house soon after six waiting to both kiss and spank you and I would love it if you have nothing else that calls, to have you stay the night. It will be nice to tuck you in and say goodnight on your birthday!" With Lash too, she seemed to find a maternal role that had been absent in her relationship with most of her own children. "A little bit of my heart seems to be with you always Joe," she wrote during the war. Eleanor became deeply involved in Lash's love affair with Trude Pratt, doing all in her power to bring them together, to erase misunderstandings between them, and to make it possible for them to find the happiness in marriage that had eluded her and Franklin. Tragically, her involvement with Lash led to one of the most bizarre and disgraceful episodes of the war. Because of Lash's involvement with the American Student Union, he was suspected of being procommunist and was placed under counterintelligence surveillance during the war. Letters between the two were opened by government agents, and even the first lady's hotel room was bugged when she went to visit Lash. As a result of such surveillance, government spies made the unfounded allegation that she and Lash were having an affair, and Lash—a soldier at the time—was sent to the Far East.

During her final two decades, Eleanor Roosevelt's children remained as much a trial as a comfort, with the possible exception of Anna. After Franklin's death, Eleanor lived at Val-Kill with Malvina Thompson, her secretary, and her son Elliott and his family. Anna and Elliott were both involved in radio and TV programs with their mother, while James and Franklin entered politics in California and New York. Among her children, only John carried out a life totally on his own. More often than not, family gatherings degenerated into bitter arguments. It was the grandchildren who brought joy—the grandchildren, old friends like Lash and Gurewitsch, and new friends like Allard Lowenstein and his young compatriots in the National Student Association, whom Eleanor befriended during the late 1940s and for the rest of her life. With Lowenstein, as with Lash and Gurewitsch, she adopted a maternal role, providing a constant inspiration to another young reformer who would try to transform America through political and social action.

As she entered her eighth decade, Eleanor Roosevelt was applauded as the first lady of the world. Traveling to India, Japan, and the Soviet Union, she spoke for the best that was in America. Although she did not initially approve of John Kennedy and would have much preferred to see Adlai Stevenson nominated again, she lived to see the spirit of impatience and reform return to Washington. As if to prove that the fire of protest was still alive in herself, in 1962 Roosevelt sponsored hearings in Washington, D.C., where young civil-rights workers testified about the judicial and police harassment of black protestors in the South.

It was fitting that Eleanor Roosevelt's last major official office should be to chair President Kennedy's Commission on the Status of Women. More than anyone else of her generation, her life came to exemplify the political expertise and personal autonomy that were abiding themes of the first women's rights movement. Eleanor Roosevelt had not been a militant feminist. Like most social reformers, she publicly rejected the Equal Rights Amendment of the National Woman's Party until the early 1950s, believing that it would jeopardize protective labor legislation for women then on the statute books. Never an enthusiastic supporter of the ERA, neither she nor JFK's commission recommended the amendment. In addition, she accepted the popular argument during the Great Depression that, at least temporarily, some married women would have to leave the labor force in order to give the unemployed a better chance. At times, she also accepted male-oriented definitions of fulfillment. "You are successful," she wrote in a 1931 article, "when your husband feels that he has been a success and that life has been worthwhile."

But on the issue of women's equality, as in so many other areas, Eleanor Roosevelt most often affirmed the inalienable right of the human spirit to grow and seek fulfillment. Brought up amid anti-Semitic and antiblack attitudes, she had transcended her past to become one of the strongest champions of minority rights. Once opposed to suffrage, she grew to exemplify women's aspirations for a full life in politics. Throughout, she demonstrated a capacity for change grounded in a compassion for those who were victims.

There was, in fact, a direct line from Marie Souvestre's advocacy of intellectual independence to Eleanor Roosevelt's involvement in the settlement house, to her subsequent embrace of women's political activism in the 1920s and 1930s, and to her final role as leader of the Commission on the Status of Women. She had personified not only the right of women to act as equals with men in the political sphere, but the passion of social activists to ease pain, alleviate suffering, and affirm solidarity with the unequal and disenfranchised of the world.

On November 7, 1962, Eleanor Roosevelt died at home from a rare form of bone-marrow tuberculosis. Just twenty years earlier, she had written that all individuals must discover for themselves who they are and what they want from life. "You can never really live anyone else's life," she wrote, "not even your child's. The influence you exert is through your own life and what you've become yourself." Despite disappointment and tragedy, Eleanor Roosevelt had followed her own advice and because of it had affected the lives of millions. Although her daughter Anna concluded that Eleanor, throughout her life, suffered from depression, she had surely tried—and often succeeded—through her public advocacy of the

oppressed and her private relationships with friends to find some measure
of fulfillment and satisfaction.

"What other single human being," Adlai Stevenson asked at Eleanor
Roosevelt's memorial service, "has touched and transformed the existence
of so many? . . . She walked in the slums and ghettos of the world, not on
a tour of inspection . . . but as one who could not feel contentment when
others were hungry." Because of her life, millions of others experienced a
new sense of possibility. It would be difficult to envision a more enduring
or important legacy.

SOURCES

The Eleanor Roosevelt Papers at the Franklin Delano Roosevelt Library, Hyde Park, New York, represent the most comprehensive collection of material available. Of particular interest are her correspondence
with Walter White of the NAACP, material about her family, especially
her father, and drafts of articles and lectures. Other relevant collections at
Hyde Park are the papers of Mary (Molly) Dewson, Hilda Worthington
Smith, and Lorena Hickok; the papers of the Women's Division of the
Democratic National Committee; and those of Anna Roosevelt Halstead.
Several collections at the Schlesinger Library, Radcliffe College, bear
directly on Eleanor Roosevelt's life: see especially the papers of Mary
Anderson, Mary Dewson, Mary Dreier, and Ellen Woodward. Of
Eleanor Roosevelt's own writings the most valuable are *This I Remember*
(New York, 1949); *This Is My Story* (New York, 1937); *Autobiography* (New
York, 1961); and *It's Up To The Women* (New York, 1933). She also wrote a
monthly column, "If You Ask Me," for the *Ladies Home Journal* from June
1941 to spring 1949 and in *McCall's* after 1949. The best place to begin
reading about her is Joseph Lash's excellent two-volume biography,
Eleanor and Franklin (New York, 1971) and *Eleanor: The Years Alone* (New
York, 1972). On Lash's personal relationship with Roosevelt, see *Love,
Eleanor: Eleanor Roosevelt and Her Friends* (New York, 1982). Other books
that cast light on the Roosevelt family include James Roosevelt, *My Parents: A Differing View* (Chicago, 1976) and Elliott Roosevelt with James
Brough, *An Untold Story: The Roosevelts of Hyde Park* (New York, 1973),
both of which offer personal views by the Roosevelt children. Even more
revealing is Bernard Asbell, ed., *Mother and Daughter: The Letters of Eleanor
and Anna Roosevelt* (New York, 1982).

Elisabeth Israels Perry

Training for Public Life:
ER and Women's Political
Networks in the 1920s

I N 1921 AN ATTACK of poliomyelitis scuttled Franklin Roosevelt's
hopes for a political career. Fearing that her husband would now lose all
interest in politics, his wife Eleanor looked for ways both to sustain his
interest and to keep the family name in the public eye. New York City
women's political organizations, of which a goodly number existed in the
postsuffrage era, were the obvious choice. Of the several she joined, three
stand out as most important to her: the League of Women Voters, which
educated voters and encouraged them to participate in the electoral process; the Women's Division of the Democratic State Committee, which
transmitted the concerns of women to the platform committees and
mobilized women party workers; and the Women's City Club, a civic
group founded in 1915 at the climax of the women's suffrage movement to
teach women how to influence political decision making. In the Women's
Division, she strengthened ties formed in the 1920 campaign with other
women Democrats. But the league and the club were nonpartisan, attracting between them thousands of women, from a variety of political camps,
who shared reform goals. Thus, by the time Franklin ran for office again
in 1928, Eleanor had met and worked closely with a large number of
politically conscious women, providing herself with a network of friends
and acquaintances she would draw on the rest of her life.

The Women's City Club offered Eleanor numerous opportunities for
leadership between 1924 and 1928. The least well known of the three
organizations she joined, it provides a unique insight into her formative
years as a public figure. Unlike the other organizations, which had limited

or partisan aims, the club investigated, debated, and then championed a broad spectrum of civic and social causes. Eleanor's relationship to its agenda helps us understand the political commitments she formed during these crucial years. It also shows how work within the women's network of New York City, by increasing her effectiveness as a political activist, trained her for the public life that was to come.

In the latter decades of the nineteenth century, large numbers of urban women formed clubs. The clubs had varying purposes, but they attracted women chiefly for the opportunities of companionship, self-improvement, and philanthropic work that they offered. During the early part of the twentieth century, some women began to look at clubs as a means of furthering specific causes. The political education of women, a concern becoming more urgent as women's suffrage seemed imminent, motivated a group of one hundred New York City suffragists to found a city club for women. Their goal was to educate members about civic and social issues of importance, teach them how government worked and how they might influence it, and orchestrate publicity and lobbying campaigns for the issues the club wished to advocate.

Once underway, the club offered some unexpected benefits. Like men's clubs, the women's club fostered the creation of networks of friendship and support that often crossed partisan lines. The networks turned out to be useful in the women's business, professional, and political lives. A second benefit was leadership experience. In mixed-gender associations, women seldom held positions of authority and usually received only token seats on committees. In single-sex clubs, where the gender issue was moot, the only criteria for holding office were the time and ability to perform club duties.

Eleanor Roosevelt profited from both of these benefits. Through the club she met a large number of politically conscious women and gained experience investigating issues and monitoring legislative action. But she did not join the club knowing these benefits would result. Rather, she considered clubs essential to women's education as voters. To a reporter in 1924, she observed that men's clubs "aren't organized for nothing." Clubs mean "getting together and learning who's who and what's what. It's harder to do that with women," she confessed, "but something akin to it must be done." Her reason was that women, even those with important welfare- or social-work positions, seldom knew how to get into "political harness." They must be shown that the thing to which they are lending all their time and efforts could be vastly speeded up by legislative action. A man knows that instinctively. If he wants something done, he'll go to his political club and talk about it, or he will write to his Congressman. A woman will organize a social or welfare group, and when that is done she will ask her husband if he can't get political pressure to bear upon her work. The vote is an unwieldy tool in her hands.

"Get into the game and stay in it," she urged women. "Throwing mud from the outside won't help. Building up from the inside will."

The founders of the Women's City Club came from backgrounds similar to Eleanor Roosevelt's: middle- to upper-class, capable of paying $120 and an initiation fee to establish the club's treasury. Later members, over eight hundred by February 1916, paid substantially less, but the amounts still limited membership to the white middle classes. In fact, although the club did not officially exclude nonwhites, for a short time it followed contemporary prejudices by limiting membership to "native-born" women. Probably the fees and dues alone would have discouraged recent immigrants from joining.

At first the club could afford only to lease a suite of rooms in the Vanderbilt Hotel as headquarters. When membership soared to three thousand after the 1917 New York election gave women the vote, the club leased, with an option to buy, an entire mansion on the corner of Thirty-fifth Street and Park Avenue. Designed by architect Stanford White, the house boasted a grand marble foyer in the Empire style and four stories of large rooms, some oval, for offices, lounges, dining, and meeting. Two years later the club bought the house for $160,000, an investment that doubled in value by 1927.

The club was determined not to be a mere social gathering place. Defined as "a civic center for women interested in municipal affairs," its interests also encompassed state and national affairs when these touched the city or women. Its first committees illustrate the range: courts, labor, city finance, housing and city planning, legislation, public safety, recreation, and social welfare. Over time, the relative importance of these committees changed. In 1916, for example, during a bitter strike in the garment industry, the labor committee, chaired by Cornelia Bryce Pinchot (wife of conservationist Gifford Pinchot), dominated club concerns. At this time the club and the Women's Trade Union League established a strong relationship, one that continued when Mary Dreier and Eleanor Roosevelt, WTUL activists, joined the club, and when in 1924 Ethel Dreier, Mary's sister-in-law, became club president.

In 1917, when the United States went to war, women's contributions to national defense came to the fore of the club's agenda, as reconstruction issues did afterward. During the early 1920s, Belle Moskowitz, an active club member then working for Democratic Governor Alfred E. Smith, got the club interested in Smith's proposals for restructuring the state administration. The club's legislation committee stayed with this issue until the proposals were implemented many years later. During the Red Scare of the early 1920s, when state legislators refused to seat duly elected socialist assemblymen and then required loyalty oaths from teachers, the club's education committee championed civil rights. And in 1924, aroused by reports of danger to young women in the city's popular dance halls, the club's recreation committee received wide publicity from a comprehensive exposé that suggested remedial legislation.

In addition to committee work, the club organized debates involving political candidates of all major parties at almost every city, state, and national election. These were well attended and widely reported in the press. The club sponsored debates, sometimes heated, on what were then seen as special "women's issues": a forty-eight-hour work week for women, the Equal Rights Amendment, child labor laws, and the dissemination of information about birth control. To facilitate lobbying in the city government, club members ran a course of lectures on how city departments worked. The better to monitor city affairs, the club organized itself into aldermanic districts corresponding to those of the city. By the fall of 1921, all this work had become too much for volunteers, and an executive staff was hired to coordinate it.

The club did not lack social amenities, although socializing was usually seen as an adjunct of more serious matters. Men had access to the dining rooms as guests of members and accompanied their spouses to receptions and meals honoring specific individuals or organized around debates. One board of directors' meeting in 1922 discussed whether the club should serve its members' noncivic needs, perhaps by arranging the purchasing of small items through the club, holding discussions of how to raise children, opening a hair dressing concession, or hiring a professional shopper and professional mender for busy career women. These ideas were not pursued: the club's leaders seemed too firmly committed to public affairs to allow more frivolous demands to distract them.

Some members, it is true, were not so interested in public affairs. Ida Reid Blair, former suffragist, businesswoman, and the club's field secretary in 1920, admitted as much when she told a reporter that many of the club's members had only "barely developed civic interests." But no one became a club leader, or stayed in the leadership for long, who lacked a background in civic affairs or a desire to learn more about them. In addition to suffragists such as Mary Garrett Hay, president of the club from 1918 to 1924, and union organizers such as Mary Dreier, professional women or women whose husbands were well known in New York City civic life dominated the board of directors and the offices. Among the early leaders were Dr. Katharine B. Davis, former city corrections commissioner; Frances Perkins, consumer activist and labor reformer; Belle Moskowitz, industrial counselor and publicist; Lillian Wald and Mary Simkhovitch, settlement-house leaders; Sadie American and Rebekah Kohut, leaders in the Council of Jewish Women; Bertha Rembaugh, lawyer; Maude Miner, probation expert; Josephine Goldmark, factory investigator; Marcia Mead, architect active in neighborhood preservation; Martha Draper, Red Cross official and education expert; Mina Bruère, charity organizer and bank manager; Rev. Marie Jenney Howe, Unitarian minister and lecturer; Virginia Gildersleeve, dean of Barnard College; Ida Tarbell, journalist; and Helen Rogers Reid, advertising manager for the *Herald Tribune*. Many of them, like Eleanor Roosevelt, had access to men of influence: Goldmark to her brother-in-law Justice Louis D. Brandeis; Bruère to her brother Henry Bruère, a founder of the Bureau of Municipal Research and a government official; Howe to her husband Frederic, a social reformer who was then immigration commissioner under President Wilson; Reid to her husband Ogden, publisher of the *Herald Tribune*. Of the women known more through their husbands' names than their own— for example, the wives of Judge Learned Hand, diplomat and financier Willard D. Straight, writers Ernest Poole and Walter Weyl, and lawyer, social worker, and political activist Raymond Vail Ingersoll—most had a particular specialty that made them prominent. Mrs. Weyl, for example, worked in the field of women's employment; Mrs. Ingersoll helped Margaret Sanger establish her programs in birth-control research.

These were all accomplished, widely known women, many of them professionals, the rest experienced volunteer activists. In 1928 club records show that among the 2,000–2,500 members were 194 teachers; 145 secretaries; 86 social workers; 73 writers; 36 editors; 35 office managers; 33 nurses; 27 physicians; 24 advertising agents; 23 lawyers; 21 each of librarians, lecturers, and artists; 18 interior decorators; 16 each of buyers and musicians; 15 institution managers; 14 each of government inspectors and insurance brokers; 12 each of bankers, dieticians, and personnel workers; 11 designers; and a handful of psychologists, actresses, architects, dentists, engineers, sculptors, real estate agents, saleswomen, office workers, researchers, importers, statisticians, printers, accountants, professional shoppers, and photographers. Some of the city's "most distinguished women," many of them involved in almost every "useful calling or profession open to women," were active members, the club boasted in a quarterly *Bulletin* of October 1928. Including a miscellaneous category of 24, the total number of professional or business women came to 982, almost 40 percent of the total membership. This made the club a lively and interesting place to be, but it also meant that most of the club's organizational work would have to fall upon the executive staff and the volunteers who had more leisure time.

One of these was Eleanor Roosevelt. Elected to the board of directors in May 1924, she immediately assumed a major role. Her first assignment was to direct the new City Planning Department, which coordinated three club committees—housing, transit, and parks and playgrounds. The committees were lumped together because each concerned an aspect of the struggle to maintain decent living standards in the city. Each gave rise to thorny issues. What should be the future of New York's Transit Commission? Should the Staten Island tunnel be open only to rapid transit? Whose land should be condemned for parks? Should parks be used for special memorials that took up precious space? How should New York's inefficient, costly, congested terminal market system be reorganized? Each question had to be researched and discussed before the club took a position. In some cases, club committees never reached agreement. Roosevelt felt keenly frustrated, for example, by the transit committee, which, although ably led by Mabel Newcomer who came down from Vassar College for its meetings, could never make up its mind to endorse a solution.

The complexity of these civic issues may be demonstrated by the city's housing problems, discussed frequently in club meetings while Eleanor Roosevelt chaired the City Planning Department. City welfare workers had long warned of a crisis in housing for the poor. Industrialization and increased immigration had driven up urban land values, forcing workers into congested ghettos of substandard housing. In the final decades of the previous century, city housing reformers and welfare workers had persuaded lawmakers to pass tenement-house laws. Designed to improve the quality of cheap apartment buildings, these laws drove building costs even higher and discouraged builders from investing in low-yield housing ventures. By the turn of the century, housing reformers were suggesting new ways to meet the shortage of city dwellings. They asked the state to finance tax exemptions and low-cost loans to builders who promised to put up workers' homes. But opposition to increasing the public tax burden to house the poor was so strong that efforts along these lines had little success before World War I.

The war caused housing conditions to worsen, as people moved into the city and the housing industry slumped. When the war ended, city rents skyrocketed, and a crisis was formally declared. One agency that tried to deal with the crisis was Governor Al Smith's Reconstruction Commission, a group of experts addressing postwar problems and formulating Smith's legislative policies. Belle Moskowitz, active in the Women's City Club, had established and administered the group. She brought its housing program to the club for endorsement and support.

While other agencies, such as New York Mayor Hylan's Committee on Rent Profiteering, grappled with the results of the housing crisis, Moskowitz's Reconstruction Commission took a new look at earlier housing reform ideas that attacked the causes. The commission argued that the state would have to intervene by extending credit to builders, allowing municipalities the right to buy and develop lands for housing, and setting up local and statewide boards to study and coordinate regional housing policies. In addition, the commission said, the state should encourage privately funded, "limited-dividend" corporations to finance large-scale, architecturally sound housing projects on lands near the city.

Some of these ideas are still controversial today, but many have been tried, and some have worked well. In the 1920s, New York's Republican-dominated legislature branded them "socialistic." Nonetheless, the Women's City Club took a strong stand in their favor. Early in 1924, before Eleanor Roosevelt took over the club's City Planning Department, the club's housing committee endorsed a state bill to extend credit through community housing corporations to builders planning projects for low-income renters. In May, the club mounted a widely publicized exhibit on an Astoria housing project being built by the City Housing Corporation. This corporation, modeled on an earlier version inspired by the Reconstruction Commission, raised money to loan at low interest to innovative builders. In 1925, Eleanor Roosevelt extended the club's efforts to support these projects. First, she organized a club meeting on the theme of regional planning in New York City, inviting Walter Stabler, from the Metropolitan Life Insurance Company, and Clarence Stein, an architect who had been housing adviser to the Reconstruction Commission and was in 1925 chairman of the State Commission on Housing and Regional Planning (recently approved by the legislature). These men debated the wisdom of providing state funding for mortgages on new apartments renting at only nine to ten dollars a room per month. Later that spring, Roosevelt led a delegation to an international congress on town, city, and regional planning. As her final effort she organized a club luncheon at which nine speakers discussed fire hazards in low-income homes being built on Long Island, where city codes did not yet apply.

Other, equally complex issues engaged Eleanor Roosevelt's time. Long a supporter of protective labor legislation for women and children, she was deeply committed to a forty-eight-hour work week. On January 31, 1924, the Women's City Club formally launched a campaign, which was to last for years, to reduce weekly working hours for women. Sara Conboy of the United Textile Workers and Frances Perkins spoke, arguing that a shorter day would mean "better motherhood and stronger women." They condemned the Equal Rights Amendment being proposed by the National Woman's Party on the ground that it would jeopardize protective legislation. A year later, the battle for shorter hours was still not won. Representing both the Women's City Club and the League of Women Voters, Roosevelt and Glendolen T. Bens went to Albany to testify on the hours bill. The hearing was stormy. Opponents warned that, if the law did not apply to men, women would lose their jobs. Speaking for the proponents, Eleanor Roosevelt argued that women, on whom future generations depended, needed government protection from inhumane conditions no matter what the cost. She also assured women that if they worked shorter hours their wages would not be reduced. Exactly how such an assurance could be made was not clear. Moreover, women continued to fear that shorter hours would make them less desirable employees than men. In the end, an hours bill passed that the Women's City Club had to oppose. Called the "Joiner" bill, it established fifty-four hours as the standard and empowered the Industrial Board to shorten work hours "under exceptional circumstances." Speaking for the club, Ethel Dreier urged Governor Smith to veto it on the basis that an Industrial Board that could shorten hours could also lengthen them. The bill, she said, was but a "gesture to stifle the accusation of broken [Republican] party pledges." Smith agreed, and in his veto of the bill called for a "real" forty-eight-hour bill and an end to such attempts to "hoodwink" the public.

While working hours and equal rights divided women bitterly in the 1920s, on another major issue—government inefficiency—there was more agreement. Here, too, Eleanor Roosevelt found the club to be a forum for her views and a school in which she learned many valuable lessons. Since the Civil War, the multiplication of state governmental duties had led to the creation of innumerable agencies, without either a master plan or a rational order to how these agencies related to one another or to the executive. By the turn of the century, New York's government—like the governments of many other states—was a hodgepodge of agencies, boards, bureaus, councils, departments, and commissions—many with redundant or overlapping jurisdictions, some permanent, others temporary, often with unclear lines of authority. Officials sometimes held terms longer than the governor's or were responsible to authorities not under the governor's control. Yet, when trouble arose, all looked to the governor to resolve it. Worse, the New York governor enjoyed only a two-year term, and the legislature controlled the budget almost completely.

The rising costs of government caused administrative reformers to argue that a more efficient structure would save money. A Constitutional Convention in 1915 proposed a reorganization plan that drastically reduced the number of state departments, rationalized their relationship to the executive, lengthened the governor's term to four years, and proposed an executive budget. But the plan, attached to a constitution the voters disliked, failed in the referendum. When Al Smith came to power in 1919, he asked his Reconstruction Commission to advise on reorganization. Under the leadership of Robert Moses, later to become one of Smith's closest associates and builder of the state's great parks and highways system, the commission produced a plan very similar to that of 1915. Once again, the ubiquitous Mrs. Moskowitz brought it to the Women's City Club for support.

From the end of 1919 until the reorganization plan was implemented—a process that began in 1926 and was not completed until the new constitution of 1937—the Women's City Club was one of its strongest advocates. In 1924, the club circularized every state assemblyman, asking that the executive budget and four-year term be passed. A year later, with Republicans locking up the relevant bills in committee, the club held a debate between Governor Smith and his lieutenant-governor, Seymour Lowman, a Republican. When Lowman accused Smith of trying to spend money like King John before Magna Carta, Smith retorted in a way he was fond of: "Behold the king of Oliver Street," he said, looking down at himself and recalling memories of his humble origins on the city's Lower East Side. After bringing down the house, he displayed a carefully constructed exhibit to show, in graphic terms, how budget reorganization would improve government efficiency. This debate made front-page news.

After becoming chair of the club's legislation committee in December 1926, Eleanor Roosevelt made passage of the reorganization plan her first order of business. In the previous fall's elections, the proposed reduction of state agencies had finally been approved, thanks largely to bipartisan advocacy led by former Governor Charles Evans Hughes, a Republican. By then, an executive budget had become less controversial: Hughes had arranged for a budget department in the executive's office, and a constitutional amendment limiting the legislature's budgetary role seemed assured of passage. Less assured was an amendment that gave the governor a four-year term, the elections occurring in presidential years. As much as he wanted the governor's term lengthened, Smith opposed the amendment on the ground that major national and state issues ought to be kept separate. Republicans favored it because traditionally they did better in presidential years, when more rural voters went to the polls.

Shortly before the fall 1927 elections, Eleanor Roosevelt dove into the thick of this controversy. She agreed to public debates with two Republican women from the City Club, Ruth Baker Pratt, first woman alderman of New York City and soon to become the state's first woman representative to Congress, and Pauline Morton Sabin, a Republican national committeewoman and later prominent antiprohibitionist. Both debates were widely covered in the press. Eleanor Roosevelt debated Pratt at the club headquarters. Pratt argued that electing a governor in a nonpresidential-election year effectively disfranchised rural voters, who, because of the long distances they must travel to the polls, tended to vote only in national elections. Roosevelt scoffed at this reasoning. If rural voters could drive ten miles every four years, they certainly could do so every two, she answered, especially when they thought nothing of driving that far to go to a movie. Major issues ought not to be lumped together, she added. It was for this reason that mayoral and gubernatorial elections had been separated, and no one had objected to that.

ER's debate against Sabin took place close to election day and over the radio. The arguments were similar, Sabin asserting that a presidential-year election would result in more voters because employers were more likely to let their workers go to the polls for a national election. Roosevelt responded with a plea not for *more* voters but for better-informed voters. After this debate, the radio station that carried it took in calls and letters to determine who won. Sabin was the victor, although Democrats called foul when stories circulated of Republican woman jamming the phone lines in an organized campaign to defeat the Democratic champion.

Housing, women's working hours, and state reorganization were only three of many issues of the 1920s that Eleanor Roosevelt studied, debated, and fought for through the Women's City Club and other women's groups. Another was child labor laws, opposed by those who thought they interfered unduly in the relation between employer and employee. Both Republican and Democratic women joined in this struggle, making it a perfect issue for Women's City Club action. Eleanor Roosevelt was at first reluctant to take a strong stand. In 1924 she had called herself a "compromiser," one who preferred to "let things go" rather than "make a fight." By 1928 *that* Eleanor Roosevelt was gone. As Women's City Club board member, she had organized large meetings, chaired board meetings, headed an important committee, studied reams of documents on major issues, and testified several times to Albany legislators. She also got her husband to write an article in the club's quarterly bulletin concerning the Democratic party's position on the tariff. In April 1925 she made her radio debut in a speech publicizing the club's activities. In this speech she called the club a "clearing house for civic ideals" to which women could turn for guidance in public matters. Most impressive was the club's practice of representing in its forums both sides of political questions and of sending members into the field to make firsthand observations of conditions. She cited the widely publicized dance-hall report, written by members who did not just investigate but actually participated in dance-hall activities to get at the truth of conditions there. By keeping an open mind, she said, club members had discovered the "fascination" and the "dangers" to girls who went to dance halls; they also noted the surprisingly "low percentage of disaster . . . in spite of unwholesome surroundings."

In recognition of her various services, the club elected Eleanor its first vice-president in May 1925. When club activities resumed after their usual summer hiatus, the pace of her efforts accelerated. Once again, she chaired meetings, represented the club to other organizations (such as the New York Council for International Cooperation to Prevent War), and helped prepare the annual spring meeting and elections for 1926. By then, she was chair of the club's civic affairs committee, an intermediate step for her between the City Planning Department and the legislation committee that she officially took over in December 1926.

Legislation was a large committee, the one that best represented the spectrum of views in the club. Consisting of the president and former president *ex officio* (Dreier and Hay), two members from the board of directors, and six members-at-large, it also seated two representatives from each "civic" committee, that is, corrections, education, public health, housing, industry, recreation, and city affairs. By sitting on the legislation committee, members of the committees could watch over bills introduced in Albany or New York that pertained to their topics, but would not have to pursue them on their own. The legislation committee would coordinate this work, selecting and rating those bills the club as a whole wished to support, oppose, reendorse, reoppose, or abandon. During the legislative session, the committee met every Monday, a considerable commitment to ask of volunteers. Once the committee decided on action, it had to submit all communications, lobbying plans, and publicity releases to either the board or its officers for approval. The committee also regularly informed the entire club membership of its plans and actions.

In spite of the club's nonpartisan nature, Eleanor Roosevelt did not hesitate to alter its 1927 legislative program to reflect Democratic party biases, as is evident from a comparison of this program before and after she became chair of legislation. The program she inherited listed the following bills for support: stricter regulation of child marriages (requiring judicial and parental consent for girls under sixteen); a "hasty" marriage bill (if under twenty-one, partners must wait five days); extension of the merit system in highly paid education appointments; and government reorganization. While opposing contraventions of the child labor laws, it reendorsed tenement fire-retardation regulations, abolition of the State Motion Picture Commission, restoration of the direct nomination of party candiates for statewide and Supreme Court offices, and the right of women to serve on juries. It reopposed permission to minors between fourteen and sixteen to go to school at night; abolition of voter literacy tests; compulsory instruction in United States history, the Constitution, civic duties, and patriotism; and proof of freedom from venereal disease before a marriage license would be issued.

In her first report (March 1927) as committee chair, Roosevelt took a different tack. She began by observing that very little was happening at Albany. The legislative personnel had changed little since the previous year, and Republicans still kept their majority in both houses. "What will happen during the few remaining weeks of the . . . session is largely a matter for hope and conjecture," she wrote, clearly without any great enthusiasm. She then introduced not the bipartisan program of her predecessors, but a list of five areas dear to only some Republicans but to many Democrats. First was the need to oppose allowing the four-year-term governor to be elected during presidential years. This "frankly favors the Republican party," she wrote, and should be "defeated in order that the way may be cleared for a fairer measure." The measure would put the election into an off year, "when state issues are not confused by consideration of national affairs and there are better chances for unbiased decisions." Secondly, she warned that "the annual drive to force the GOP to carry out its forty-eight hour week campaign pledges" might result in the club's accepting a compromise recommended by the Industrial Survey Commission. This permitted a week of forty-nine and one-half hours for working women and minors, with a possible seventy-eight hours of overtime during a year. The difficulty of enforcing such a measure, however, led Roosevelt to warn that the club's industry committee would have to watch it "with sharp and untiring interest." Roosevelt's third area of concern was the executive budget and making the governor head of the executive department of the state. This she merely mentioned, passing on to the fourth area—a "particularly vicious" item—the Truman-Miller bill, which threatened to lower the minimum working age of boys from fourteen to twelve and allow them to work until 8 p.m. on days when school attendance was not required. "Too many evasions of the child labor laws are possible now," Roosevelt warned. This bill entailed "a most regrettable backward step." Finally, the yearly "crop" of bills seeking to weaken the continuation-school law must be defeated. These "lessen the opportunities for children who must work to receive further schooling."

Roosevelt's program contained several of the bipartisan issues agreed upon the previous year, but ignored others and put the emphasis clearly on Democratic goals. Her next report (June 1927), considerably toned down, reflected the club's broader interests. She listed eight bills the club as a whole had supported, half of which had become law or been passed to be sent to the voters for referendum. The latter included the "hasty" marriage and executive budget bills, and another increasing workmen's weekly compensation for disability. Bills that failed included a stricter continuation-school bill, the extension of the merit system into educational appointments, child marriage, and the off-year election of the governor. Of the bills the club opposed, the Truman-Miller bill failed, and a compromise forty-eight-hour bill passed, a "step in the right direction," Roosevelt wrote, but by no means a battle won. All in all, she found the session disappointing and not meriting any particular elation. Still, the partisan language of her first report was now totally gone, suggesting that she had been criticized or had realized herself that such tendentiousness was out of place.

Eleanor Roosevelt's last year of active work at the Women's City Club was 1928. By the fall, her husband was running for governor, and New York's Governor Smith was running an uphill, and finally futile, race for the presidency. At year's start, however, other issues seemed more important, although, with one exception, not particularly dramatic. Roosevelt's legislation committee, "with painstaking care," had selected eight bills to support that spring: the child marriage bill; a dwellings bill, providing more light and air for apartments in large cities; an occupational diseases bill, extending workmen's compensation to cover disabling diseases contracted through employment; the merit bill in educational appointments, covering those that carried permanent tenure and high salaries; two bills correcting "vicious" special laws affecting salaries and promotions in a bureau of the Education Department; a bill making voter registration more convenient; and, the dramatic exception, a birth-control bill amending the Penal Law to allow physicians to dispense contraceptive information to any married person.

This last was dramatic because the legislation committee decided to organize a club debate and referendum to determine the membership's wishes. No other issue had received such treatment. Two physicians were invited, Ira S. Wile, who had debated in favor of birth control at the club in 1916, and Charles A. Gordon, who spoke for the opposition. The contents of the debate, held on November 14, 1927, remained secret until the referendum results were published on January 5, 1928. A transcript is preserved in the club archives.

Wile opened by tracing the development of civilization from abortion and infanticide to the conscious control of conception. Abortion was a "horror" to him, but the mortality rates of illegally obtained abortions were equally horrifying. Man was not a "breeding" animal, he said. The desire to regulate the timing and number of offspring was natural; it was even encouraged in contemporary public-health pamphlets which, unfortunately, were not allowed to tell women how to do it. Although illegal, birth-control information, the "last step" in women's emancipation, was spreading on its own as mores and customs changed. Twenty years ago, Wile concluded, he could not have mentioned the word "sex" in a meeting of this kind; fifteen years ago he escaped arrest at a meeting in Boston's Faneuil Hall only by quoting Scripture.

Gordon's side of the argument stressed the theme that "Nature exacts an awful toll of those who interfere with its orderly processes, and payment is always exacted." He advised that while birth-control propaganda was now widespread, science should not leap to adopt its claims. The birth rate was already falling, prenatal care had improved, and giving birth was no longer the potentially frightening event of the past. Further, the claims for birth control had been exaggerated. Contraception had not prevented women from seeking abortions, contraceptive use in early life might lead to sterility, and no "absolutely safe and certain" method existed. If women knew the extent to which the medical profession opposed birth control, he concluded, they would wait.

Contemptuous of these arguments, Wile in his rebuttal pointed out that modern society had not lived "according to nature" for a long time. While professional medical organizations were against birth control, individual physicians were not. Admitting that medical treatments did sometimes fail, he urged his listeners not to give up on them and ended with an impassioned plea for "conscious procreation."

This plea had its desired effect on the club's membership, which overwhelmingly defeated Gordon in the mailed ballot. Their decision made press headlines throughout New York State, as well as across the nation. In many of these articles, Eleanor Roosevelt's photograph appeared as a "club leader." Whether she was pleased to be so identified in such a controversial decision, she did not say, but she did remark in her next committee report that the publicity helped the club gather support for its program.

Eleanor Roosevelt published her last committee report in the club's

Bulletin for June 1928. She praised the committee members for a faithfulness that surprised her in light of the legislature's lackluster year. Sadly, not a single bill supported by the club had passed: neither voter registration nor child marriage; not dwellings, birth control, occupational diseases, or appointments according to merit. Roosevelt urged the club to take a more active interest in city affairs. The club should retain its interest in state bills, she said, but it could accomplish more by "closer contact with city problems." To this end, the club had asked the League of Women Voters representative who attended city hall sessions to share her reports with the club.

In her two years as chair of the legislation committee, Eleanor Roosevelt had worked with women outstanding in the public service tradition of her day. Several were lawyers, a profession barely open to women and thus attracting particularly hardy, committed types. Caroline Klein Simon, a Republican activist in the League of Women Voters, became a New York secretary of state and a judge in the state court of claims. Bertha Rembaugh, a Republican active in the Progressive party in 1912, was the first woman to run for a municipal judgeship (1919); she remained active in politics as an expert in prohibition enforcement and water power. Dorothy Kenyon, a left-wing Democrat, fought discrimination against women throughout her life in active association with the League of Women Voters, the National Woman's Party, and the American Civil Liberties Union.

Susan Brandeis, the Supreme Court justice's daughter, had been a suffragist in Boston, argued before the Supreme Court (1925), and then was a special assistant in the United States District Attorney's office for the Southern District of New York. Two physicians, Eleanor Conover and Helen Montague, brought, respectively, expertise on hospital administration and children's mental health to the club's public health campaigns. Mary (Molly) Dewson, involved in Democratic party politics, already had enjoyed a distinguished career in reforms to improve the lives of working women and children. Dewson had come to the club as civic secretary in 1924, keeping the post for only a year but doing the best job ever of organizing the club's work. Her successor, Clara Tead, wife of industrial expert Ordway Tead, eventually became a junior college dean and president. Grace H. Childs, wife of industrialist and civic leader Richard S. Childs, was treasurer of the Women's Trade Union League. Grace La Fetra, a businesswoman in real estate, developed through the club an interest in housing reform that led her, with Dorothy Rosenman, to found the National Committee on Housing. Maria L. Hoyt was chair of the Manhattan League of Women Voters. Katharine L. Potter was active in girls' club work. Harriet Townsend was a social worker and lecturer at Teachers College, Columbia University. Bertha Backus Brown, active in Brooklyn civic life, was the wife of Roscoe C. E. Brown, professor at the Columbia University School of Journalism. Protestant, Catholic, Jew; Democrat, Republican, Progressive, Prohibitionist; volunteer, professional—they were an impressive group who in spite of their differences worked together on issues of significance to them and their city.

In December 1928 Eleanor Roosevelt resigned her club positions and prepared to move to the governor's mansion in Albany. There, she expected to join the Albany Women's City Club and continue the same sort of work she had done before. The New York club begged her to stay even though she could not attend meetings; in January the board reluctantly accepted her departure. They feted her twice—once at a luncheon for her, Ruth Baker Pratt (just elected to Congress), and Edith Lehman, wife of the new lieutenant-governor, and later at an informal dinner. We have no transcript of these events, where the speeches and her responses formed a valedictory for an epoch in her life now closed. The newspapers reported only the first event, attended by seven hundred members and guests. Here, they focused on Congresswoman Pratt, whose accomplishments at the time must have appeared more outstanding (reelected in 1930, she was defeated in the Democratic landslide of 1932). Regarding Eleanor Roosevelt, the newspaper reported only that she reminded her clubmates to praise government officials when they did well, and not just to criticize them, a remark perhaps reflecting her new status as the wife of a newly elected governor.

In her memoir *This I Remember*, Eleanor Roosevelt calls the years 1921 to 1927 a "private interlude" for her and her family. The deceptiveness of this label should now be apparent. As a result of her experiences in the women's political networks of New York City, she had become an accomplished, widely known, and admired public figure in her own right.

SOURCES

The main sources for this essay are at the New York Women's City Club. They consist of bound copies of the club's executive board minutes, reports of the civic secretaries, occasional committee minutes, scrapbooks containing the club's quarterly bulletins, other ephemeral publications, and newspaper clippings. Original correspondence from the period has been destroyed. Newspapers, especially the *New York Times*, were a second major source. Material on New York legislative issues of the 1920s can be found in Gov. Alfred E. Smith, *Public Papers* (Albany, New York, 1920–28), and in the reports of his Reconstruction Commission of the State of New York. For a scholarly treatment of the Smith era in state politics see Paula Eldot, *Governor Alfred E. Smith: The Politician as Reformer* (New York, 1983).

Susan Ware

ER and Democratic Politics:
Women in the
Postsuffrage Era

ELEANOR ROOSEVELT STOOD futilely outside the door of a smoke-filled room in June 1924 at the Democratic national convention while the platform committee refused to consider a plank on women's issues that she had hoped would be endorsed. At the 1940 Democratic national convention, acting almost single-handedly, Eleanor Roosevelt calmed rebellious delegates and thereby assured the nomination of Henry A. Wallace as Franklin Roosevelt's vice-president. In 1920, Eleanor Roosevelt was so unknown as the wife of the Democratic vice-presidential candidate that a newspaper published a picture of another woman cropped from a Roosevelt family portrait, mistakenly identifying her as the candidate's wife. In 1956, now a person of international stature, Eleanor Roosevelt played a crucial role in Adlai E. Stevenson's nomination and run for the presidency.

In Eleanor Roosevelt's rise to national power and prominence, her participation in Democratic women's politics in the 1920s and 1930s proved especially important to her political education: these years served as an apprenticeship for the position of power she later wielded on the national and international scene in the 1940s and 1950s. On a broader level, Eleanor Roosevelt's activities in the interwar years also reflect the new political roles that women were playing in twentieth-century American life. Eleanor Roosevelt typifies the vanguard of women who entered political life after 1920 in the wake of the Nineteenth Amendment. Her career reflects the priorities that women brought to politics and government in the postsuffrage era and suggests how new entrants to the political arena

[46]

defined and maintained roles of their own. For Democratic and Republican women alike, the 1920s and 1930s represented a time of apprenticeship, of trying, often unsuccessfully, to make their voices heard on the state and national levels. But women were learning to play the political game too, and Eleanor Roosevelt is only the most outstanding example of women's expanding contributions to the tenor of public life in twentieth-century America.

What would women do once they had the vote? This was a weighty and highly charged question for American citizens in the 1910s and 1920s. Women and men alike had always seen politics as a male preserve. They associated the political process with male institutions such as the club, the saloon, the factory, and the docks, places where "ladies" would never dare to enter. That women now demanded access to this world was a radical notion indeed.

Equally unsettling were predictions about the changes that women would bring to the political process once they got the vote. Many politically ambitious women were certain that women's politics would be different from men's. Men, they argued, entered politics for selfish reasons such as the quest for power, publicity, and personal aggrandizement. Women, they argued, entered the political system to work for measures that would benefit their families, communities, and society as a whole. Women's distinctive approach to political participation was largely derived from traditional definitions of women's sensibilities and responsibilities. As Eleanor Roosevelt once said, "When all is said and done, women *are* different from men. They are equals in many ways, but they cannot refuse to acknowledge their differences."

To a certain degree, Eleanor Roosevelt's remarks are supported by the history of women's participation in American politics in the years after suffrage was obtained. Women's politics were often different from men's. For example, an issue-oriented approach to politics characterized women's political activity throughout this period. Furthermore, women established a tradition of working for their political goals not only through the two-party system but also through nonpartisan voluntary associations and reform groups. Eleanor Roosevelt worked in the League of Women Voters, the Women's Trade Union League, and the Women's City Club of New York concurrently with her extensive participation in women's Democratic politics in the 1920s. She did not draw great distinctions between these organizations: sometimes the Democratic party offered the best mechanism for accomplishing her goals, other times a nonpartisan group of concerned citizens was more effective.

Women also held a broader conception of the kinds of issues appropriately addressed by the political process than men ordinarily did. Instead of the usual political concerns—such as patronage or the location of new courthouses—women wanted the political system to tackle such issues as peace, an end to poverty, women's rights, education, the problems of youth, and social reform. Women derived this broader and more ambitious political agenda from their identification with the concerns of home and family which, broadly enough construed, could cover everything from pure milk and better sewers to job security, the minimum wage, and unemployment compensation. In many ways, the agenda that these women brought to politics in the postsuffrage era anticipated the larger role of the federal government that has become the hallmark of the modern welfare state.

At the base of this new issue-oriented approach to politics was a commitment to increased public interest and attention to the political questions of the day. This, of course, applied to male voters as well as female, but women wanted most of all to reach ordinary women who traditionally had not been interested in politics. The need for a concerned citizenry took on special force during the 1930s, but even before the Great Depression, women entering politics had hoped to move society toward a more humanitarian and socially interdependent viewpoint. "Perhaps," Eleanor Roosevelt commented, "we are going to see evolved in the next few years not only a social order built by the ability and brains of our men, but a social order which also represents the understanding heart of women." In her view, women constituted a vanguard for social change: "The attitude of women toward changes in society is going to determine to a great extent our future in this country. Women in the past have never realized their political strength. Will they wake up to it now?"

Eleanor Roosevelt's earliest experiences with partisan politics were hardly auspicious. Her participation in the 1920 campaign was limited to a month-long trip as the vice-presidential candidate's wife. She was the only woman on the campaign train, and she did little to hide her disapproval of the late-night card games and other male high jinks. The one saving grace of this trip was the beginning of her friendship with Louis Howe, one of

her husband's most trusted political advisers, who remained her loyal
supporter until his death in 1935. Howe saw something behind this shy
and lonely woman, and he imparted to her his practical knowledge of
politics: how to read a newspaper, how to write a good letter, how to give
a good speech. "Say what you have to say and sit down," he instructed his
willing pupil.

The Eleanor Roosevelt whom Howe tutored was a woman searching for
new directions, a quest that had begun even before her husband was
struck by infantile paralysis in the summer of 1921. Her casting about for
useful work took on new dimensions when, at Howe's insistence, she
became her husband's stand-in after 1921 in politics and public life. Somehow everyone (including ER) found it easier to deal with her widening
public activities when they were placed in the conventionally acceptable
framework of "doing it for her husband."

Eleanor Roosevelt always said that if women were going to succeed in
politics, they had to do it from the inside. Taking her own advice, she
devoted six years to the Women's Division of the State Democratic Committee of New York State. As finance chairman, she raised funds for the
Women's Division budget each year, giving Democratic women a valuable
financial independence to pursue their own goals. She helped to start and
edit a Democratic women's newspaper; she attended both state and national political conventions. At the request of Governor Al Smith, she
lobbied in Albany on issues of interest to Democratic women. Most far-
ranging of all was her organizing of women throughout New York. She
and Caroline O'Day divided the state in half each summer and visited
leaders in every county; since they switched every other year, Eleanor
soon had contacts with politicians throughout the state. Starting off with
the modest goal of serving as her husband's stand-in, by 1928 Eleanor
Roosevelt was a political personage in her own right. In fact, she was
probably better known among New York Democrats than her husband.

She still met disappointments, however. In 1924 Cordell Hull, chairman of the Democratic National Committee, asked Eleanor to head a
committee to submit planks from women's organizations to the Democratic national convention to be held in New York City that June. But the
convention delegates had so little interest in women's issues that the
planks were never formally put before the platform committee. Another
disappointment grew out of what at first seemed like a major break-
through: the winning of equal representation for women on all state

Democratic committees in 1926. The women soon found, however, that the real decisions were made not in open committees, but behind closed doors. Even though New York women had constructed the most effective women's political organization of any state in the country, they remained outsiders to real power.

Despite these setbacks, the experiences of Democratic women in New York foreshadowed the major outlines of women's politics for the next several decades. One of the most important lessons learned during this apprenticeship was the importance of grass-roots organization—something the suffrage movement had heavily stressed. Most of Eleanor Roosevelt's female co-workers in the Democratic party had worked in the women's suffrage campaign and were skilled in its techniques. Frances Perkins, a suffrage veteran who worked in state government under Al Smith in the 1920s, recognized the links between the suffrage campaign and women's politics: "The women's organizations around New York and in some other states too, with a hard core of the same group that were for suffrage, have followed the same methods of organizing wherever they have gone into politics. That is, they've done a grass-roots organizing job and haven't depended upon big, overall banners and slogans, although they haven't been ashamed to use them and have been perfectly able to get up a big meeting. But they have known that the real work was done in smaller meetings, in the house-to-house visitation, and in the organizing."

Such tactics, developed first in the women's suffrage campaign and then refined in the 1920s, had a great impact on women's politics during the New Deal: practically every one of Democractic leader Molly Dewson's innovations in the 1930s had its roots in New York in the previous decade or in women's suffrage. Personal contact with individual Democratic leaders, grass-roots organizing with an emphasis on small towns and rural areas, a newspaper to keep women informed, fact sheets at election time, and a commitment to year-round political organizing were staples of politics at the Women's Division of the State Democratic Committee in the 1920s long before they were used in the New Deal.

The New York experience in the 1920s also illustrates the interconnections and networks that often characterized women's approach to politics. Eleanor Roosevelt learned her way in public life from other women—Esther Lape and Elizabeth Read at the League of Women Voters, Rose Schneiderman and Nelle Swartz at the Women's Trade Union League, and Nancy Cook, Marion Dickerman, Elinor Morgenthau, and Caroline

O'Day in Democratic politics. Good friends as well as political associates, these women worked together on a broad agenda of reform issues, not just for the election of the next Democratic candidate. A good example of their cooperation was the Joint Legislative Conference, an informal coalition of women's organizations that pooled its lobbying efforts in Albany throughout the 1920s. As chair of this group during the mid-1920s, Eleanor Roosevelt lobbied for such causes as the minimum wage for women, an eight-hour day, and stronger child labor laws. She and her associates wanted to make the political system more responsive to the general welfare; partisan politics was but one means to this end.

The high point of Eleanor Roosevelt's early years in Democratic politics came during the 1928 presidential campaign, which also marked a turning point in her own political career. She had become so well known for her work in New York that Belle Moskowitz asked her to head women's work in the national campaign for Democratic presidential candidate Al Smith. Eleanor Roosevelt proved an excellent administrator and organizer, feeling entirely at home in the frantic atmosphere of the campaign. She threw herself into her work so completely that she could not participate in her husband's bid for the governorship of New York. How far things had come since Louis Howe had nudged Eleanor Roosevelt to serve as her husband's stand-in! Now she had her own political career.

Despite her efforts, the campaign did not produce a national Democratic victory at the polls in 1928. Franklin, on the other hand, narrowly won the New York election, immediately raising questions about Eleanor's future in politics. She had always insisted that once her husband's health permitted his return to politics, she would bow out. Yet the personal growth and satisfaction she had derived from her political work by 1928 made this clearly impossible. Instead, her political career went into a period that Joseph Lash has aptly characterized as "experimental adaptation." She resigned from the board of the Women's Division of the Democratic State Committee; she no longer gave political speeches or lobbied for civic organizations. But far from leaving politics, she learned to operate in a new, less publicly visible way that ultimately gave her more power over political matters than would otherwise have been possible. Working behind the scenes and through trusted lieutenants, as the governor's wife Eleanor Roosevelt developed the political style she would raise to an art form during the opportunities presented by the New Deal.

Eleanor Roosevelt always downplayed her political power. "Consciously, as I have said, I never tried to exert any political influence on my husband or on anyone else in the government." "However," she continued, "one cannot live in a political atmosphere and study the actions of a good politician, which my husband was, without absorbing some rudimentary facts about politics." The assumptions she brought both to politics and marriage made it convenient to perceive her activities within this limited framework.

It was during her husband's tenure as governor of New York that Eleanor refined many of the techniques that she had learned during the previous ten years. She keenly understood the importance of having accurate factual information, and as her husband's reporter and observer, she acquired an enormous amount, much of it useful for her own purposes. The technique of the fact-finding tour, which she honed during those four years, became one of her staples during the New Deal, when she toured coal mines, Puerto Rican sweatshops, and WPA sewing rooms, and during the war when she visited GIs abroad. This represented one of her most effective means of keeping in touch with her public.

She was also careful to further the interests of women in state politics and government. She played a role, for example, in the appointments of Frances Perkins and Nelle Swartz to state posts. She maintained close touch with politically active women in the state, and opened the governor's mansion to her women friends from the Joint Legislative Conference whenever they came to lobby in Albany.

One person who came to fill an important place in Eleanor Roosevelt's political life during these years was Mary (Molly) W. Dewson. Dewson was a product of the same New York social welfare networks as Eleanor, and they had first met through the Women's City Club. Unlike Eleanor, Dewson had stayed aloof from partisan politics during the early 1920s and did not take an active role until 1928, when she was asked by Eleanor to help out in Al Smith's midwestern campaign headquarters. For the next twelve years, no national campaign was run without Molly Dewson in charge of women's activities.

Eleanor and Molly instantly hit it off: both were organizers rather than spellbinding speakers, both shared similar commitments to responsible government and social change. Dewson always felt free to speak her mind, and she got along famously with Franklin as well. More significantly, Dewson began working with Eleanor Roosevelt just as Eleanor was redefining her political role in light of her husband's victory in the New

York gubernatorial election. While Eleanor, now the governor's wife, reduced her overt political activities and sought a lower profile, Dewson became increasingly visible in women's campaigning. She helped deflect the limelight from Eleanor, who could then work more effectively behind the scenes. In FDR's drive for the presidency, ER and Molly Dewson had back-to-back desks at headquarters, although Eleanor's name never appeared on the official Women's Division masthead. As Dewson observed with classic understatement, "Having through Mrs. Roosevelt a direct line to the Governor, to Louis [Howe], and to Jim [Farley], and having such a sympathetic operator, was an incalculable time saver."

Eleanor Roosevelt had never wanted her husband to be president, and she feared the captivity of the White House. But once installed in Washington, she was able to continue, indeed dramatically expand, the scope of her activities through just the kind of techniques that she had been developing in Albany. In politics, Molly Dewson was out front, but she and Eleanor Roosevelt were working in tandem behind the scenes. On social welfare issues, which had taken on even greater urgency in the deepening depression, ER was able to use the office of the first lady, as well as her access to the president, to promote the causes she believed in. And she soon found that she could command attention for her views in her own right. The public in the 1930s at first resented this outspoken and untraditional woman in the White House: Why doesn't she stay home and take care of her husband and family? people complained. But gradually, Eleanor Roosevelt won a larger measure of public support for what Joseph Lash has called her "politics of conscience."

Several factors facilitated the widening power that Eleanor Roosevelt commanded in the 1930s. First, the severity of the depression forced the federal government to take unprecedented steps: America's modern welfare state was born during the 1930s. Many of the new programs administered from Washington were ones that public-spirited women like Eleanor Roosevelt had been advocating since at least the 1920s. These women naturally played a role in their implementation and often spoke out in favor of even more extensive government intervention. Eleanor Roosevelt consistently held a more radical vision of social change and economic redistribution than her husband's New Deal ever embraced.

Another factor in ER's widening influence was her enormous capacity to inspire loyalty and trust in those who came into contact with her. Women knew they had a friend in the White House, someone who would look out for their needs. While not specifically identifying herself as a feminist, Eleanor Roosevelt made women's rights one of her priorities, especially in the early New Deal. She arranged tea parties for women executives at the White House, and broke precedent by holding press conferences open only to women reporters. Whenever possible, she made sure that women's needs were not overlooked.

Eleanor Roosevelt also possessed a tool that worked like a magic wand for her friends and political colleagues: access to the White House. Enormously generous in lending both her name and the aura of the White House to support issues she cared deeply about, she took the office of the first lady, a position without any concrete institutional responsibilities, and turned it into a base of independent power. She presided over White House conferences on consumers, the emergency needs of women, and camps for unemployed women; in each case, her presence provided just enough publicity to break the bureaucratic stalemates afflicting the program. She often invited women administrators to her press conferences to discuss their work, thereby providing a public forum for their efforts. She could provide access to the White House on an individual level as well. "When I wanted help on some definite point," Molly Dewson recalled, "Mrs. Roosevelt gave me the opportunity to sit by the President at dinner and the matter was settled before we finished our soup."

Given the wide scope of Eleanor Roosevelt's activism in the 1930s, it is sometimes hard to separate her partisan actions for the Democratic party from her more general activities: so many of her activities were political in the broad sense embraced by women in the postsuffrage era. Yet she devoted a significant amount of time to women's Democratic politics in the New Deal. She played a key role in convincing her husband and James Farley to make the Women's Division of the Democratic National Committee a full-time, year-round operation with an adequate budget, and she persuaded Molly Dewson to take on the job as its director. From then on, Eleanor Roosevelt served as an intermediary between Dewson and the men at the Democratic National Committee; her intercession was especially invaluable in winning increased patronage for women. During the New Deal, Molly Dewson built the Women's Division into one of the most active and effective components of the Democratic party, yet she could never have done it without Eleanor Roosevelt's continuous support.

The first term proved the peak of ER's involvement in women's politics during the New Deal. After the successful 1936 reelection campaign, she told Molly Dewson that her days of active organization work were over. By the late 1930s, she was moving toward a public stance that was more independent of her husband. As she noted in her autobiography, by the second term people began to see her less as a mouthpiece for FDR and more as a person with her own point of view. Increasingly, she used her public position to tackle her own particular concerns, such as youth, antifascism, and the growing threat of war in Europe. At the same time, she began to participate more in Democratic politics as a whole, not just Women's Division activities.

In general, Eleanor Roosevelt's participation in politics can best be understood as evolutionary, with the 1920s and 1930s serving as an apprenticeship for the wider political influence she commanded in the 1940s and 1950s. The first stage occurred between 1921 and 1928, when she functioned openly and effectively in women's organizations and women's state politics. Then, with her husband's election in 1928, she entered a new stage that lasted until late in the New Deal. She used her position as the wife of an elected public official to work effectively behind the scenes, mastering the political system and the bureaucracy on behalf of the causes she believed in. Her impact grew dramatically in this period, as did her self-confidence. By 1940, Eleanor Roosevelt was entering the final stage of her political career, where she began to function independently in the Democratic party itself. This, of course, had always been the goal of women in politics: organize women as a group so they could then gain the skills necessary to succeed in the male world of politics.

Several examples from the post-1940 period illustrate her emergence as an independent force in the Democratic party even before her husband's death in 1945. Eleanor Roosevelt helped to launch the political career of California Congresswoman Helen Gahagan Douglas in 1939 and 1940. She also played a significant role in the selection of Henry Wallace for vice-president in 1940. The delegates to the 1940 Democratic convention in Chicago were in a rebellious mood: they were willing to accept the unprecedented third term for FDR, but were flexing their muscles on the vice-presidential nomination. By all accounts, ER's hurried flight to Chicago at the suggestion of Frances Perkins and her speech to the boisterous delegates calmed the convention and saved the Wallace nomination. This episode foreshadowed the role that she would play at the United Nations and in Democratic politics during the 1950s, once she was, in her words, "on my own."

There is an understandable tendency among historians to put Eleanor Roosevelt into a category all her own. She was, without doubt, the country's most widely respected female public figure from the 1930s on; she touched more lives personally and symbolically than any other woman in this century. Yet by making Eleanor Roosevelt into a larger-than-life figure, we lose sight of how representative she was of the attitudes and experiences women brought to public life in the postsuffrage era. It does not diminish Eleanor Roosevelt to place her within these broader patterns—in many ways, it makes her accomplishments in forty years of public life even more impressive.

On one level, Eleanor Roosevelt's experiences, and those of the circle of women she worked with in the 1920s and 1930s, suggest that opening the political process to women did make a difference. Writing in *Good Housekeeping* in 1940, ER assessed the positive changes that women's suffrage had brought to public life:

> . . . on the whole, during the last twenty years, government has been taking increasing cognizance of humanitarian questions, things that deal with the happiness of human beings, such as health, education, security. There is nothing, of course, to prove this is entirely because of the women's interest, and yet I think it is significant that this change has come about during the period when women have been exercising their franchise.

Roosevelt answered the critics who said suffrage had no effect (What have men done with their votes? she asked) by showing that women's participation had altered the tenor of public life. She did not claim a revolution in public or political mores, but she did believe that credit should be given where credit was due. Eleanor Roosevelt remained too modest, however, to include her own pathbreaking role in promoting this fundamental shift in political and governmental priorities.

More broadly, the experiences of women like Eleanor Roosevelt tell us a great deal about the fate of feminism in the postsuffrage era. The activities of Democratic women in New York in the 1920s, and women in the New Deal in the 1930s, working through networks that intertwined social welfare, politics, and women's issues, suggest that feminism did not die after women won the vote. Women like Eleanor Roosevelt, who were consciously forging new roles for women in politics and government, show the survival of a feminist impulse in these decades. To be sure, no mass movement pushed women's claims, but individuals and networks of women kept women's issues on the public agenda.

No clear consensus has yet emerged on the definition of feminism in the postsuffrage era; the relation between women's issues and a more general commitment to social reform has been a major point of debate. Eleanor Roosevelt's experiences in politics help to clarify the issue. Roosevelt represents a pattern of mainstream or liberal feminism that stretches from the suffrage movement to the revival of feminism in the 1960s. In seeking to include women in the dominant political system rather than demanding a dramatic restructuring of politics and society, liberal feminists claimed a heritage stretching back to the Enlightenment and to such nineteenth-century thinkers as John Stuart Mill. While winning acceptance in the public sphere is not the only objective that feminism seeks to address, it remains a central goal on any feminist agenda.

The evolution of Eleanor Roosevelt's career mirrors the patterns of liberal feminism in the period after 1920. In the 1920s and 1930s, she battled for women's inclusion in the political and governmental system. She did not insist on major changes in the prevailing system: she believed that if women did a good job, individual success would gradually break down male resistance. Although Roosevelt's attention to women's issues was deflected to some degree in the 1940s and 1950s, when her interest shifted to issues of peace, international understanding, and civil rights, she never stopped raising women's issues. Her farewell speech to the United Nations addressed the political rights of women. And in one of her final public acts, she chaired the 1961 Presidential Commission on the Status of Women.

Many forces came together in the 1960s to fuel the revival of feminism, and feminist activism took new forms that went beyond merely integrating women into the mainstream. But the women's rights branch of the new women's movement (represented by Betty Friedan and the National Organization for Women) was an important element in the general revival, and the presidential commission served an important catalytic role. Although too ill to attend many of the commission's meetings, Eleanor Roosevelt's involvement symbolically linked the efforts of new feminists in the 1960s with the efforts of earlier generations of public-minded women in the 1920s and 1930s.

To link Eleanor Roosevelt with the patterns of liberal feminism is not to suggest that this approach to feminism is without flaws. In fact, Eleanor Roosevelt's experiences in politics show some of liberal feminism's more troubling limitations. By putting so much stress on integrating women into the dominant political system, women like Eleanor Roosevelt often failed to question the structural and cultural factors that kept women out in the first place. One good woman in politics, or even a hundred good women, could not change centuries of prejudice that kept women from being taken seriously. Moreover, training women in grass-roots organization did not automatically guarantee access to the traditional sources of party power higher up. It was a rare woman like Eleanor Roosevelt who was able to make the transition from women's politics to national prominence.

Probably the greatest failing of women in politics in this period was their inability to institutionalize their gains. Women remained dependent, financially and otherwise, on the good will of the men in power. In certain periods, like the 1930s, historical conditions proved ripe for progress. In that decade, women in politics gained ground because of the depression, the weak status of the Democratic party at the outset of the New Deal, Molly Dewson's political astuteness, and unflagging support from Eleanor and Franklin Roosevelt in the White House. During wartime, however, Dewson's issue-oriented approach had nowhere to go. After the war, the Women's Division struggled on under Truman, but was abolished completely in an economy move after the 1952 election. Since the Women's Division had always depended on the men in the Democratic National Committee for its budget, Democratic women had no way to counter this move; by the 1950s Eleanor Roosevelt and Molly Dewson were no longer available to intercede. Unfortunately, women of Eleanor Roosevelt's stature remained few and far between.

At the same time, liberal feminism had certain advantages that perhaps outweighed its drawbacks in this period. Given the lack of an organized women's movement in the 1920s and 1930s, it was up to individuals like Eleanor Roosevelt to keep feminism alive. Her willingness to work within the political system increased her effectiveness in the public sphere, especially as she learned to make the system work for her values and goals. Few could aspire to the kind of power and influence she possessed as the wife of the president, but her presence in the White House proved an inspiration to women in Washington and across the country. Through her travels, her daily newspaper column, and her speeches, she represented a model of public-spirited womanhood that exemplified what suffrage leaders had in mind when they battled for the vote.

Eleanor Roosevelt's political career has one final relevance for understanding women's fortunes in public life in the post-1920 period. The number of women elected to office or a headcount of women on party committees is not the only measure of political power: women may not hold half the positions in public life and politics, but they often exercise power nonetheless. In general, women's political power in the twentieth century has tended to be more decentralized than men's: women have often worked through informal networks and channels rather than institutional or bureaucratic structures. Furthermore, women have often approached power differently than men, looking to politics not just for personal gain and advancement but for the implementation of ideals of humanitarian and social reform. The gender gap is not an invention of the 1980s.

The 1960s saw the introduction of a "new political history" that turned away from party elites and politics at the national level to examine voting patterns and ethnic alliances in local politics. Women's history is now at a stage where a "new political history" may be developing, but one of an entirely different sort. This new outlook casts its net widely in the post-suffrage era to find examples of women exercising power in politics and public life. In doing so, it looks not just at elected or appointed officials, but at lobbyists, reformers, and public-spirited community volunteers. It seeks a cooperative approach to power and is on the lookout for networks. It wonders how women in public life have used the tools at hand to work for the causes they believe in. In constructing this new political history of women, there is no better place to begin than with the career of Eleanor Roosevelt.

SOURCES

Eleanor Roosevelt left extensive published sources depicting her participation in politics and public life, and these provided much of the material for this essay. For her attitudes on women in public life, see Eleanor Roosevelt, *It's Up to the Women* (New York, 1933); *My Days* (New York, 1938); *If You Ask Me* (New York, 1946); "Women in Politics," *Good Housekeeping* (January, March, April, 1940). The first two volumes of her autobiography, *This Is My Story* (New York, 1937) and *This I Remember* (New York, 1949), provide her impressions of the 1920s and the White House years. They should be supplemented by Joseph P. Lash, *Eleanor and*

Franklin (New York, 1971) and *Eleanor: The Years Alone* (New York, 1972), which also proved indispensable in providing a detailed account of Eleanor Roosevelt's political participation in these years. Also of interest is Lash, *Love, Eleanor: Eleanor Roosevelt and Her Friends* (Garden City, New York, 1982). For general background on women in politics in this period, see Susan Ware, *Beyond Suffrage: Women in the New Deal* (Cambridge, Massachusetts, 1981); William H. Chafe, *The American Woman: Her Changing Social, Economic, and Political Roles, 1920–1970* (New York, 1972); and Eleanor Roosevelt and Lorena Hickok, *Ladies of Courage* (New York, 1954). For biographical material on individual women mentioned in this essay, see *Notable American Women, 1607–1950* (Cambridge, Massachusetts, 1971) and *Notable American Women: The Modern Period* (Cambridge, Massachusetts, 1980).

PART 2

THE POLITICS
OF CONSCIENCE

Winifred D. Wandersee

ER and American Youth:
Politics and Personality
in a Bureaucratic Age

T HE DECADE OF THE 1930s witnessed an economic, military, and moral crisis of overwhelming proportions in which the modern state emerged with the potential for total domination. In at least one case, that of Nazi Germany, that potential was carried to its logical extreme, resulting in the massacre of millions of people. In the United States, the reaction to the crisis was the New Deal, a hodge-podge program of reform that has received ample criticism from the Left and the Right, but can only be characterized as "moderate" and "gradualist" in comparison to the changes wrought by the dictators of Europe.

Led by Franklin Roosevelt, a man who labeled himself "a Christian and a democrat," the New Deal was nonideological, intellectually shallow, sometimes contradictory, and even old-fashioned. Roosevelt's greatest gift was his ability to touch people personally and make them feel that he cared about them. In an age of personal alienation and bureaucratic detachment, the extent to which the American people felt that they had a friend in the White House is quite astonishing. But the friend was not always Franklin: sometimes it was his wife. Eleanor Roosevelt was also "a Christian and a democrat"; beyond that she was a compassionate woman—a humanitarian who both exemplified the best of the New Deal and played a large role in creating it.

Eleanor Roosevelt made her mark on many aspects of the New Deal, and for that reason received from her contemporaries a great deal of criticism, much of it quite insulting. Nevertheless, she played an extremely vital role as an intermediary between the president and the people. ER has been called FDR's "eyes and ears," but she was more than

[63]

that: she was his conscience. She forced him to deal with the hard, human issues, sometimes pushing him further than he wanted to go and at times providing him with the leverage to bring others with him. Consciously or not, she often acted as a lightning rod for Franklin's policies. In the later years of the New Deal she provided a vital link between the political left and the administration by befriending people and supporting movements that would have been politically dangerous for Franklin to support. Her relationship with the American youth movement provides an excellent opportunity to explore the nature of her political role, the extent to which it reflected her husband's political needs, and the degree to which it expressed her own personal needs, arising not only from her compassion for others but also from her search for love, friendship, and recognition.

Eleanor's relationship with the youth movement has to be evaluated in the context of her attitudes toward young people and her attempts to encourage and influence youth programs and policies within the New Deal. Likewise, the attempts by congressional leaders and right-wing critics to smear the youth movement and the first lady must be viewed against a backdrop of conservative reaction to the New Deal and the attempt to roll back the reforms of that administration. Getting at Eleanor was a way of getting at Franklin. Also, more than any other New Dealer, Eleanor was determined to protect and expand the social welfare reforms of the New Deal, even as the nation began the process of retooling for war.

Eleanor Roosevelt's response to the problems of young people during the Great Depression was a product of her private life and personal philosophy intertwined with her public activity. Personal feelings played a large part in influencing her political objectives, and it is sometimes hard to separate the two. Her political philosophy was based upon a simple but intense desire to do good toward those in need. Joseph Lash, her major and most sympathetic biographer, notes in the introduction to *Eleanor Roosevelt: A Friend's Memoir*:

> That conscience of hers was like a steady Gulf Stream of goodness radiating out from the White House through all the ambits of New Deal power and along all its coasts of ambition, gentling them to beneficent purpose.

Even the more detached biographers have admired her "goodness" though belittling her intellect. James Kearney, in *Anna Eleanor Roosevelt:*

The Evolution of a Reformer, observes that she was at her best in calling attention to abuses, but that she had no workable solutions. According to Kearney, she did not know economics or law; her grasp of history, philosophy, and public administration was very limited; and she never really understood the difficulties of business and financial institutions. Yet she communicated a concern for the "human factor" that the "tough-minded realists" with their command of economic and legal expertise failed to do. With all her weaknesses, Eleanor Roosevelt was "the personification of virtually unblemished kindness, generosity, and in the best sense of that over-used word—goodness." Her concerns were also a reflection of personal needs that she carried into the public arena. Many actions taken on behalf of others reflected her desire to be loved and needed—her desire for friendship.

Along with these subjective factors that were to create a bond between Eleanor Roosevelt and the young people of the 1930s was the objective reality of the Great Depression. However brutally it may have affected adults, the depression had its greatest impact upon young people, who suffered the highest rates of unemployment, lost their youth to the grinding poverty of those years, and saw the opportunities and the joys of young adulthood—school, careers, marriage, homes of their own—pass them by.

The New Deal began to lay the groundwork for an overall philosophy with respect to youth that encompassed several areas of major concern, including child labor, education, family environment, and youth employment. But employment was clearly the most important issue. Although accurate statistics on the unemployment of youth are difficult to obtain, George P. Rawick, who has done the most thorough analysis of the statistical data, estimates that at any one time during the 1930s, at least twenty to thirty percent of those between the ages of sixteen and twenty-four were unemployed.

Unemployed young people were seen as a serious social problem. Some saw them as the breeding ground for revolution; others feared the deadening effects of discouragement, disillusionment, and apathy. Eleanor Roosevelt feared the loss of a generation in the midst of a depression caused by adults. She carried the guilt of her own generation, which she accused of neglect and indifference, and she pushed for a youth program to rectify the situation. Throughout the 1930s, she believed that the government was responsible for providing not only jobs, but a *cause*, an ideal through which young people could see themselves as useful members of a national community.

One of FDR's first actions during the "hundred days" was to establish the Civilian Conservation Corps. The CCC was never seen as the answer to the youth problem, nor was it conceived for that purpose. Roosevelt saw in it the dual possibility of relieving unemployment and establishing a long-range conservation program. It was originally intended for adult men, but it became a bastion for unemployed youth because the regimented lifestyle that it promoted was neither appealing nor practical for adults. It placed men in camps away from their families and paid them an arbitrarily low wage, of which a large portion was sent home to their dependents.

The CCC was unappealing to adults, but it also failed to meet the needs of youth. It discriminated against blacks and entirely ignored young women; those youths who did participate were forced to live under emergency conditions in an authoritarian structure. They responded by simply leaving the camps before their service was completed. One out of every five young men who entered the CCC could not adjust to the life of the camps: about fourteen percent deserted and another seven percent were discharged for disciplinary reasons.

Eleanor Roosevelt was interested in the concept of a universal youth service as a substitute for war and a way to satisfy what she saw as the need of young people to serve in some cause that went beyond themselves. But she objected to the military administration of the CCC camps, and she saw the need for a much broader program. The program that emerged— the National Youth Administration (NYA)—was partly the product of her concerns and ideals, but it was also an idea whose time had come.

Interpretations differ regarding the role that Eleanor Roosevelt played in the origins of the NYA. Joseph Lash assigns her a leading role, claiming that she not only had the ideas, but that she had to sell Harry Hopkins, Aubrey Williams, and the president himself. But there were pressures from other New Dealers. David Walsh, the chairman of the Senate Committee on Labor and Education, and Frances Perkins, secretary of labor, fed into the climate of opinion that called for action.

Lash claims that although ideas for a youth agency were floating around, Hopkins and Williams of the Works Progress Administration were reluctant to present their proposal to the president because they feared the potential political repercussions stemming from an agency that might seem to regiment American youth in a manner similar to German youth. Eleanor Roosevelt was recruited to carry the proposition to the president, but first she had to convince Hopkins and Williams that the need for a program outweighed the dangers.

A more recent (1983) account by John A. Salmond is less generous in attributing influence to Eleanor Roosevelt. Although agreeing that she was probably important in educating her husband on the dimensions of the youth problem, Salmond argues that by May 1935, FDR was already committed to a program of some kind and had several blueprints of how to accomplish it. He had, for example, already recieved proposals from: Katherine Lenroot of the Children's Bureau, backed by Frances Perkins; John Studebaker, the federal commissioner of education; and Aubrey Williams of the WPA.

FDR turned these various ideas over to a private group headed by Charles Taussig, president of the American Molasses Company, who was later to become chairman of the National Advisory Committee to the NYA. Taussig was a close friend of Eleanor Roosevelt, with whom he shared a common interest in the youth problem. In April 1935, he and ER, Owen D. Young, chairman of General Electric, and David Sarnoff of RCA met to discuss the alternatives that had been proposed.

The plan that came out of this group was closest to the Perkins-Lenroot model, which advocated scholarship aid at the college and high school levels and a work-relief program administered by a youth division of the WPA and assisted by an advisory committee of community leaders. FDR turned this plan over to Hopkins and Williams, who evolved a plan containing all the elements of what would become the NYA.

The only serious opposition to the NYA came from John Studebaker of the Office of Education. He vigorously opposed the creation of a new federal agency, and proposed to place the program under the auspices of the Office of Education. Although his proposal received little serious attention, Studebaker continued to oppose the NYA even after its establishment; the ongoing feud between the NYA and the Office of Education was one factor leading to the demise of the youth program in the 1940s.

According to Salmond's account, Williams and Hopkins discussed the proposal with Roosevelt before presenting it to the president, but did this partly out of courtesy, partly because she was a member of the Taussig group, and partly because they respected her judgment. ER then talked about the plan to the president, which led to the idea that she had "sold" the NYA to a reluctant president. Salmond argues that by May 1935, she was preaching to the converted, and that the president, by submitting the draft proposal to Hopkins, had already indicated who would administer it.

On the other hand, Joseph Lash recounts a conversation that took place much earlier, though he does not date it, during a dinner at the White House. On this occasion, Eleanor was pushing Franklin on the need to provide for young people and on the limitations of the CCC in fulfilling that need. Franklin was unwilling to discuss the issue, but Eleanor persisted. He finally responded by agreeing to talk to some of her friends, Charles Taussig in particular. It is possible that this discussion laid the groundwork for the establishment of the Taussig group. In any case, it seems obvious that Eleanor exerted a strong influence. If Franklin was converted to the idea of a youth agency by June 1935, this was due to the pressure of several people who had access to him, including Harry Hopkins, Aubrey Williams, Frances Perkins, David Walsh, Charles Taussig, and Eleanor. Certainly the most influential and the most persistent of these people was the president's wife.

Whatever her initial contribution, Eleanor Roosevelt's continued interest activated the National Youth Administration and provided it with protection and inspiration. The program had some difficulty in getting started, especially with respect to the leadership of Aubrey Williams, who divided his time between the WPA and the NYA until 1938. She literally adopted the NYA as at least a partial solution to the employment problems of youth, and saw its potential for becoming a far broader and more effective, perhaps even permanent, organization. ER was continually asking for information about the agency, attempting to place people within it, and making policy suggestions. She entertained members of the advisory committee, kept in contact with Taussig, and maintained a regular correspondence with Williams. By November 1935, she was writing about delays in the vocational guidance program and about a library project in Oregon. She visited projects and described them to Williams; in fact, she made it her business to know as much about the NYA as possible.

The relationship between Eleanor Roosevelt and Aubrey Williams is quite characteristic of the type of friendship that she often established through her public activities. She and Williams, working as a team, reinforced each other, pushing for similar goals and expressing the same concerns. The friendship, which lasted until her death in 1962, was the most important relationship that Williams developed during his years in Washington. He continued to seek her advice and support after he left government service. On one occasion he called her "the greatest person I have ever known."

Indeed, it was Eleanor Roosevelt's intense interest and Williams's great regard for her that spurred him on after a rather slow start during the first year of the NYA. He tried to answer all her inquiries himself and to act upon as many of her suggestions as possible. In order to keep himself sufficiently informed, he had to involve himself in many administrative details. Once he terminated his connection with the WPA in 1938 and moved over full-time to the NYA, he was able to give youth affairs even more attention. By this time he was pushing the agency in a new direction—toward job training for defense needs.

The NYA proved to be a relatively successful and popular New Deal program, although its accomplishments were limited and its acceptance was not universal. Aubrey Williams sent Eleanor Roosevelt a report on January 16, 1936 that enumerated the activities of the five programs under the auspices of the NYA: student aid, which had a $27 million appropriation; work projects, to which $20 million was appropriated; vocational guidance and junior placement in selected communities; camps for unemployed women, of which forty-five were opened between July and November 1935; and finally, apprenticeship training, which was set up in forty-three states. The program of the NYA was quite comprehensive, and it was subjected to almost constant criticism from both sides of the political spectrum. It also experienced considerable internal controversy, partly due to the problems that Williams had in dealing with his staff and with the public. In particular, Williams had a reputation for left-wing radicalism that left him open to red-baiting from the Right. Roosevelt protected the agency from outside criticism, she wrote about it in her column, and she tried to smooth over tensions within. She acted as a channel through which Taussig and Williams could communicate with the president and she mediated disputes between the NYA and the National Advisory Committee. Finally, she maintained close contact with state administrators, visiting them and inviting them to Hyde Park for occasional picnics.

Eleanor Roosevelt never envisioned the NYA as the total answer to the problems of youth. Throughout the 1930s, she kept in touch with other groups and agencies, and she continually advanced the idea that unemployed youth was not simply a depression phenomenon. Even after recovery, young people would have special needs. In fact, as Lash points out, Eleanor Roosevelt began to feel that public-service employment might become a permanent feature of the American system. She supported proposals made in 1936 to establish a Department of Education, Social Welfare, Health and the Arts. She wanted a youth-service division to be included that would unite the NYA, CCC, and government-sponsored apprenticeship training programs. But 1936 was an election year, and the NYA was already under attack from those who felt that it spent too much money and undermined the morale of youth.

FDR was sensitive to criticism on the Right, especially in an election year. Eleanor Roosevelt, although aware of the political realities confronting her husband, was even more sensitive to unrest on the Left, especially among youth. Her awareness that the New Deal in general and the NYA in particular were primarily stopgap measures made her eager to keep an open line of communication to young people, even those who seemed alienated from the American system and the New Deal administration. This fact, more than any other, explains her tolerance of the leftist activities that were to characterize the American Youth Congress and the American Student Union.

The First American Youth Congress was held in 1934, the brainchild of Viola Illma, a young woman who edited a magazine called *Modern Youth*. Illma saw herself and her journal as a clearinghouse of information for young people, and in fact, she established a Central Bureau for Young America in an attempt to initiate a movement that would address their major problems. In the summer of 1934, Illma sent the first lady a program of the projected American Youth Congress to be held in cooperation with New York University. Roosevelt was interested, but unwilling to commit herself to sponsoring the event. She simply responded with a letter indicating her interest and asking for follow-up information.

The tumultuous First American Youth Congress reflected the wide-ranging political spectrum of youth in the 1930s. There was, by this time, a great stirring among various constituencies, especially among the religious youth movement and among campus leaders. Also, radical organizations, including the Young Communist League, the National Students' League, and the Student League for Industrial Democracy, were becoming revitalized.

A National Conference of Students in Politics had been held in Washington, D.C., in the previous year. The Student League for Industrial Democracy was a major force behind the conference; but its appeal was far broader, and representatives of socialist, communist, liberal, and religious groups also attended. An impressive list of progressive reformers lent their names as advisers, including Charles Beard, John Dewey, Philip LaFollette, and Senator Robert Wagner. Although President Roosevelt refused official White House support of the conference, ER delivered what proved to be the keynote address. She spoke before the National Student Federation of America, a liberal student organization, and urged them to put aside selfish interests and devise new ways of working together on the big issues.

The conference set the tone for student politics in the 1930s. The liberal students did not have a clear-cut position, nor did they have a sense of what they wanted to accomplish. The socialists and Communists, in spite of factionalism and infighting, and their vaguely collectivist rhetoric, were able to control the atmosphere and the content of the conference. This was to be the basic pattern of the youth conferences sponsored by the American Student Union and the American Youth Congress for the rest of the decade.

By 1934, when Viola Illma was ready to carry out her plans for the first American Youth Congress, the leftist organizations were prepared to exert their influence far more effectively than other youth groups. Illma, typical of most nonleft youth, had no clear-cut conception of what she intended to accomplish with a youth congress. Basically, she wanted to pull young people together to discuss their common problems under the guidance of prominent adults. What actually resulted was a leftist takeover of the congress, which politically isolated the groups led by Illma.

The congress adopted a series of resolutions opposing the NRA, the major New Deal agency, demanding the abolition of the CCC because it was a step toward militarism and fascism, calling for the right of workers to join trade unions of their choice, favoring social security legislation, and demanding militant antiwar activity on the part of American youth. Although the congress took a hostile tone toward the New Deal, most of its resolutions were, in fact, based upon a broad consensus of opinion. The antiwar resolution, in particular, reflected the isolationist mood that cut across the political spectrum. The congress also set up a committee empowered to create a permanent organization. Although many youth organizations were represented on the executive board, the Young People's Socialist League and the Young Communist League were in control.

The history of the youth movement of the 1930s is best understood by tracing the rise and fall of the American Youth Congress in the context of the New Deal and as a significant wing of leftist politics during these years. The role of Eleanor Roosevelt, on the other hand, could be characterized as that of a leader of the "leftist New Dealers." She and a group of like-minded New Dealers, including Harry Hopkins, Aubrey Williams, and Charles Taussig, were concerned with finding a democratic solution to the youth problem. They were devoted to the NYA because they saw it as a way of heading off radicalism by making genuine reforms, and they supported the American Youth Congress because they believed its leaders would accept those reforms.

Eleanor Roosevelt remained tolerant of AYC leftist activities longer than any of her colleagues because of a compassion, characteristic of her, that colored her politics and sometimes her judgment. This caused her to interpret the actions of youth and her actions on their behalf as a kind of partnership, pulling the people and their government together in actual friendship. Lash, in his account of his own friendship with the first lady, noted her response to a letter that she had received from a woman whom she had never met, but who had come to look upon her as a reliable friend in times of trouble. "The feeling of friendship," ER wrote, "the feeling that in the house where government resides, there also resides friendship, is perhaps the best safeguard we have for democracy."

It was on the basis of this philosophy that Eleanor Roosevelt befriended all the groups that were disadvantaged and alienated from American society: the sharecroppers, the unemployed, blacks, and young people. The two youth organizations that benefited most directly from her support were the American Youth Congress and the American Student Union. They were the bodies most representative of the youth movement, at least in terms of organizational strength. The American Youth Congress was an umbrella organization, thus enabling it to overstate greatly its numerical strength, claiming that it represented some four and a half million young people. These were not individuals, of course, but people who belonged to some sixty affiliated groups, ranging from the YWCA to the American League for Peace and Democracy. It is doubtful that many of these youth even knew they were linked to the American Youth Congress, but the numbers were nonetheless impressive enough to grant the organization an audience. The American Student Union, on the other hand, was more tightly organized. Created in 1935 by a merger of Communist and socialist youth groups, and always under strong Communist influence, it never had more than a few thousand members.

The Second American Youth Congress, held in Detroit in July 1935, was not much broader than the bounds of the socialist and Communist youth movements and their close allies. At least 14 of the 40 members of the National Council were either open members of the Young Communist League or consistent fellow travelers. Another 8 to 10 members worked consciously with the Young Communist League, although the evidence here is more circumstantial. Almost all of the members of the smaller and more important National Administrative Council, composed primarily of paid functionaries, were clearly part of the bloc led by the Young Communist League. This group appointed all committees, put out all publications, and acted as liaison officers with national and regional organizations and public and government figures.

Crucial figures in this group included Waldo McNutt, William Hinckley, and Reverend Jack MacMichael, the three chairmen of the American Youth Congress from 1934 to 1942; Joseph Cadden, the executive secretary, Abbott Simon, the legislative secretary, and Miriam Bogarad and Frances Williams, the administrative secretaries. Although none of these can be identified unequivocally as members of the Communist Party or the Young Communist League, all of them consistently followed the Communist line from 1935 to 1942. They supported the New Deal and the collective-security foreign policy when the Communists did, and attacked the New Deal and accused it of imperialism when the Communists did. Joe Lash, executive secretary of the American Student Union, was also a member of the executive board of the American Youth Congress. He was part of the Communist bloc within the youth movement during the heyday of the Popular Front, although he was never actually a member of the Communist party. All of these young people—in particular, Hinckley, MacMichael, Cadden, Simon, and Lash—became correspondents and personal friends of Eleanor Roosevelt. She was the vital connection between the Left and the New Deal through her relationship with youth leaders.

From 1936 through 1938 the Communists solidified their hold upon the American Youth Congress and American Student Union by moving toward complete support of both the foreign and domestic politics of the

New Deal. This involved a certain amount of in-fighting among socialists and Communists that left the socialists isolated, but the outcome was the coopting of both the American Youth Congress and the American Student Union by the Popular Front. Many of the youth leaders involved in the Popular Front were very idealistic about what they hoped to achieve. Lash and James Wechsler, editor of the *Student Advocate*, envisioned themselves as the nucleus for a group of "genuine Popular Fronters" who were not interested in advancing the cause of the Communist party, but who wanted to prove to the world that Communists and socialists, pacifists and Quakers, single-taxers and civil libertarians could work together against reaction. To these hopeful reformers, the Popular Front offered a potential turning point in political history.

The movement toward a pro-New Deal stance began at the Third American Youth Congress in 1936. In a letter to President Roosevelt, the American Youth Congress leaders asked for a letter of greeting. Acting on the advice of Aubrey Williams, FDR responded with a positive statement on the importance of young people coming together to seek solutions to complex problems. ER also made initial contact with the American Youth Congress in 1936. She addressed the National Council in January when it met in Washington to lobby for the American Youth Act, a bill which had been drawn up by the National Council in 1935. The bill provided for a wide range of government-sponsored programs for youth, including vocational training and employment on public enterprises, a system of supporting students, and an employment program on college campuses. The provisions of the American Youth Act were far more generous than those of the National Youth Administration. The youth leaders themselves acknowledged that it would cost about $3.5 billion a year in comparison to the NYA budget of $50 million. Critics estimated the cost at $20 billion.

The American Youth Act was written up as a direct challenge to the limitations of the National Youth Administration. In June 1935, NYA officials had approached Walter McNutt, chairman of the American Youth Congress, asking for an endorsement of the newly established youth agency. Instead, McNutt laughed and derided the NYA as a "sop." The American Youth Congress then turned to writing its own program. Thus, when Eleanor Roosevelt arrived at the National Council meeting in January 1936, she was introduced to a company of young people who were hostile toward the government and all of its representatives, including Eleanor herself. Barbed questions were directed toward her. On the defensive, she acknowledged the shortcomings of the NYA and sympathized with the impatience of youth, but she told them that the American Youth Act was too expensive and had not been thought through, especially with respect to its administration.

In this first direct encounter with American Youth Congress people, Eleanor Roosevelt was patient and tactful. She maintained that approach throughout her working relationship with them, even though they were not always as tolerant toward her and did not necessarily respect her position or her intellect. One of the participants was Joe Lash, who several years later was to change his views of the first lady considerably. On this occasion in a letter to a friend, he described her as "a good woman utterly lacking in knowledge of social forces and systems and why good men are helpless without organizations." He continued that she thought she could reform "capitalists" by "inviting them to the White House for dinner and a good talking to." Not all of the delegates were so condescending, however, and on the whole, Eleanor Roosevelt's appearance was a success. At the end of the year, she was invited to serve on the advisory board of the American Youth Congress, but she turned it down on the grounds that she was too busy and that their political stance was not realistic.

The American Youth Congress moved closer to the New Deal in 1937. A revised American Youth Act was introduced in the House, and in February 1937, the American Youth Congress mobilized four thousand young people in Washington, D.C., for a weekend of lobbying. The activities included visiting with congressional representatives, listening to speakers, and marching down Pennsylvania Avenue to the White House to present to President Roosevelt a petition calling for the passage of the American Youth Act. While waiting for the president, some of the young people sat down on the White House lawn. Two of them, William Hinckley and Abbott Simon, were arrested, but were later released when the White House intervened.

A friendly gathering in the afternoon included a delegation from the congress, President Roosevelt, the first lady, Aubrey Williams, and several other New Dealers. Although the Roosevelts did not sympathize with the more dogmatic of the young people, the demonstration strengthened the efforts of the administration to enlist congressional support for its youth program. By 1937–38, both the president and the first lady were beginning to see young people as potential allies against an increasingly recalcitrant Congress. Stalemated in Congress by a coalition of Republicans and southern Democrats and unable to find support for his policies through the Democratic party, FDR began to look for support on the Left. ER, with her natural sympathy for the underdog and her tolerance for political heretics, became the spokesperson for the New Deal and the vital link between the Left and the administration. Her move to the Left brought her in touch with groups such as the American Youth Congress, the League of Women Shoppers, the National Negro Congress, the NAACP, the trade unions, the Southern Tenant Farmers Union, and the Southern Conference for Human Welfare. These were connections that she wanted to make, but they were also politically useful to the president. She was able to show a concern and sympathy for controversial issues without necessarily implicating the administration.

The Fourth American Youth Congress, held in Milwaukee in July 1937, was a self-conscious effort to make youth part of a Popular Front, pro-New Deal alliance. For the next two years, until the Nazi-Soviet pact of 1939, the American Youth Congress acted as a lobby for New Deal programs at home and collective security abroad. This was the period of Eleanor Roosevelt's closest involvement with the movement.

The World Youth Congress, which was held at Vassar College in August 1938, was heavily supported by the New Deal administration. Mayor LaGuardia and Assistant Secretary of State Adolph A. Berle, Jr. greeted the delegates when they arrived in New York City. Eleanor Roosevelt and Aubrey Williams addressed them during the Vassar sessions, and Charles W. Taussig spoke twice to the congress. The president was unable to attend, but he met after the congress with Abbott Simon of the American Youth Congress and Elizabeth Shileds-Colling, the English head of the World Youth Congress movement. As a result, a friendly letter from FDR was included in the final report of the Second World Youth Congress.

Eleanor Roosevelt was completely taken by the congress. The young people seemed to be messengers of the future, especially in their concern for other parts of the world, such as Latin America, Africa, and Asia, and in their progressive stance on domestic issues. A few weeks later, when she attended the *New York Herald Tribue* forum, she talked enthusiastically about "youth's contribution in keeping the mind of the nation young." She urged her contemporaries, especially her husband, to listen to young people, and she consciously used the American Youth Congress as an ally in her efforts to win Franklin over to a more extended youth program. But Eleanor was wise enough to recognize the political realities that stayed her husband's hand, and she tried to interpret them to her friends in the Youth Congress. If they really wanted to bring about change, she pointed out, they should work with public opinion in the districts from which the unsympathetic congressman hailed. In other words, if Eleanor used young people to pressure her husband, she also used them as political allies of the New Deal.

By 1938, when the New Deal reigned in both the American Youth Congress and the American Student Union, Eleanor Roosevelt had become the patron saint of the youth movement. On February 21, 1939, she was the guest of honor at a banquet in New York City where she gave the major address of the evening—a coast-to-coast broadcast in which she scoffed at charges that the American Youth Congress was Communist-dominated. She was backed by Charles Taussig, chairman of the National Advisory Committee of the NYA. Taussig, like her, was sincerely interested in youth and was reluctant to believe that the movement was a leftist front. In June 1939, he held a luncheon in New York City in honor of Eleanor Roosevelt to introduce the American Youth Congress leaders to a group of people who might be helpful to them. Taussig wrote her later:

> There is considerable evidence that our luncheon at India House was successful. How much money the American Youth Congress will be able to get as a result of the luncheon I do not know but some of our guests have already indicated that they will make contributions. . . . As far as those who attended our luncheon are concerned, I think we successfully laid [sic] the ghost of Communism. Your remarks particularly were most helpful.

Taussig's comments underlined a significant aspect of Eleanor Roosevelt's relationship with the youth movement: her support lent it credibility. Indeed, some of her contemporaries felt that without her support the American Youth Congress would have faded out of existence much sooner than it did. She tried to sell the ideas and the importance of youth not only to the president, but also to others.

As the New Deal and the youth movement moved toward a closer and more supportive relationship, the American Youth Congress dropped its sponsorship of the American Youth Act and instead became a conscious lobby for the NYA. The National Council of the American Youth Congress abandoned the fight for the American Youth Act entirely in February 1939. It cautioned the members of the American Youth Congress against being too radical and declared that the task of the American Youth

Congress was to educate the citizens through local discussion of community and national issues. Thus, in less than two years, the American
Youth Congress had moved from opposition to total support of the youth
program of the New Deal. In return, the youth leaders had the illusion of
being close to the centers of power. Abbott Simon, Joseph Cadden, and
William Hinckley were in close touch with New Deal figures, especially
in the NYA. They occasionally lunched with the president, they presented their views on youth programs, and they were accepted as a responsible lobby for youth.

George Rawick, who has studied the youth movement in detail, suggests that it is incredible that the Advisory Committee of the NYA accepted at face value the change in the approach of the American Youth
Congress. They seemed unaware that every other communist-front organization was also becoming conservative and respectable and that the
line of the Communist party had changed. At a meeting of the National
Advisory Committee of the NYA in February 1939, Charles Taussig
pointed out the advantages of working with young people—even the most
radical of them: it would encourage the responsible ones, whereas ignoring them might allow the development of an irresponsible group. "I am in
favor myself of working with any of these groups who have the energy to
get out and act to do something for youth," he declared.

The pro-youth New Dealers were taking a stance not unlike that of
many intellectuals and political activists of the 1930s. They were "duped"
only to the extent that others, perhaps philosophically more sophisticated
than themselves, were duped. Like most liberals of the 1930s, they saw
fascism as the threat, not communism, and there was a good, objective
reason to do so. Eleanor Roosevelt fit perfectly into this pattern. Although
she has been accused of being naive and gullible regarding the youth
movement, she was, in fact no more naive than many others who saw
themselves in a far more pretentious light. The archetypal anticommunist
liberal, she saw the danger not in communism itself, but in the conditions
that led to unrest and alienation. But her anticommunist stance did not
cause her to let events in the Soviet Union or critics at home keep her
away from organizations in which Communists were active. Furthermore,
on issues of domestic reform, her sympathies were clearly with the political Left.

The American Youth Congress of July 1939 was the high point of the pro-New Deal youth movement. New Dealer participants, such as Harold Ickes, Aubrey Williams, and Eleanor Roosevelt, were highly visible. The three thousand young people who attended were enthusiastic and well-informed, nearly perfectly in step with the ideals of the first lady. They attacked the U.S. Congress, but it was the anti-New Deal Congress that had killed the Federal Theatre Project and slashed the WPA and PWA appropriations. They demanded an extension of the New Deal: a nationwide program of apprenticeship training, federal aid to education, and an expanded NYA. The American Youth Congress also called for the establishment of a $500 million loan fund to help young people finish their schooling, establish homes, and get started in life.

The culmination of the congress was the adoption of a creed and a resolution condemning all dictatorships. It made a positive pledge to serve the country and mankind, to progress through social pioneering within the American system, and to the free worship of God. Eleanor Roosevelt called the creed the finest thing that she had seen come out of any organization. She sent it and the resolution on dictatorships to many people who were critical of the American Youth Congress.

Cooperation between the youth movement and the New Deal came to an abrupt end with the signing of the Nazi-Soviet Pact of 1939. The American Student Union and the American Youth Congress, in spite of internal conflict and turmoil, followed the flip-flop in the Soviet party line and went from a pro-New Deal, collective-security position, to an anti-New Deal, isolationist position.

In the middle of this ideological switch, the House Un-American Activities Committee, headed by Martin Dies of Texas, held hearings on the American Youth Congress and the American Student Union. The public hearings in November 1939 received a great deal of publicity. Several former members of the Young Communist League testified that the American Student Union and the American Youth Congress were Communist-controlled. The leaders of these organizations also testified. Hinckley and Cadden denied being members of the Communist party and denied that the American Youth Congress was Communist-controlled. In fact, they lied—at least on the latter point. Joe Lash of the American Student Union had a difficult task, because he was in conflict with the Young Communist League in the American Student Union; but he did not want to be a turncoat and open himself up to the charge of red-baiting.

His testimony was evasive, confused, and at times, flippant; his discompo-sure was obvious enough to attract the attention, and eventually the sup-port and friendship, of Eleanor Roosevelt.

From the very beginning, Roosevelt took an active role in the Dies Committee proceedings. She had met the young people at the train on November 29th and urged them to testify openly and honestly. She also appeared at the hearings, sat with Hinckley, MacMichael, Cadden, and Lash, and was highly protective of the civil liberties of her protégé. At one point, when she considered the line of questioning to be unfair, she went over to the press table with a pencil and paper as if she were going to report it in her newspaper column.

ER also invited six of the young people to the White House for lunch during the hearing. Later she invited the same six for dinner and to spend the night. Not everyone at the dinner shared her sense of trust in the youth leadership. Aubrey Williams, one of the guests, knew of their leftist connections and feared that they would disappoint his friend, Eleanor. As the young people, out of earshot of the Roosevelts, began a litany of praise for Eleanor's courage and steadfastness, Williams fixed the group with a piercing look and said, "Don't let her down; it will break her heart."

At the conclusion of the hearings, ER stated to the press that she had done her own investigation of the American Youth Congress long before the Dies Committee and had found nothing to indicate that it was Com-munist-controlled. Few liberals took the Dies Committee seriously any-way, but her supportive public testimony enhanced the credibility of the American Youth Congress, at least in this sector of public opinion.

The Dies Committee hearings were also significant in that Eleanor Roosevelt's relationship with American Student Union leader, Joe Lash, became a genuine friendship that was to become very close over the next several years. Lash has written extensively of this relationship, and little can be added except to note that the friendship was not atypical of the intense relationships that Roosevelt occasionally developed through her political interests. In the years from 1939 to 1945, her interest in youth began to take a much more personal focus on Joe Lash himself and his friend (later, his wife) Trude Pratt. This friendship reflected not only ER's feelings for Lash and her concern for the personal and political turmoil that he experienced during these years, but also seemed to be a result of the deep personal disappointment that she experienced when the youth movement dramatically changed its policy line in 1939–1940.

The new Soviet-line policy of the American Youth Congress was openly demonstrated in February 1940 at a mass pilgrimage to Washington, D.C. This project had originally been authorized as a demonstration in support of the New Deal in the summer of 1939, before the Nazi-Soviet Pact. It had been projected as a "citizenship institute," emphasizing civic education rather than militant demonstrations. By February, however, the intent of the pilgrimage was very different: to oppose the foreign policy of the Roosevelt administration as "prowar," and to inaugurate a new campaign for the American Youth Act.

In spite of charges and countercharges of Communist domination, Eleanor Roosevelt expended all of her energies in supporting the pilgrimage. She spent hours on the telephone arranging to put up American Youth Congress leaders at the homes of prominent Washingtonians. She invited fifteen members of the National Council to stay at the White House. She also arranged to have the Army at Fort Myer, Virginia, provide housing and breakfast to many of the young people, and she persuaded hotels to give them three hundred rooms at one dollar a night; one delegate even slept on the couch in her study.

But the Washington pilgrimage was to bring what Lash called "the first real jolt to her confidence." What had been originally planned as a citizenship institute was transformed through Communist manipulation into an anti-Roosevelt, antiwar demonstration. Eleanor Roosevelt sensed the shifting mood of the congress, but rather than Communist manipulation, she saw an honest expression of how young people felt. Certainly, she had some factual basis for her perceptions. Many liberals and leftists felt that FDR's preoccupation with the war crisis endangered civil liberties and the continuation of the New Deal. Insiders such as Harold Ickes and Aubrey Williams had similar fears. Antiwar feelings were widespread, and ER's own son John had voiced his concern about his father's interventionist policies. It was therefore easy for her to interpret the mood of the pilgrimage as representative of how young people regarded the approaching crisis rather than as a conscious policy of manipulation. Certainly the young people who sincerely opposed the war did not see themselves as tools of international communism.

In addition to making arrangements for living quarters, Eleanor Roosevelt held a congressional reception at the White House, where American Youth Congress leaders pressed for action on the American Youth Act. She helped the Youth Congress obtain a government auditorium and speakers from the administration, and she persuaded the president to speak to them from the rear portico of the White House.

Roosevelt's speech to the delegates represented the official break between the New Deal and the youth movement. The delegates had paraded down Pennsylvania Avenue with signs, placards, and floats denouncing "imperialist war" and calling for the passage of the American Youth Act. It was a cold, rainy day, and the president kept them waiting, wet and miserable, for the prime-time broadcast of his speech at 12:30. Then, to the chagrin of the youthful demonstrators and the discomfort of the first lady, FDR delivered what has since been termed "a verbal spanking." Instead of congratulating them on their activism, he sternly reminded the youth of the achievements of the New Deal. He made the unfortunate remark that young people had opportunities for employment no worse today than they had had ten, twenty, or thirty years ago. Finally, he directed his most severe criticism at the resolution passed by the New York City Council of the American Youth Congress, by a vote of one thousand to five, condemning a U.S. loan to Finland. American sympathy was ninety-eight percent behind the Finns, he declared, and it was "axiomatic" that the United States wanted to help with loans and gifts.

The speech encountered a sullen silence interspersed with boos and hisses, a response that led columnist Walter Lippmann to refer to the audience as "shockingly ill-mannered, disrespectful, conceited, ungenerous, and spoiled." Others did not agree, particularly John L. Lewis of the CIO, a confirmed Roosevelt-hater. When the Youth Congress delegates returned to the Labor Department auditorium, Lewis met them with a powerful oratorical indictment of the Roosevelt administration, its employment policy, its youth policy, and its foreign policy. The young people applauded wildly, while Eleanor Roosevelt sat on the platform, knitting, her face impassive.

The atmosphere remained charged on Sunday night as Eleanor Roosevelt brought the institute to a close with a question-and-answer period. She faced a hostile audience for two hours, patiently answering their questions and gaining, if not their agreement, at least their respect. The debate between the first lady and the American Youth Congress has been described in several accounts; perhaps the most moving is a recent description by Michael Straight, a left-wing student activist of the 1930s who had become a New Dealer by 1940:

She spoke in a whisper. She was very pale. A few of us tried to give her some
support by applauding her. Once again, she held up her hand to silence us.

She could have said that the president of the United States needed no defen-
ders. She chose instead to defend everything that he had said and done. Her
endorsement of him came as a heavier blow than his own speech, for none
could question her courage or concern.

It was a fearful ordeal, and both she and the audience were exhausted at its
end.

The audience was not too exhausted to give the speaker a standing
ovation. Nonetheless, the experience left ER deeply hurt. She had been
annoyed at the tone of her husband's speech, but was even more disappointed at her young friends for their lack of respect for the presidential
office. For several months after the institute, she continued to hope that
the American Youth Congress leaders would respond to reasoned argument. She encouraged the organization of a liberal caucus inside the congress to fight the Communist influence, but was disconcerted to discover
that the officers of the congress were hostile to such a caucus. She continued her financial help, but also pointed out to the leadership that the
American Youth Congress position on the Communist issue had to be
cleared up.

Several months after the February institute, Eleanor Roosevelt wrote an
introduction to Leslie Gould's official history of the American Youth
Congress. Although Gould sharply attacked President Roosevelt for his
prowar foreign policy, ER was nonetheless gentle in her criticism and
highly complimentary of the American Youth Congress. In fact, she
strained to accommodate the American Youth Congress during the spring
of 1940, because she felt that with her support the liberal group might win
out over the Communist elements. She invited a group of fifty young
people to the White House to talk to the president over dinner. FDR sat
for three hours and answered their questions. He refused to be baited by
their attempt to imply that he had turned reactionary. After he left the
gathering, Williams, Hopkins, and Mrs. Roosevelt spoke to them for
several more hours.

She also requested a friend, Ed Flynn, to lend his home for a fundraising meeting of the American Youth Congress, but there was no real

turnout because people distrusted the organization in spite of her endorsement. It was becoming more and more clear to her that unless the American Youth Congress could clarify its position by condemning the aggressions of Hitler and Stalin, it would be unable to get funding in the future.

The Sixth American Youth Congress was held at Lake Geneva, Wisconsin, in July 1940, but Eleanor Roosevelt refused to attend. She was dismayed and disillusioned by the antiwar, isolationist stance of organized youth in the face of what she viewed as a perilous international situation. She continued to write long letters to American Youth Congress leaders, trying to educate them about what she perceived to be America's defense needs, and trying to convince them that the Youth Congress had to clear itself of the charges of Communist domination. Publicly, Eleanor Roosevelt continued her support of the American Youth Congress. In the face of opposition from several Jewish youth groups, she declared that she "would go on working with the American Youth Congress even if there were more Communists in it than I think there are as long as they continued to work for the same ideals for youth that I believed in. . . ."

There were some Communists in the organization, she admitted, but they did not control it. Even after studying the reports of the Sixth American Youth Congress, she still tried to maintain cordial relations. Whether she was unwilling to admit that she was wrong, or simply unwilling to deny her friends, not until the fall of 1940 did she finally repudiate the American Youth Congress: its opposition to military conscription was in her words, "stupid."

Foreign policy was the issue that finally divided Mrs. Roosevelt from the young people whom she had trusted. She had shifted her own position during the late 1930s from pacifism to collective security, from antiwar to pro-Allies. She was disappointed that young people could not see the dangers of the international situation, and that the policies of youth groups were being manipulated by a small clique of pro-Communist supporters who were interested less in a strong youth movement than in following the Soviet party line. Most of all, she was deeply hurt because she had been deceived. Eleanor Roosevelt said in later years that her experience with the youth movement taught her how to deal with Communists in the United Nations. But there is no doubt that she felt great disappointment over what she saw as a betrayal.

The American Youth Congress continued its opposition to the

Roosevelt administration until July 1941. Even Eleanor Roosevelt suffered its barbs: Joe Lash was denounced as her "lackey"; her interest in work camps was seen as a plan for militarizing young people, and she was challenged to a debate on the subject. But suddenly, in July, at its Seventh Congress, the American Youth Congress adopted a pro-New Deal, prointervention line. The Germans had invaded Russia and the American Youth Congress was ready to support what was now seen as a "democratic war." But it was too late to win back the first lady. She had moved on to other concerns. The American Youth Congress and the American Student Union existed into 1942 and then quietly disappeared as the young went off to war.

The youth agencies of the New Deal, the Civilian Conservation Corps and the National Youth Administration, also met their demise, victims of a policy of all-out war, full employment, and the efforts of a conservative Congress to roll back the New Deal. Eleanor Roosevelt, in spite of the tremendous criticism that she had received through her youth activities, continued her public life, though with a somewhat different emphasis. Her official support of youth shifted to the International Student Service. This organization had been formed in 1920 to assist European students who were refugees of World War I. Through the 1920s and 1930s it organized conferences which emphasized a foreign policy that had a bias in favor of the League of Nations. She encouraged the International Student Service to expand its activities to assist young people who were looking for an alternative to the Youth Congress and Student Union. Joe Lash became active in this organization, and the woman he was later to marry, Trude Pratt, was instrumental in shifting its emphasis.

As a member of the board of the International Student Service, Eleanor Roosevelt gave the keynote address at a conference entitled "Students and the Future of Democracy." She faithfully attended board meetings, many of them held in her New York apartment. She also helped raise money and gave her own generous contributions. In the summer of 1941, at the invitation of the two Roosevelts, the International Student Service held a leadership institute at Campobello. Though she had given up on the American Youth Congress, the first lady had certainly not given up on youth.

The war years took the first lady in a different direction beyond the scope of this paper, but her work in civilian defense reflected the same humanitarian goals. She was determined not to lose the New Deal during the war, and she saw Civil Defense as a way of preserving it. During the postwar era, she sought to expand the New Deal through her work in the Democratic party. Her experience with the Communist element in the American Youth Congress mader her less tolerant of communism. Along with Joe Lash and other New Deal liberals, she was instrumental in establishing the Americans for Democratic Action.

In the end, despite Eleanor Roosevelt's sympathy and support, and despite a strong organizational base, American youth was unable to make any really permanent programmatic gains during the New Deal. Certainly the war and the conservative reaction in Congress to the New Deal were important factors preventing further gains. Young people themselves had to share some of the blame. Depending upon one's political perspective, they either "sold out" to the New Deal during the Popular Front period or were too ideologically tied to the Communist party. In any case, they were not able to use the political opportunities that seemed to present themselves.

It is tempting to point to Eleanor, as so many historians have pointed to Franklin, and say that she had no theoretical framework in her approach to youth problems; that she was an "intellectual lightweight"; that she missed the "main chance" by failing to embrace the Left and turning instead to the anticommunism of the later New Deal. But Eleanor was not Franklin. She had neither his power nor his responsibility. She was able to move further to the left than he was able to do, but in the end, like her husband, she was "a Christian and a democrat" who rejected the ideological stance of the political Left. But she was also a dedicated humanist. In a bureaucratic and totalitarian age, Eleanor Roosevelt responded to the needs of the individual and played a large role in keeping the New Deal close to the people, and the youth of America close to the New Deal.

SOURCES

The most essential readings on Eleanor Roosevelt and American youth are the four books by Joseph P. Lash: *Eleanor Roosevelt: A Friend's Memoir* (New York, 1964), *Eleanor and Franklin* (New York, 1971), *Eleanor: The Years Alone* (New York, 1972), and *Love, Eleanor: Eleanor and Her Friends* (New York, 1982). Taken together, these offer a deeply personal account of ER's activities and friendships. The most important and complete study of the youth movement is George Rawick's unpublished dissertation, *The New Deal and Youth: The Civilian Conservation Corps, the National Youth Administration, and the American Youth Congress* (University of Wisconsin, 1957). John A. Salmond's recent study, *A Southern Rebel: The Life and Times of Aubrey Willis Williams, 1890–1965* (Chapel Hill, 1983), is invaluable for an understanding of the National Youth Administration.

There are several other useful biographies of Eleanor Roosevelt, including James R. Kearney, *Anna Eleanor Roosevelt: The Evolution of a Reformer* (Boston, 1968), and Tamara K. Hareven, *Eleanor Roosevelt: An American Conscience* (Chicago, 1968). In addition, see two books by ER, *The Autobiography of Eleanor Roosevelt* (New York, 1937) and *This I Remember* (New York, 1949).

The youth movement of the 1930s is the focus of a recent study by Eileen Eagan, *Class, Culture, and the Classroom: The Student Peace Movement of the 1930s* (Philadelphia, 1981). In addition, there is an interesting contemporary account of the politics of the movement by Hal Draper, "The Student Movement of the Thirties: A Political History," in *As We Saw the Thirties*, Rita James Simon, ed. (Chicago, 1967). Leslie A. Gould's *American Youth Today* (New York, 1940) is the "official history" of the American Youth Congress. On the Dies Committee and the politics of red-baiting, see Walter Goodman, *The Committee: The Extraordinary Career of the House Committee on Un-American Activities* (New York, 1964).

The most important primary sources are at the Franklin D. Roosevelt Library in Hyde Park, New York. The papers of Eleanor Roosevelt are extensive: especially valuable is her correspondence with Charles Taussig, Aubrey Williams, and several of the youth leaders, particularly Joseph Lash, Trude Pratt, Viola Illma, Jack MacMichael, and Abbott Simon. The papers of Taussig and Williams are useful for the National Youth Administration. The Records of the National Youth Administration and the Records of the Civilian Conservation Corps, in the National Archives, Washington, D.C., contain correspondence with ER about youth programs. Finally, her column "My Day" contains comments and insights on youth, as well as other relevant issues.

Joanna Schneider Zangrando
and Robert L. Zangrando

ER and Black Civil Rights

\\ THIS IS A TIME when it takes courage to live," Eleanor Roosevelt told a meeting of the Americans for Democratic Action in April 1950. She might as well have been describing her entire life as an advocate of human rights. She had shown courage in her commitment to civil rights, in her personal convictions about the importance of human dignity, in her involvement with civil rights organizations fighting for minority opportunities. She had played symbolic and educational roles for the entire nation and, subsequently, for the world as a representative to the United Nations. She exemplified the belief that human dignity, the democratic ethic, and civil rights were inseparable.

Eleanor Roosevelt's career and the movement for civil rights in the twentieth century evolved concurrently and mutually reinforced each other. By the 1940s she and civil rights had become inseparable, to critics and supporters alike. Eleanor Roosevelt and civil rights advocates shared a commitment to the American Dream: they worked with equal enthusiasm for social justice within an established system of redress; and their sense of personal responsibility, service to others, and democratic convictions shaped their public visions. Their aspirations for America depended upon a coalition of civic, labor, ethnic, liberal, social gospel, women's, and civil libertarian groups. This coalition took political shape during the New Deal and became an essential reformist legacy by mid-century. An international depression, World War II, and the Cold War convinced them that public issues could no longer be addressed solely within the boundaries of the continental United States. Both found their way, therefore, into international affairs, and both perceived the United Nations as an

[88]

instrument for global reconciliation and the liberation of Third World peoples.

Little in Eleanor Roosevelt's background suggested that she would someday become a leading advocate of civil rights for black Americans. The patrician culture in which she was reared, it is true, mandated service to others. She recalled her mother explaining that as a member of that culture "you were kind to the poor, you did not neglect your philanthropic duties . . . you assisted the hospitals and did something for the needy." Eleanor Roosevelt fit this pattern well: she joined the New York City Junior League in her late teens, worked at the Rivington Street Settlement House, and participated in the National Consumers' League. For Eleanor Roosevelt, however, as for many upper-class women of her generation, service was more than a matter of noblesse oblige, it was a great educational experience. The previous generation had often defined service in religious and denominational terms. It was organized religion that set the standards for obligatory work performed for society's benefit, and it was women most of all—denied full participation in church and civil governance—who rendered such service. By the 1890s, however, religion was losing much of its authority to a new, scientific-industrial order, and service increasingly embraced the defense of a secular democratic ethic in a pluralistic setting. Eleanor Roosevelt and the Progressive Era in which she came to her young adulthood "discovered" political reform, the needs of workers, urban sanitation, women's suffrage, and civil rights. Although it retained a tinge of Judeo-Christian responsibility, service to others became largely secularized—as Eleanor Roosevelt's career was to demonstrate.

A similarly deep transformation occurred within the civil rights movement. Black Americans had long aspired to equal rights and constitutional guarantees, but a bitterly racist reaction had foreclosed the gains of the Civil War and Reconstruction. Already victimized by white brutalities, the Afro-American community suffered the added restrictions of Jim Crow, a practice whereby southern and border states from 1890 onward revised their constitutions and enacted statutes to segregate blacks in every area of public life. Elsewhere, discriminatory customs and attitudes prevailed, making racism a truly national phenomenon.

Yet even during these bleak years changes were taking place that would produce major new social upheavals during the first half of the twentieth century. Large numbers of black men and women were moving from the rural South to the cities of the North, the Midwest and (by World War II) the Pacific Coast. This relocation exposed them to the same secularized, urban experiences that nurtured the Progressive movement. As a growing concentration of black residents, and voters, began to demand their share of American democracy, the issue of civil rights appeared on the reformist agenda. No longer isolated in a rural setting, blacks sought and got assistance from white liberals, and together they created organizations to pursue an interracial American Dream. Among these were the National Association for the Advancement of Colored People (NAACP), founded in New York City in 1909, and a companion body, the National Urban League, launched two years later. A mobilized civil-rights movement dedicated to working within the law and the established political system was emerging at just the time when Eleanor Roosevelt and her liberal peers had begun to formulate their vision of a comprehensive, pluralistic democracy. In racism they would find a common enemy.

Racism is the attribution of inferiority or an attitude of hostility directed toward an entire group of people based solely on an observation of their external physical differences. Racism can exist only if the racist wields arbitrary power: raw power in the form of lynching or race riots; economic power to control employment, promotion, and job benefits; political power to prevent the enfranchisement and political participation of the target group; cultural power to discount the existence or validity of another people's heritage. And power can exist only if it has the sanction of the law. Racism is not an individual problem, but a social reality: victims who seek to escape its burdens cannot succeed by their own individual efforts alone, but must work within an institutionalized solution—a movement.

Eleanor Roosevelt seldom dealt with the full implications of racism's configurations, for hers was largely an appeal to individual behavior. In her last book, *Tomorrow Is Now*, published posthumously in 1963, she argued that

> there is no more liberating, no more exhilarating experience than to determine one's position, state it bravely and then *act boldly*. Action brings with it its own courage, its own energy, a growth of self-confidence that can be acquired in no other way. . . . The individual is the spur to public action.

Invoking the style of nineteenth-century reformers and their expectations of a better world, she admonished whites to exhibit fairness and exhorted blacks to demonstrate excellence. She was, accordingly, an advocate of equal opportunities rather than a social critic or an architect of structural change. This neither discredits her personally nor undervalues the enormous contributions she made to interracial justice. It merely points out the limitations as well as the concern that she displayed.

There were reasons for these limitations. Eleanor Roosevelt and her cohorts—who came to positions of authority and influence from the 1920s to the 1950s—had been reared in the late-nineteenth and early twentieth-century presumptions of racism, in which theories of racial hierarchies abounded. White Anglo-Saxon Protestants from northern and western Europe were assigned superior positions; people from southern and eastern Europe, Asia, the Caribbean, and Africa were deemed inferior. These views affected policymaking in public and private sectors alike, so that any changes that Eleanor Roosevelt and the liberals of her generation sought later to invoke had to be weighed against a legacy of conventional wisdoms learned in their younger years.

As they questioned and challenged social injustices, Roosevelt and her contemporaries came to value "tolerance," "reform," and "brotherhood" in pursuit of the American Dream. Accordingly, they looked with suspicion upon the programs of Marcus Garvey and of the American Communist party. In the 1920s Garvey's black nationalism, economic separatism, racial pride, and back-to-Africa movement seemed incompatible with Eleanor Roosevelt's emerging enthusiasm for American pluralism. In similar fashion, the Marxist critique of a capitalist, class-based society appeared too extreme to a majority of Americans, even during the depression years. Relying upon the moderate, procedural instruments of a progressive liberalism, Eleanor Roosevelt embraced the New Deal-type solutions that became synonymous with her public behavior.

Certainly she was not the first white woman of the twentieth century to wage a campaign for civil rights. Settlement-house workers Jane Addams, Mary White Ovington, Lillian Wald, and Florence Kelley, each a member of the NAACP board of directors, preceded her in this area. Roosevelt had worked with women like them on urban issues. During the 1920s, while her husband recovered from his polio attack, she involved herself with Rose Schneiderman and the National Women's Trade Union League and with Molly Dewson and Democratic party politics. By the close of that decade, Eleanor Roosevelt had achieved a public reputation in her own right and considerably expanded her perceptions of America's needs. In addition, several crucial developments affected her. A coalition of liberal reformers, labor-union advocates, and urban-based, ethnic constituencies had begun to transform the Democratic party. Northern blacks would soon move into this coalition. Franklin Roosevelt's victories in 1928 and 1930 as governor of New York and his election to the White House in 1932 would permanently transform Eleanor Roosevelt's life, putting her in a position where personal inclinations to service could respond to the urgent demands for reform. Civil rights was one of those, and she had the courage to react in an energetic and supportive manner.

She was the first president's wife thus to be fully engaged in public affairs, and the first openly to espouse a concern for civil rights. In this, she was far ahead of her husband. He argued that he could not promote civil rights because he needed the cooperation of southern Democrats, first for economic recovery measures and later for defense expenditures. As Roy Wilkins of the NAACP observed, the president let Eleanor Roosevelt " 'run interference' . . . on the Negro question" to the administration's benefit. Black leaders regularly turned to her when they could not gain access to the chief executive, a fact amply confirmed by her correspondence at the Roosevelt Library in Hyde Park.

Early in the New Deal, the National Negro Press Association asked her to help it get blacks appointed to high office, and she tried without success to include a black reporter at her weekly press conferences. She helped place her friend, black educator Mary McLeod Bethune, at the National Youth Administration in 1936; she met with black sharecroppers; she held numerous strategy sessions with black leaders at the White House and in the field. She repeatedly made inquiries about civil rights to such high-ranking officials as Secretary of the Interior Harold Ickes, Secretary of Labor Frances Perkins, Secretary of Agriculture Henry A. Wallace, presidential adviser Harry Hopkins, and officials Aubrey Williams and Will Alexander, among others. Civil rights activist Pauli Murray and black author Richard Wright found her a sympathetic if not always a compliant correspondent. Despite criticism, she invited such organizations as the National Council of Negro Women to hold meetings in the White House and, unlike her predecessors, allowed herself to be photographed regularly with black Americans. If none of this seems exceptional in the 1980s, it is precisely because Eleanor Roosevelt had helped throughout her career to educate Americans to the need for interracial reform in both personal and public behavior. She set a standard for courage and conviction in welcoming blacks to participate at the highest national levels.

Nothing more clearly indicates both the strengths and weaknesses of her position than the drive in the years 1934 to 1940 to secure a federal law against mob violence. With the prevalence of racism and of one-party political control throughout southern and border states, lynching had claimed the lives of over 3,300 black men and women in the period from the early 1880s to the early 1930s. This was but the crudest and most visible form of social control the dominant white majority employed to intimidate Afro-Americans in a biracial society. Since local white officials and the white electorate who kept them in office proved wholly indifferent to lynching, the NAACP argued that only federal intervention would induce the states to prosecute lynchers and end the practice of mob violence. Eleanor Roosevelt thought so too, and the NAACP papers at the Library of Congress and her own materials at Hyde Park affirm the close working relationship that ensued between NAACP Executive Secretary Walter White and Eleanor Roosevelt in this endeavor.

Their compatibility is readily understandable, if one recalls that White and other NAACP officials shared with her the same progressive enthusiasm for public service and social responsibility. They emphasized interracial justice as part of a democratic ethic, and fully endorsed constitutional rights and opportunities in pursuit of that justice. Neither White nor Eleanor Roosevelt could sanction black nationalism; each became impatient with Marxist militancy; and both were utterly contemptuous of the fascist extremes that rocked Europe and threatened the United States before World War II. Theirs was a harmonious partnership of commonly held views and aspirations.

Under floor sponsorship by New York Democrats Joseph Gavagan in the House and Robert F. Wagner in the Senate, the antilynching bill passed the lower chamber in 1937 and again in 1940. This reflected the emerging potential of the black urban vote in northern and midwestern industrial states and the willingness of New Deal legislators to respond to it. It also marked the flowering of the NAACP coalition that Walter White and others had been nurturing among black activists, liberal politicians, labor leaders, reform-minded churches, civil libertarians, and certain ethnic and women's organizations. Despite strong liberal support, however, the bill was turned aside in the Senate by a southern-led filibuster or threatened filibuster and never became law. The NAACP tried vainly to revive the issue as part of President Harry Truman's so-called civil-rights package in 1947–49, but entrenched segregationist power from the one-party South, abetted by conservative Republican legislators from the North, once again prevailed.

In an effort to get her husband's endorsement for an antilynching law, Eleanor Roosevelt arranged a lengthy, informal discussion between him and Walter White on the veranda of the White House one Sunday in May of 1934. It gave the civil-rights leader and the president an important opportunity to explore the topic at length and without interruption. Prior to the meeting Eleanor Roosevelt had warned White that "I do not think you will either like or agree with everything that he [the president] thinks, [so] I would like an opportunity of telling you about it, and would also like you to talk to the President. . . ." Nothing much was changed by the face-to-face session, but it indicated clearly the entrée that civil rights leaders would enjoy in the Roosevelt White House because of Eleanor Roosevelt's initiative.

Several weeks later when southern senators prevented the bill from coming to a vote, White expressed his keen disappointment but reaffirmed his appreciation for what Eleanor Roosevelt had done. In the following weeks and months the two of them frequently discussed the bill's prospects. White kept her closely informed about civil rights strategies, and he explained the delicate negotiations then under way with representatives of the Atlanta-based Commission on Interracial Cooperation and its special working unit, the Association of Southern Women for the Prevention of Lynching.

The president and his advisers were determined to avoid the antilynching issue. On occasion they sought refuge in southern appeals to states' rights, with FDR claiming that an informed public opinion would ultimately resolve the matter locally. Eleanor Roosevelt, nonetheless, passed White's letters on to him with a scribbled request that he "[r]ead . . . marked parts." Such persistence eventually wore on her husband's patience and that of his immediate advisers. One of them, Stephen Early, sent a "PERSONAL AND CONFIDENTIAL" memorandum to Malvina (Thompson) Scheider, Eleanor Roosevelt's personal secretary, in August 1935. Its function was to discredit White and deflect Eleanor Roosevelt's support of the NAACP and its antilynching measure. It failed, and she remained steadfast in her endorsement of civil rights and of Walter White. In her response to Early, Roosevelt admitted that White had "been a great nuisance with his telegrams and letters . . . . However, reading the papers in the last few weeks, does not give you the feeling that the filibuster on the lynching bill did any good to the situation and if I were colored, I think I should have about the same obsession that he has." She subsequently promised Walter White that she would talk again with the president to see what might be done about moving civil rights questions forward: "I am deeply troubled about the whole situation as it seems to be a terrible thing to stand by and let it continue and feel that one cannot speak out as to his [sic] feeling."

Her involvement in civil rights, however, was not restricted to the NAACP alone. In the summer of 1938 the National Emergency Council submitted its *Report on the Economic Conditions of the South* to President Roosevelt. Meanwhile, a white southerner named Joseph Gelders had proposed the need for a regional meeting on civil liberties. Acting on the advice of Lucy Randolph Mason, a southern official of the Congress of Industrial Organizations, Eleanor Roosevelt introduced him to the president, whose encouragement prompted Gelders to convene the Southern Conference for Human Welfare that November in Birmingham, Alabama. The SCHW was a focal point for several interests: the president wanted some group to work for the liberalization of southern politics; civil rights supporters hoped the group would challenge the poll tax; southern liberals welcomed a fresh, regionally based initiative; and organized labor looked upon the conference as a wedge for its organizational drives. Eleanor Roosevelt addressed the first three annual meetings of the conference and retained her interest in the group's progress into the mid-1940s. Her courage was particularly symbolized at the 1938 session when she refused to comply with a Birmingham ordinance that required segregated seating for the delegates.

The more widely publicized incident in which Eleanor Roosevelt demonstrated her commitment to equal rights occurred the following year. The Daughters of the American Revolution had refused to permit the noted black contralto, Marian Anderson, who had sung at the White House three years before, to perform at Constitution Hall in Washington, D.C. Roosevelt—a long-time DAR member—announced in her "My Day" column on February 27, 1939, that the Daughters had "taken an action which has been widely talked of in the press. To remain as a

member implied approval of that action, and therefore I am resigning."
Her public stance prompted the Department of the Interior to arrange a
Marian Anderson concert at the Lincoln Memorial on Easter Sunday,
1939, for a crowd estimated at 75,000. The NAACP acknowledged
Eleanor Roosevelt's role by inviting her to present its prestigious Spingarn
Medal to Anderson in July 1939.

Her efforts for civil rights intensified with the approach of World War
II, as the American economy shifted to full employment under the stimuli
of defense contracts and military conscription. Congress enacted several
preparedness measures, going so far as to institute the nation's first
peacetime draft in the fall of 1940. In that setting the question of civil
rights took on added meaning. Would black men and women have equal
opportunities in the expanded defense industries? Would blacks enjoy
access to military service on anything other than a discriminatory basis?

In July 1940 Eleanor Roosevelt's friend Mary McLeod Bethune, director of the Division of Negro Affairs at the National Youth Administration, supplied her with considerable documentation about the inequities
that black workers faced in defense plants, and Roosevelt protested these
realities at the White House. Ten months later she appealed to Sidney
Hillman in the Office of Production Management about the disabilities
that confronted black workers. Meanwhile, A. Philip Randolph of the
Brotherhood of Sleeping Car Porters, Walter White, and other black leaders had approached the president about defense mobilization and black
rights. Here again, Eleanor Roosevelt served as a go-between, although
she took a less militant stand than did Randolph and his emerging March
on Washington Movement. She worried that a massing of 100,000 black
demonstrators in the capital might evoke violence from southern racists
and undermine the entire civil rights cause.

Her candor in expressing these fears to Randolph and White seemed to
have jeopardized neither their respect for her nor their willingness to rely
upon her as their link with the White House. Indeed, after the president
had issued Executive Order No. 8802 on June 25, 1941, establishing the
Fair Employment Practices Commission, White telegraphed her "VERY
WARM THANKS FOR THE MAJOR PART YOU PLAYED IN . . .
[THE] APPOINTMENT . . . OF BOARD TO INVESTIGATE AND
CORRECT RACIAL DISCRIMINATION IN NATIONAL DE-
FENSE PROGRAMS." In a subsequent letter, he affirmed "how grateful
every Negro and every member of other minorities which have been

discriminated against should be to you, the President, and [New York City's] Mayor [Fiorello] LaGuardia." And when Randolph asked her to cochair a committee on job opportunities for black locomotive firemen on southern railroads, it was clear that she had not lost her credibility. Besides, they still needed her. In early 1942, White and Randolph sought her help in trying to salvage the FEPC from the bureaucratic obscurity to which the president seemed likely to consign it.

Just as surely as Eleanor Roosevelt played a constructive role in the question of black employment opportunities, she also sought a solution to discrimination in military service. She urged her husband to include black civilians on local draft boards and pushed him to respond affimatively when civil rights leaders wanted White House discussions in the fall of 1940 on the role of blacks in military service. In her wartime visits to England, the Caribbean, and the South Pacific, she met with black troops as a demonstration of her concern about their status, and blacks turned to her about conditions in the Army and Navy. A black officer wrote her, anonymously, to complain about the racist conditions at Fort Huachuca in Arizona. In mid- and late 1943, when Walter White sought clearance to visit military theaters of operation in England and North Africa, he invoked her assistance to facilitate his investigation of conditions facing black troops overseas. In 1944 Mabel Staupers, executive secretary of the National Association of Colored Graduate Nurses, met with Eleanor Roosevelt to discuss the discrimination her members faced in military placement. The irony, of course, was that wartime casualties put an added strain on the availability of nursing service at all battle fronts, and yet black nurses were denied the opportunity to serve fully. Thanks to Eleanor Roosevelt's intervention, and to pressures applied by the civil rights movement in general, these conditions were eventually altered. In January 1945, the Army Nurse Corps ended its racial quotas and the Navy Nurse Corps opened its ranks to black women.

In the spring of 1944, the NAACP honored Walter White for his quarter-century of dedicated service. At a banquet in the grand ballroom of New York City's Hotel Roosevelt, the featured speakers included Wendell L. Willkie, Eleanor Roosevelt, Arthur Garfield Hays of the American Civil Liberties Union, Hollywood actress Jean Muir, and author and literary critic Carl Van Vechten, among others. In her praise of White, Eleanor Roosevelt might well have been commenting on her own experience:

I know perhaps better than most people how disheartening it is to work as Mr. White has worked and stand up under defeat over and over again and pick the pieces up and start again and always hope that each defeat means some victory and a step forward. I think that takes great courage, and for that reason tonight I want to congratulate Mr. White, not on the personal courage which he showed when he was young, but on the courage which it takes to accept temporary defeats in order that you may eventually win and never to acknowledge that you really are defeated. That is a very fine kind of courage and Mr. White has it.

Because she was years ahead of most white Americans in her defense of blacks, Eleanor Roosevelt needed a reserve of that same courage she attributed to Walter White. Her commitment to civil rights opened her to public and private attacks. Segregationists accused her of undermining a southern "way of life." They often distributed pictures of Eleanor Roosevelt escorted by black males, conferring with black civil rights leaders, or otherwise socializing with Afro-Americans in ways that seemed compromising to southern traditions. (The use of photographs to discredit her brings to mind the same tactics employed by racists in the 1960s to damage the reputation of Dr. Martin Luther King, Jr.)

Stories in publications like the *Georgia Woman's World* augmented a host of verbal rumors about alleged improprieties on Eleanor Roosevelt's part. Widely circulated reports told of so-called Eleanor Clubs designed, it was said, to promote rebellion among black domestic workers in the South. Opponents of the New Deal such as the Liberty League, a business-financed and ideologically conservative organization, portrayed Eleanor Roosevelt's civil rights activities as a negative feature of the New Deal, and the Republican party sought in more muted terms to do the same. Nor did she escape criticism from some blacks, mostly militants suspicious of the procedural reforms that she, the NAACP, the National Urban League, and similar civil rights advocates were trying to advance. Even certain members of the New Deal administration were impatient with her. White House advisers Stephen Early and Marvin McIntyre resented her importunities in behalf of Afro-Americans; Secretary of the Army Henry L. Stimson denounced "Mrs. Roosevelt's intrusive and impulsive folly" in advocating expanded rights for blacks in the Armed Forces; and so close a friend and sympathizer as Harry Hopkins recognized the difficulties she could create within the administration:

This incident [her appeals for clemency in the case of the condemned black sharecropper Odell Waller in the summer of 1942] is typical of the things that have gone on in Washington between the President and Mrs. Roosevelt ever since 1932. She is forever finding someone underprivileged and unbefriended in whose behalf she takes up the cudgels. While she may often be wrong, as I think she was in this case, I never cease to admire her burning determination to see that justice is done, not only to individuals, but to underprivileged groups.

Walter White staunchly defended her. To those who claimed to support her objectives but not her means he pointedly asked what methods they suggested she employ:

Silence? Let us look at the things Mrs. Roosevelt has asked for the Negro. Freedom from lynching and mob terrorism, jobs, the right to participate in government on the same basis as others. I wonder if the so-called resentment against Mrs. Roosevelt is not due in large measure to the fact that being the great humanitarian she is and, also, being the wife of the President, her statements about the South cannot be brushed off lightly.

And yet, Eleanor Roosevelt's background of traditional humanitarianism as well as her role in the White House induced a cautionary stance on civil rights. She knew, as her husband's political aides often reminded her, that she spoke not only as a private citizen but for the president and the Democratic party. There were times, she admitted in *This I Remember*, when her husband's reluctance to commit himself or to take a stand on political issues "annoyed me very much." Though she ultimately deferred to his wishes, she recalled that she wanted

to get all-out support for the anti-lynching bill and the removal of the poll tax, but though Franklin was in favor of both measures, it never became "must" legislation. When I would protest, he would simply say: "First things come first, and I can't alienate certain votes I need for measures that are more important at the moment by pushing any measure that would entail a fight."

Because of her husband's political considerations and those of the Democratic party, she confessed, "I frequently was more careful than I might otherwise have been."

After the particularly brutal Claude Neal lynching at Marianna, Florida, in October 1934, Walter White wanted her to speak at a protest rally in New York City. At the President's request she declined. In early 1935, the NAACP, in cooperation with the College Art Association, sponsored an Art Commentary on Lynching that included contributed works from over three dozen artists—Peggy Bacon, George Bellows, Thomas Hart Benton, Reginald Marsh, and Hale Woodruff among them. White hoped that Eleanor Roosevelt might play a prominent part in the exhibit's New York City opening, but the president thought that imprudent. Once again she declined, although she did visit the exhibit in an unobtrusive fashion to show support for its message. In June of 1941 she allowed herself to be used as the president's agent in an attempt to forestall A. Philip Randolph's threatened march on the capital.

Quite apart from any deference to the president's wishes, Eleanor Roosevelt had her own cautious side. After trying without success to raise the question of segregation with Secretary of the Navy Claude Swanson in 1935, she replied to a black newspaper editor who had complained about government practices that "these things come slowly and patience is required in all great changes." Reflecting something of the conformist attitudes that often accompany a national crisis, she applauded a January 1943 *Reader's Digest* article that took black editors to task for allegedly excessive race militancy in wartime. Now it was Walter White's turn to complain about her reactions. In October 1943 her own essay for the *Negro Digest* urged blacks "not [to] do too much demanding."

None of this should have been too surprising. In the May 11, 1942 issue of the *New Republic* she had already observed that people could not be forced "to accept friends for whom they have no liking, but living in a democracy it is entirely reasonable to demand that every citizen of that democracy enjoy the fundamental rights of a citizen." She knew it was trite to urge black Americans to be patient, but "that is what we must continue to say in the interests of our government as a whole and of the Negro People; but that does not mean that we must sit idle and do nothing." Those who would move black Americans forward were the "great group of educated Negroes who can become leaders among their people, who can teach them the value of things of the mind and who qualify as the best in any field of endeavor."

In this regard, Eleanor Roosevelt voiced the progressive, elitist traditions of the early twentieth century. Like so many liberals with whom she came to adulthood, she had an inordinate belief in the prospects of progress and the ability of rational discussion and fair-mindedness to make a difference. But all of that took time. The world, meanwhile, was changing rapidly. NAACP lawyers might still make significant strides in such Supreme Court decisions as *Brown v. Board of Education* in 1954, but a series of larger events after World War II had begun to transform the landscape of interracial concerns. The Cold War, America's global defense of "Freedom," and the Third World's drive for decolonization drastically altered the style of international diplomacy, while the advent of mass movements on the domestic scene would eventually displace the neatly conceived, predictable tactics of lobbying, litigation, and high-level negotiations on which civil rights leaders had come to rely.

The postwar decolonization movement among Third World peoples put the question of race in an entirely new light, one that many traditional white Americans found unsettling. Decolonization efforts provided Afro-Americans with models of initiative that challenged existing racial assumptions and jeopardized long-standing racial arrangements that whites had taken for granted. To her credit, Eleanor Roosevelt had already recognized the negative implications of international racism, for she and Pearl Buck had explored them as early as 1941. Roosevelt's impressions were further reinforced by such civil rights leaders as Walter White, who saw the matter from two intersecting perspectives. On the one hand, race reform at home and abroad was a matter of simple justice and equity. On the other, the independence movement created Third World nations that both the Soviet Union and the United States courted as client states in a bipolar struggle for world dominance. Accordingly, race could never again be a question of second-order priority.

In 1945 Eleanor Roosevelt had become a member of the NAACP board of directors. Two years later she joined Walter White, Senator Wayne Morse of Oregon, and President Truman in addressing a plenary session of the NAACP annual conference held at the Lincoln Memorial in Washington. Introducing her, White told the audience that "after thirteen years as the First Lady of the Land [she] is now the First Lady of the World." In her speech, Eleanor Roosevelt emphasized the United Nations' concern for human equality and noted that America's posture on human rights (i.e., civil rights in that setting) was under scrutiny by the entire world. It was, therefore, simultaneously a moment of NAACP celebration and of recognition that civil rights had now to be seen in an international context. Subsequently, Eleanor Roosevelt admonished the Americans for Democratic Action that "We have . . . to make sure that we have civil rights in this country . . . . [because] it isn't any longer a domestic question—it's an international question. It is perhaps the question which may decide whether democracy or communism wins out in the world."

Ironically, the issue of communism cut in both directions simultaneously: the Cold War and McCarthyism imposed a certain conformist mentality on all Americans, even while their eagerness to improve America's international image intensified a concern for racial reform. This contradiction also appeared in the postwar career of Eleanor Roosevelt. At a top-level seminar on civil rights held in September 1950 at the Connecticut home of Walter and Poppy Cannon White, Eleanor Roosevelt acknowledged the hesitation and fear that Cold War attitudes had imposed throughout American life. And yet, as a member of the American delegation to the UN, she had steadfastly refused to introduce the NAACP's 1947 *Appeal to the World*. Prepared by the eminent scholar Dr. W.E.B. Du Bois, this was a stinging indictment of American race relations and a request for UN monitoring of racial injustices. Roosevelt worried that the document would damage America's international reputation, and she resented the fact that its introduction would throw the spotlight on American domestic behavior while leaving that of the Soviets untouched.

According to Du Bois, in a memo prepared specifically for the NAACP board of directors in September of 1948, the American delegation to the United Nations had "refused to bring the curtailment of our civil rights to the attention of the General Assembly [and] refused willingly to allow any other nation to bring this matter up; if any should, Mr. [sic] Eleanor Roosevelt has declared that she would probably resign from the United States delegation." So, the woman who gained international stature in helping to produce the famous United Nations Declaration on Human Rights was herself reluctant to bring the issue of America's racial policies before the world body.

A similar conflict surfaced over the 1956 Democratic national platform and selection of a presidential candidate. She chastised Roy Wilkins, Walter White's successor at the NAACP, for suggesting that blacks might not support Adlai Stevenson for the presidency. Her displeasure was so strong that she threatened to withdraw from the board of the NAACP on which she had served for more than a decade. The issue in 1956 was a simple but nearly fatal one for the civil rights coalition. Four years before, Adlai Stevenson had run as the party's nominee on a ticket with John Sparkman of Alabama and a platform that seemed to civil rights leaders considerably milder than the 1948 Truman defense of civil rights. Meanwhile, the Supreme Court had issued its school desegregation ruling. In response, 19 of the 22 senators and 77 of the 106 representatives from the congressional delegations of eleven Deep South states issued their famous "Southern Manifesto," which urged the citizens of their states to resist the implementation of the *Brown* decision. It was apparent that reactions to civil rights threatened to disrupt the Democratic party along regional lines.

In light of its White House aspirations, what would the party do about a civil rights plank in 1956? The Stevenson forces, backed by Eleanor Roosevelt, waffled on the issue in a search for party unity. There was genuine concern about losing the South, since Dwight Eisenhower had carried four southern states in 1952 and was likely to repeat that success. The civil rights coalition, of course, wanted the Democrats to return to a strong endorsement of minority goals. In this instance, Eleanor Roosevelt took a relatively conservative stance in deference to her support for the nomination and election of Adlai Stevenson. It cost her a considerable amount of respect among civil rights advocates. It also helped to convince a number of young black militants that the New Deal forces of the 1930s and the progressive, reformist mentality of the early twentieth century—which Eleanor Roosevelt so amply represented—were not wholly reliable.

Until the late 1940s, Eleanor Roosevelt had appeared to be a great race-relations pioneer, and indeed she was, for her time. But her experiences as an American delegate to the United Nations, during the Truman administration, forecast that the likelihood of constructive change was more complex and its realization more tenuous than she, and most Americans, had imagined. She persisted, nonetheless, in her hope that common sense might prevail. She argued in a 1954 edited volume, *it* [sic] *Seems To Me*, that "those of us who have prejudices will have to make every effort to overcome them, since the only hope for peace in the world is to understand and like people of different religions and nationalities and races." Clearly her emphasis was on individual initiative and goodwill, and she counseled moderation and patience.

> I doubt if "lighting into" people ever does much good but I think the time has come when we ourselves must stand up and be counted for our beliefs. If we can say quietly that we think the attitude that someone is taking is harmful to the co-operation between people of different races and religions and will not help to promote peace in the world, and explain very calmly why we think

so, we may plant a seed in even a prejudiced mind, which may of itself bear fruit someday.

Perhaps Eleanor Roosevelt had lived too long in the privileged world of the upper classes; perhaps she had worked too long in the give-and-take of American political compromise; perhaps she knew too little—because she really had no sustained contact with them—about the everyday realities of life among the black poor, the white underprivileged, and the racists of all socioeconomic classes. All of which makes it even more remarkable that she devoted herself so extensively and so long to the cause of civil rights for black Americans. Perhaps she was genuinely incapable of believing that goodwill would not ultimately prevail.

New civil rights activists, engaged from the mid-1950s onward in the dramatic techniques of massive, nonviolent, participatory demonstrations, may have doubted the efficacy of Eleanor Roosevelt's procedures and priorities, but she proved an abiding advocate of their objectives nonetheless. Two things, after all, made her sympathetic toward Martin Luther King, Jr. and the Southern Christian Leadership Conference that he organized in 1957, and toward the Student Nonviolent Coordinating Committee and the Congress of Racial Equality. They all shared her devotion to an interracial society defined by constitutional liberties, and they abhorred the violence that the Ku Klux Klan and other racists employed. In the spring of 1962 Eleanor Roosevelt chaired an *ad hoc* Commission of Inquiry into the Administration of Justice in the Freedom Struggle and was appalled at the disclosures. In *Tomorrow Is Now* she noted that civil rights workers "were the people who suffered indignity, danger, arrest on preposterous charges; people who are even now facing incredibly long prison sentences; people who, in some cases, were treated with a brutality that sickens one to think of." "It takes courage," she told an NAACP chapter meeting in Spring Valley, New York, "to stand up the way they [black activists] are doing in the South, trying to prevent bloodshed, working with Gandhi-like patience." They might invoke a confrontational style that she had tried throughout her life to avoid, but civil rights workers of the early 1960s and Eleanor Roosevelt had the same aspirations for a humane and equitable world.

Whatever her behavior in individual instances, Eleanor Roosevelt remained an advocate of civil rights throughout her long career. Customarily self-effacing, she could be assertive when challenged. In her 1958 book, *On My Own*, she recalled a rare moment of exasperation that prompted her to tell a Soviet UN delegate, who had criticized the United States's treatment of blacks, that: "I had spent a good part of my own life fighting against discrimination and working for educational and other measures for the benefit of Negro citizens of the United States." And so she had. She embodied the American moral conscience in its finest sense. By personal example—in her writings, her speeches, her travels throughout the United States and the world, her access to President Roosevelt, and her role as UN delegate—she publicized her commitment to personal service and her belief in the democratic process as the means of achieving equality for black Americans.

They recognized and valued her contributions. At her death in November 1962, the black community mourned her. "A hushed silence fell in Negro homes across the nation as families heard the sad but expected news that Eleanor Roosevelt, First Lady of the World, had died. . . . They knew they had lost the most outstanding champion of Negroes in the nation," the Chicago *Defender* declared. And they fully understood how instrumental she had been: "Though her husband, as President, was given credit for sympathizing with the plight and aspirations of Negroes, it has since become apparent that it was she who made him conscious of the social injustices existing in the country," the Pittsburgh *Courier* reported; while the New York *Amsterdam News* observed that "Whether in praise or criticism millions credit Mrs. Roosevelt with being a major inspiration and force in the improvement of the status of Negroes over the past 30 years." The Kansas City, Missouri, *Call* referred to her as "our Eleanor," and the Baltimore *Afro-American* noted in a first-page headline that "We have lost a great friend."

The NAACP board of directors lamented its loss, because she had always given "Negro Americans an understanding of their individual worth and capabilities and their rights and responsibilities as American citizens." In his last book, *How Far the Promised Land?*, published posthumously in 1955, Walter White had already taken her measure:

> Especially stirring was the moral leadership of Mrs. Eleanor Roosevelt on human rights. Her enemies and critics used every device of criticism and slander to stop her, but, undaunted, she continued to speak and act as her conscience dictated. She gave to many Americans, particularly Negroes, hope and faith which enabled them to continue the struggle for full citizenship.

And with full justification, so street-savvy a black novelist as Claude Brown dedicated his 1965 best-seller *Manchild in the Promised Land* "To the late Eleanor Roosevelt, who founded the Wiltwyck School for Boys. And to the Wiltwyck School, which is still finding Claude Browns." Perhaps Martin Luther King, Jr. said it best for his generation when he wrote in the *Amsterdam News* of November 24, 1962 that "The courage she displayed in taking sides on matters considered controversial, gave strength to those who risked only pedestrian loyalty and commitment to the great issues of our times."

SOURCES

The best primary sources on ER and civil rights for black Americans are the Eleanor Roosevelt Papers at the Franklin Delano Roosevelt Presidential Library, in Hyde Park, New York, and the Papers of the National Association for the Advancement of Colored People at the Manuscript Division of the Library of Congress in Washington, D.C. Other letters and memoranda may be consulted in the Franklin D. Roosevelt Papers at Hyde Park, the Papers of the Brotherhood of Sleeping Car Porters at the Library of Congress, and the personal papers of Walter White and of Poppy Cannon White at Yale University's Beinecke Rare Book and Manuscript Library in New Haven, Connecticut. There are also some pertinent documents at the Harry S. Truman Presidential Library in Independence, Missouri, especially for Eleanor Roosevelt's term as an American delegate to the United Nations.

Eleanor Roosevelt published extensively. In addition to her syndicated newspaper column "My Day" she also wrote a monthly piece that appeared in *The Ladies' Home Journal* from 1941 to 1949 and, thereafter, in *McCall's*. These columns deal infrequently with civil rights, except when major issues, such as the antilynching bills of the 1930s, the question of race relations during World War II, or the international implications of racial patterns in the United States commanded her attention.

Of the various books that she wrote, the following have helpful passages on race and civil rights. Three of these are autobiographical: *This Is My Story* (New York, 1937); *This I Remember* (New York, 1949); and *On My Own* (New York, 1958). An edited collection of questions and answers from her magazine columns appeared as *it* [sic] *Seems to Me* (New York,

1954), and a volume of social commentary, *Tomorrow Is Now* (New York, 1963), was published posthumously.

Of the scholarly biographies, Joseph Lash's two-volume study, *Eleanor and Franklin* (New York, 1971) and *Eleanor: The Years Alone* (New York, 1972), is the most comprehensive, providing fairly detailed coverage of civil rights matters. See also Tamara K. Hareven, *Eleanor Roosevelt: An American Conscience* (Chicago, 1968). Other useful books include: Jason Berger, *A New Deal for the World: Eleanor Roosevelt and American Foreign Policy* (New York, 1981); Ruby Black, *Eleanor Roosevelt: A Biography* (New York, 1940), which has neither footnotes nor bibliography; and James R. Kearney, *Anna Eleanor Roosevelt: The Evolution of a Reformer* (Boston, 1968).

Of special interest are: Jervis Anderson, *A. Philip Randolph: A Biographical Portrait* (New York, 1972); Herbert Garfinkel, *When Negroes March: The March on Washington Movement and the Organizational Politics for FEPC* (New York, 1969); Thomas A. Krueger, *And Promises to Keep: The Southern Conference for Human Welfare, 1938–1948* (Nashville, Tennessee, 1967); Walter White, *A Man Called White: The Autobiography of Walter White* (New York, 1948), and *How Far the Promised Land?* (New York, 1955). Also useful is an essay by Darlene Clark Hine, "Mabel K. Staupers and the Integration of Black Nurses into the Armed Forces," in John Hope Franklin and August Meier, eds., *Black Leaders of the Twentieth Century* (Urbana, Illinois, 1982).

Black newspapers and serial publications contain valuable, if scattered, references to Eleanor Roosevelt and civil rights. Chief among those used are the Baltimore *Afro-American*, the Chicago *Defender*, the Kansas City, Missouri, *Call*, the New York *Amsterdam News*, and the Pittsburgh *Courier*. *The Crisis*, monthly magazine of the NAACP, and *Opportunity*, published by the National Urban League, provide some information about Eleanor Roosevelt, as does the *New York Times*.

Blanche Wiesen Cook

"Turn toward Peace:"
ER and Foreign Affairs

The newspapers these days are becoming more and more painful. I was reading my morning papers on the train not so long ago, and looked up with a feeling of desperation. Up and down the car people were reading, yet no one seemed excited. To me the whole situation seems intolerable. We face today a world filled with suspicion and hatred. . . . We can establish no real trust between nations until we acknowledge the power of love above all the other power. . . . You laugh, it seems fantastic, but this subject [love] will, I am sure, have to be discussed throughout the world for many years before it becomes an accepted rule. We will have to want peace, want it enough to pay for it, pay for it in our own behavior and in material ways. We will have to want it enough to overcome our lethargy and go out and find all those in other countries who want it as much as we do.

THOSE WORDS BEGIN and end Eleanor Roosevelt's 1938 "little book on peace," *This Troubled World*. The book is dedicated to Carrie Chapman Catt, "who has led so many of us in the struggle for peace," and develops many of the themes that were to remain constant as Eleanor Roosevelt's vivid presence in global politics unfolded.

Passionately committed to peace, Eleanor Roosevelt was not an absolute pacifist. She called herself a "realistic" pacifist and meant by that support for both military preparedness and conscription. "In a world that is arming all around us, it is necessary to keep a certain parity," she wrote in 1938. Actually Eleanor Roosevelt believed in power. She understood power, sought power, and, more than any other contemporary woman in public life, influenced policy from positions of power. She believed in bold and vigorous action. As she wrote, "Faint heart ne'er won fair lady, nor did it ever solve world problems!" She understood the complexities of colonial privilege and revolution; the vagaries of competition and compromise. She was a practical idealist; an American internationalist, specifically an internationalist whose values were profoundly American. She was committed to the precepts of America as codified in the Declaration of Independence and the Bill of Rights.

Eleanor Roosevelt believed in liberty, democracy, and freedom. But she believed that no individual, community, or nation could be truly free so long as others were fettered. With courage and simplicity she personally carried her commitment for human rights into tiny villages as well as into the citadels of power. As "First Lady of the World" she touched the imagination of people everywhere because she included in her vision people of all economic and social classes.

Inevitably, she was also vilified, scorned, abused and hated. Not only reactionaries like the frankly fascist Father Coughlin considered her subversive; liberal Republicans like John Foster Dulles thought her positively dangerous and sought her removal from the United Nations Human Rights Commission. But her vision—which evolved slowly over time and in response to new learning and experience—remains today what it was for her in 1938, an alternative to "acknowledging that we are going to watch our civilization wipe itself off the face of the earth." As she observed in 1938, humanity must either "recognize the fact that what serves the people as a whole serves them best as individuals," or abandon the goal of moving "forward except as we have moved in the past with recourse to force," continually suspicious and violent toward each other.

Throughout her public career, Eleanor Roosevelt had the support of and worked with like-minded women and men who also operated from positions of privilege, influence, and power. On issues relating to international peace and civil rights, where her stands were often far bolder than her husband's, she had from the beginning the support of a group of political women who were to become her life-long friends and whom she credited with "the intensive education of Eleanor Roosevelt." Esther Everett Lape, a crusader for national health care and a leader in the fight for American participation in the World Court, and attorney Elizabeth Read introduced her to the women's movement for international peace and to such World War I-era peace and feminist activist as Agnes Brown Leach, Carrie Chapman Catt, and Jane Addams.

Although Eleanor Roosevelt subsequently became identified with the activist peace movement that Jane Addams guided until her death in 1935, during World War I ER was associated with the interventionalist, pro-Allied sentiment spearheaded by her uncle, Theodore Roosevelt, and her husband, Franklin Roosevelt, who then led the preparedness movement in Woodrow Wilson's cabinet. As undersecretary of the Navy, Franklin Roosevelt bitterly opposed such administration pacifists as Secretary of State William Jennings Bryan and his immediate superior, Josephus Daniels, who equated navalism with imperialism. He hoped they would both resign and free him to pursue the teachings of his hero, Alfred Thayer Mahan, who popularized the notion that seapower was the key to world power. While ER was not so scornful of Bryan or Daniels, and acknowledged that she admired their principled courage, she had nothing to do with such organizations as the American Union Against Militarism (which became the ACLU) or the Woman's Peace Party (which was re-named the Women's International League for Peace and Freedom), led by her later friends and allies.

Throughout the early years of the war, Eleanor Roosevelt's thoughts ranged from despair to outrage. On May 14, 1915, she wrote a German friend and Allenswood classmate, Carola von Passavant: "This whole war seems to me too terrible. Of course it brings out in every nation wonder-ful, fine qualities . . . self-sacrifice and unselfishness. . . . [But] war also brings out in all nations certain qualities which are not beautiful and I wish it could be wiped from the face of the earth. . . ." There is no evidence that in 1915 Eleanor Roosevelt was even aware of the activities of the Woman's Peace Party organized by Jane Addams, Lillian Wald, Crys-tal Eastman, and others to keep the United States neutral, to encourage the neutral countries to mediate a peace without victory, and eventually to introduce a peace program that was to become the basis for Woodrow Wilson's Fourteen Points—a future of world stability enforced by a League of Nations.

When, in April 1917, the United States entered the war to make the world "safe for democracy," Eleanor Roosevelt plunged into war work deeply aware of a "sense of impending change" that would transform the more stable world of her birth. In full uniform, she spent the war years administering a Red Cross canteen and a knitting brigade. She helped to found the Navy Relief Society and was considered "the dynamo" behind the canteen service that greeted as many as ten troop trains a day at Union

With son, Elliott, at Campobello, 1917.
—*Franklin D. Roosevelt Library*

Eleanor Roosevelt in 1920.
—*Franklin D. Roosevelt Library*

Meeting of League of Women Voters at Hyde Park, October 14, 1927. Eleanor Roosevelt, Mary Garrett Hay, and Carrie Chapman Catt.—*Keystone-Underwood*

Eleanor Roosevelt and other members of the Committee on Legislation, 1927–1928, of the Women's City Club of New York.—*Women's City Club of New York*

Eleanor Roosevelt with Elizabeth Christman and Rose Schneiderman at the National Women's Trade Union League, Washington, D.C., May 5, 1936.—*Underwood & Underwood*

Eleanor Roosevelt awarding a medal to Marian Anderson in 1938.
— *Marian Anderson*

Eleanor Roosevelt, with Mary McLeod Bethune, addressing second National Conference on Negro Youth, Washington, D.C., January 12, 1939.—*World Wide Photos, Inc.*

Eleanor Roosevelt, Melvyn Douglas, and Helen Gahagan Douglas visiting a Farm Security Administration Camp, while Helen Gahagan Douglas was National Committeewoman, in California, 1940.—*Western History Collections, University of Oklahoma Library*

Eleanor Roosevelt holds a poster of the Declaration of Human Rights, Lake Success, New York, November 1949.—*United Nations*

Eleanor Roosevelt, with Fala and "Tamas" at Val Kill, Hyde Park, 1951.—*Franklin D. Roosevelt Library*

Eleanor Roosevelt in 1957.—*Franklin D. Roosevelt Library*

Press conference at Hotel Jayhawk, Topeka, Kansas, April 1959.
— *Franklin D. Roosevelt Library*

Arriving in Washington, D.C., 1960.
—*Franklin D. Roosevelt Library*

PART
3

POLITICAL FRIENDSHIPS

Martha H. Swain

ER and Ellen Woodward:
A Partnership for Women's
Work Relief and Security

"TO ME TWO PERSONS stand out as living examples of what women can accomplish," wrote the head of the Oklahoma Women's Division of the Works Progress Administration in 1939. "They are Mrs. Franklin D. Roosevelt and Mrs. Ellen S. Woodward." As a state director of women's relief-work activities, the Oklahoma administrator could well appreciate that the measure of equity given to women in successive relief administrations since their inception in 1933 was due primarily to the fact that Eleanor Roosevelt had cared very much about women when the New Deal began. She had insisted that women be included in the jobs programs. She had collaborated with Ellen Woodward who, as the assistant administrator of the Federal Emergency Relief Administration, the Civil Works Adminstration, and the WPA, devised and supervised work projects that assisted more than 500,000 "forgotten women." The compatible partnership between the two women continued after Woodward left the WPA to assume a position on the Social Security Board in December 1938. Thus for more than twelve years the two humanitarians worked to insure to women an equitable distribution of federal funds and benefits.

Ellen Woodward was not among the network of social workers, Democratic activists, and reformers who were known to the Roosevelts in the prepresidential years. It is unlikely that the two women ever met prior to the Democratic convention of 1932, where a social function for the Roosevelts attended by national committeemen and committeewomen provided an opportunity for at least an introduction. As the new Democratic committeewoman from Mississippi, Woodward was one of the

[135]

many party leaders who corresponded with Eleanor Roosevelt regarding postconvention plans to mobilize female voters, but there is nothing in the exchange that indicates a personal friendship. Their paths did not cross again for more than a year, when circumstances brought them together to begin their endeavors to extend the New Deal to American women.

Ellen Woodward was a Mississippian, born in Oxford in 1887 as the daughter of William Van Amberg Sullivan, a prominent trial lawyer who served for a short time at the turn of the century as a Mississippi congressman and United States senator. As a young girl, Ellen lived in Washington, returned to high school in Oxford, and attended for a year Sans Souci, a small seminary for women in South Carolina. Like the young Eleanor, her formal schooling ended early; at age nineteen, shortly after her social debut, she married Albert Young Woodward, a rising Mississippi attorney. As a young matron she participated in community and federated club affairs in Louisville, the small central Mississippi town that became her permanent home and legal residence. By her own admission, she was "one of those organizing women." She spearheaded a drive to convert an old frame schoolhouse into a community center, conducted a city beautification program, and managed her husband's successful campaign for the state legislature.

After his death in 1925, which left her a widow at age thirty-seven with a teenage son, Ellen Woodward announced her candidacy for the legislature, trounced her male opponent, and became the second woman to serve in the Mississippi House of Representatives (1925–1926). At the end of one term, she left the legislature to join the staff of the new Mississippi State Board of Development and soon became its executive director. By 1932 she had a reputation in Mississippi as a woman who had done as much to develop economic programs and to promote industrial growth and diversity in the state as had any man. She was also recognized as a gifted politician, astute in dealing tactfully but resolutely with sensitive issues. In 1931 she was designated by Mary (Molly) W. Dewson, the new director of the Democratic women's division, to organize Mississippi women for Franklin D. Roosevelt's coming candidacy. Years later Frances Perkins remembered that Woodward had been "very, very useful in convincing delegates, not only in her state, but of other border states to whom she had access." Named as a state committeewoman in 1932, and tapped by James A. Farley, party chairman, to conduct the drive in Mississippi to help pay the party's postelection debt, Ellen Woodward was no stranger to the Democratic men who summoned party loyalists to Washington to take posts under the New Deal when the new administration took shape.

Relief for the unemployed and the destitute held first place among the New Deal planners as they drafted legislation during the "First Hundred Days" to overhaul the modest emergency relief measures of the prior administration. When the Federal Emergency Relief Administration (FERA) began in the spring of 1933, Eleanor Roosevelt cautioned the relief directors and bureaucrats not to forget that recipients should be dealt with as human beings who preferred to work rather than go on the dole. She knew from her mail that women were in want. Thousands of letters—more than 300,000 by the end of the year—poured across her desk. In August 1933, in the first of a two-year series of monthly pages she wrote for the *Woman's Home Companion,* she told her readers, "I want you to write me. . . . I want you to tell me about the particular problems which puzzle or sadden you." The responses came from single women who were unable to support themselves or their dependents, from married women who were the only able breadwinners in their families, from widows, and from mothers whose children were ill or disabled.

Fearing that women would be overlooked as work programs were set up, Eleanor Roosevelt moved quickly to convince Harry L. Hopkins, head of FERA, that activities must be created for women. Hopkins consulted his old friend Frank Bane, then the commissioner of public welfare in Virginia, about a woman who could direct a women's division within FERA. Bane told him of the Mississippi woman whose agency had only recently sponsored a Brookings Institution study of the state's fiscal structure. He described Ellen Woodward as competent, progressive, humane, and innovative, familiar with welfare administration and knowledgeable about existing emergency relief programs. She had served as executive director of the Mississippi Conference on Social Work from 1928 to 1930 and had then joined the five-member executive committee of the State Board of Public Welfare, which had been created in 1932 when emergency funds had first been appropriated to the states. From 1924 to 1929 she had served as a trustee of the state charity hospital and since 1928 she had been the only woman trustee of the Mississippi Children's Home Society. In early August, Hopkins notified the Mississippi Development Board chairman that he wanted the services of its executive director. On September 1, 1933, Woodward became the director of the newly created Women's Division of the Federal Emergency Relief Administration.

When Woodward assumed her duties, about fifty thousand women were working on relief projects, chiefly in canning and sewing centers or in clerical jobs, but the projects lacked coordination and were extremely limited in the assistance they offered. Much more imagination had to be brought to bear if work programs were to employ the types of women who wrote Eleanor Roosevelt pleading for jobs. State FERA offices, which attempted to deal with the problems of needy women, did so with staff temporarily assigned from other tasks or who simply worked at two administrative jobs. Woodward's priority was to assemble a staff in each state to direct the work projects, which, she and Hopkins intended, would go far beyond the neglected and often slipshod existing programs. When Hopkins officially notified each state relief director, on October 10, of the new women's division, he directed each to appoint a qualified woman who should devote herself full-time to the women's program. They were to be women acquainted with social and civic agencies, employment services, and the status of the current relief programs. There were also practical and political considerations. The appointees should be loyal to the purposes of the New Deal, a requirement that excluded Republican partisans. Both Eleanor Roosevelt and Molly Dewson submitted names to Woodward although it was not mandatory that she approve of them if investigation revealed a lack of experience and skills.

Having taken the initiative to inaugurate a women's program, the first lady continued to nurture it. In essence, she became a self-appointed chief adviser to Woodward's division. In November 1933, she conceived the idea of a White House Conference on the Emergency Needs of Women to focus the attention of prominent leaders of women's organizations and social service agencies on the new program and to invite their cooperation in dealing with the plight of jobless women. Working through ER's secretary Edith Helm, Woodward and her assistant Dr. Chloe Owings sent telegrams to fifty-nine women leaders whose names had been suggested by Eleanor Roosevelt's office. Those invited included national club presidents, executive directors of private charities and social service centers, the heads of government bureaus whose functions affected women and children, and all of the congresswomen. Quickly planned and executed, the conference proved to be a stimulating forum where women from every part of the country exchanged information on the extreme difficulties women faced in finding work. The Women's Bureau representative reported that in New York City there were 250,000 unemployed women in "all degrees of distress," while in the southern city of Birmingham there were six thousand unemployed clerical workers alone. When a new department story in that city announced seventy-five job openings, it had received five thousand applicants. And so the accounts ran.

Eleanor Roosevelt, in her customary role of facilitator, turned the conference over to Harry Hopkins, who reported that an estimated 300,000 to 400,000 women, many of them homeless, required immediate assistance through direct relief, shelter, food, medical care, or simply "decent attention." More importantly, they needed to be put to work in imaginative but practical jobs that would be socially constructive and thus acceptable to the community. It would not be an easy task, he admitted, because most women who were gainfully employed worked in factories, service industries, and in domestic jobs in the home, areas where employment opportunities were most diminished. He challenged the audience to conceive of projects in public service for the 300,000 to 350,000 women whom he hoped to have at work within a month. Woodward, who presided over the afternoon session, described the work already underway in seventeen states and two territories, where women directors were "on the firing line." She emphasized the gravity of the problem, particularly in industrial states where one-fourth of those persons who registered for work were women, and she warned of the constraints that confronted the architects of a women's relief program. Women could not be employed on mass projects such as construction, which provided work for thousands of men on one project alone; nor could they work on projects that competed with the private sector. Eleanor Roosevelt added another caveat. Unlike men, women could not be expected to leave behind their families and dependents to accept employment; they would have to work on projects in their own communities. Although it would be much more difficult to create a half-million jobs for women than four million jobs for men, she insisted that relief administrators be told to allocate jobs and funds to the women's program. Later, when Woodward prepared her file on the White House conference, she labeled it "Where the Women's Division was born."

The women who convened that November day at Eleanor Roosevelt's invitation were expected to return to their home states and implement the decisions reached at the White House conference. Their cooperation was essential if programs were to be created at the local level, where grassroots support was absolutely necessary. From the very beginning of the

FERA projects for women, the men who were the state directors of the Emergency Relief Administration resisted the allocation of staff and money to a program for women. The Mississippi director complained that he was "bombarded" by letters from club women suggesting "silly programs," and the story was no different elsewhere. When the FERA administrator in Massachusetts protested that there was not enough money to provide jobs for women, ER intervened. She recommended to Woodward that a definite work order be given. One day later, Woodward informed her, a field representative sent to Boston had reported that the "confusion" regarding the eligibility of women's projects had ended and women would be put to work at once. Very soon ER extended her good offices again when she invited Woodward to her press conference to answer questions about women's work relief. It was at that time that the first lady publicly condemned the work-relief policy of paying women less than men.

By the end of 1933, state directors of women's divisions had received sixty-seven FERA issuances describing hundreds of work activities to absorb unemployed professional women, such as nurses, dental technicians, librarians, teachers, and home economists. Projects provided work also for the unskilled in the production of garments, mattresses, and household items to be distributed to needy families certified for relief, and in gardening and canning projects that supplied food. Many projects had a double purpose of providing both employment and desperately needed goods and social services—for example, library projects that focused on the extension of services to rural areas, and housekeeping-aides projects that provided home care to relief families where there were working mothers, young children, or ill or aged members.

Although Eleanor Roosevelt had no day-to-day involvement in the administration of projects, she expressed a keen interest in developing projects related to her own interests, especially in furniture-making, weaving, and handicrafts. Handicrafts, in particular, seemed to provide an opportunity to preserve a traditional craft. She often received samples of needlework from women who hoped that she could help in marketing their work, and in one case she purchased a hooked rug that she admired. Projects sometimes stemmed from recommendations sent to the White House, particularly from professional women in the field of child care and health services. In the fall of 1933, after conversations with the actress Eva Le Gallienne and the artist Edward Bruce, and because of her own knowledge of the plight of jobless actors and artists, Mrs. Roosevelt urged that Hopkins create work projects for the unemployed in those fields.

The work program under the FERA had scarcely been launched in the fall of 1933 when it was threatened by the Civil Works Administration (CWA), created in November with the clear intent of putting men to work during the winter months, primarily on construction projects. The Women's Division faced a new challenge in its determination to have women's projects declared eligible for CWA funds under its Civil Works Service branch. Woodward did not have to inform Eleanor Roosevelt that opportunities for women had been curtailed. Women from around the country wrote to the White House of their rebuffs. "I should like to know why it is that men can be placed so easily and not women," asked one; "I understand that the CWA cannot help unemployed girls," said another. "Why should men be allowed to work, and women with identical responsibilities be forced to stand in line for endless hours and beg for every mouthful?" was a common complaint. An Indiana woman asked the essential question: "Is there a place for us anywhere in America?" After ER discussed the matter with CWA administrator Hopkins and his assistant Aubrey Williams, both already troubled by the discrimination against women, directives flew to state relief heads. By the late winter of 1934, Woodward was able to report to her White House mentor that more than 300,000 professional and unskilled women were at work on CWA projects.

The demise of the CWA in the spring of 1934 ended one troublesome aspect of the relief-work business, but after the woes of winter came shortages in some areas from summer drought, and mounting surpluses elsewhere. Woodward expanded mattress and bedding projects that used surplus cotton, increased beef- and food-canning programs that would supply winter needs, and transferred professional women on former CWA projects to new white-collar projects that paid them higher wages. "Will you criticize very frankly my work and my plans and give me those suggestions that have come from your first-hand contacts during the summer," she wrote to Eleanor Roosevelt who had begun a practice of inspecting the women's projects as she traveled about the nation. In 1934, ER began to send her itinerary to Woodward so that she could recommend projects to be visited along the way.

More and more, Eleanor Roosevelt heard of the deprivation and anguish of the American people from those who looked upon her as a court of last resort. Correspondence in the Eleanor Roosevelt Papers at the Roosevelt Library at Hyde Park, in the FERA and WPA records at the National Archives in Washington, and in the Ellen Woodward Papers at the Mississippi Department of Archives and History attest poignantly to the circumstances of those who, through no fault of their own, were down on their luck. "I have been placed at my wit's end and know not what to do next," wrote one woman. Many of the letters, written on tablet paper, came from the uneducated and barely literate. Others, articulately written on embossed paper, came from middle-to-upper-class women whose incomes had now vanished and whose savings were depleted. "What, dear Mrs. Roosevelt, is an educated, experienced, cultured woman of background, travel, and poise to do when she is hungry, penniless, footsore, and weary?" wrote a Philadelphia matron, who added that Meridel LeSueur had written of her type, in her article entitled "Women Are Hungry," in the March 1934 *American Mercury*. This woman and thousands like her, Woodward pointed out to Eleanor Roosevelt, had had no preparation for placement in one of the professional projects and yet could not accommodate themselves to the training programs for unskilled, "blue collar" occupations. When Woodward transmitted to a local caseworker a moving letter to Eleanor Roosevelt from an elderly Salt Lake City woman, she asked that the woman's problems be held confidential because "her pride must not be hurt." ER also understood the humiliation felt by a man certified as unemployable, when work relief was provided to his wife. "I'm called a kept man," a Connecticut husband and father confided in one of many such letters. The correspondence reveals, too, that the first lady, her daughter Anna Boettiger, and their staff handled the letters with discretion, channeling them to the most appropriate New Deal agency that could investigate the cases and expedite relief. Those involving women and children were sent to the Women's Division, where Woodward's staff conducted investigations to verify the authenticity of the letter or to evaluate the soundness of the need. Often Eleanor Roosevelt knew of the disposition of the case within a week or two.

Woodward's office served as an intermediary also for a number of private charities and social agencies that appealed to the White House when their resources were exhausted. Investigation proved that the District of Columbia Little Sisters of the Poor genuinely needed the commodities they requested for their care of the aged. On the other hand, a women's service center in St. Louis was denied assistance after investigation indicated that its statement of need had been grossly exaggerated and its past performance inefficient.

Complaints about the insensitive actions of local relief authorities drew prompt and thorough investigation. The letter from an unmarried Kansas City woman complaining of her difficulty in finding work struck a responsive chord, for ER had a special concern for single women. "They say they can't place me as I do not have a family. What are we single girls going to do?" the woman asked. Her letter to the White House, referred first to Mary Anderson in the Women's Bureau and then to Ellen Woodward, was forwarded to the director of women's work in Kansas and then to Kansas City relief authorities. The case, closed when jobs were found for both the young woman and her sister, typified those handled by Woodward's division. Investigation by the Women's Division revealed that the tattered underwear distributed to an Alabama child and then sent to Eleanor Roosevelt along with a bitter letter was the "charity" of a church group and not the doing of the Emergency Relief Administration. Roosevelt heard, too, from a Missouri woman whose pregnancy was criticized by the relief official to whom she applied for aid. The woman eventually received an apology after Missouri authorities identified the official. When a Georgia woman wrote that "if I could only explain to you and the president the way Welfare help is carried on heare it would be a book," her letter prompted an investigation. Both Roosevelt and Woodward were aware that they were sometimes victims of fraudulent complaints and schemes. Even their attempts to prevent deception, however, led to criticism from correspondents who thought that their confidence had been betrayed or who faced recriminations from local relief authorities who resented interference from Washington. "No matter how carefully we try to guard the handling of relationships with certain kinds of persons," Woodward wrote to her friend in the White House, "there are heartaches."

Eleanor Roosevelt contributed personally to many of the people who appealed to her. When a Missouri mother requested a graduation suit for her son, for whose schooling the family had made sacrifices, ER asked Woodward to make inquiries so that "something to help them out" might be sent. When ER learned that a ten-year-old Florida boy was giving up his daily milk to his pregnant mother and that a Tucson relief client needed hospital care, she sent funds to meet the needs. Doubtless the records merely hint at her personal generosity to needy women and children over the years. The mere fact that she had cared enough to visit the depression-ridden made an impact on the lives she touched. After she accompanied the president to the Tennessee Valley Authority region in the fall of 1934, a deaf-mute mother of eight wrote to her, "You all come back again."

Women wrote to the first lady not only to ask for the funds, encouragement, or intercession that she could offer, but also to extend assistance. Some described property they wished to donate for the use of the women's projects or resident centers. Others wrote to suggest useful projects for the Women's Division, particularly in the fields of nursing and education. When Mary E. Williams, the director of public health nursing at Tuskegee Institute, sent her an extensive plan for a rural health center, Alabama relief programmers eventually revised the plan for implementation. Because the White House mail and her frequent trips to the hinterlands kept Roosevelt apprised of relief needs, she often communicated those needs to relief administrators. "The need for clothing everywhere seems to be becoming much greater," she wrote to Woodward during the winter of 1935. Was it possible, she asked, to employ white-collar workers in clothing-collection projects as well as to use surplus textiles for the production of garments for women at Camp Jane Addams (a resident camp for unemployed women)? Could surplus commodities be provided for the nursery school at Arthurdale (a resettlement community in West Virginia that she had virtually founded)?

Eleanor Roosevelt's long experience in Democratic politics and her wide association with women in the Northeast were invaluable to Woodward as she wrestled with the personnel problems that were a constant factor in keeping the women's programs on an even keel. The extensive projects in both New York State and New York City, like those elsewhere, depended on competent leaders who could deal with the myriad details of the projects and the incessant criticism that came from private industry, particularly garment manufacturers and retailers of household goods. The complaints, aimed at the New York project directors, the White House, and the New York congressional delegation, that the clothing projects were devastating to private enterprise, could not go unanswered and were a continuing irritant to the New York women's work director. When it was finally necessary to remove an ineffective and politically indiscreet director in New York, even though she had the support of the congressional delegation, Roosevelt and Woodward consulted one another to find a replacement who would not provoke political recriminations that might wreck the projects. They collaborated also to prevent the New York relief programs from being exploited by Republican opponents of Congresswoman Caroline O'Day, a strong supporter of the WPA and a close friend of them both. ER astutely handled other potentially dangerous matters. Whenever WPA critics came to her, whenever she learned of informants planted on work projects as opposition spies, and whenever she learned of dissension within a project, she notified Woodward.

On more than one occasion, Eleanor Roosevelt had to referee the fractiousness that existed among a handful of powerful Democratic women leaders. In Pennsylvania, national committeewoman Emma Guffey Miller, as authoritative as she was effective, fought tirelessly to remove the state director of the women's projects, who was not sympathetic to the political considerations that motivated Miller. Impressed by the director's competence, Woodward defended her to ER and managed to resist Miller's pressures. In these protracted disputes, she never countermanded Woodward's decisions on matters relating to her administration of the Women's Division.

While the new Works Progress Administration was being planned in early 1935, Woodward once again turned to her White House ally. "Won't you please ask the President to emphasize in his talk . . . that employable women on relief will receive their fair proportion of jobs in the new program. . . . You are always on the alert to safeguard the welfare of needy women." Authorized by an executive order in May 1935, the WPA was intended to replace the last vestiges of the dole with a massive jobs program that went beyond either of its predecessor work programs. Soon after the WPA was begun, Woodward took the spotlight at the first lady's weekly press conference to announce that women were to be given equal consideration with men under the new program. She was, nonetheless, frustrated during the early months of the WPA in meeting her goal of putting to work the half-million women who had been certified as bona fide heads of families. New WPA regulations required a larger local sponsorship of the nonlabor costs of projects. This made it difficult to continue many of the women's activities that had been partially funded by women's organizations or state social agencies, whose revenue sources were limited. The additional stipulation that fewer nonrelief supervisory personnel could be employed undercut many of the efforts made in the earlier FERA and CWA women's programs. It appeared that only the sewing projects were compatible with the concept of mass employment that dominated the thinking of the WPA engineers, and that the state directors of women's work were in danger of losing the autonomy within the state relief organizations that Mrs. Woodward had won for them. Woodward and Roosevelt worried that the projects providing both work for professional women (teachers, librarians, and nurses, among others) and training programs for unskilled women would suffer as the new directives went into effect. By pooling their efforts the two women saved the earlier, well-integrated program of women's work; in 1936 the Women's Division reached its peak with 460,000 women employed. That May, ER greeted the state and regional directors, who came to Washington for a conference at the Mayflower Hotel and for a large exhibit of the services and goods flowing from an enormously productive women's program.

In July 1936, with her powerful friend's blessing, Woodward received jurisdiction over Federal One, which included the WPA Art, Writers', Theater, and Music Projects. A year earlier she had become the director of the Women's and Professional Projects. The scope of her efforts was thus greatly enlarged, especially by the addition of the arts projects, and now embraced programs for women (and men) of widely varying abilities, from artists to housemaids.

It was for the less-skilled of them that Eleanor Roosevelt had a special compassion, for she knew that the depression had taken its greatest toll among the women least able to cope. Since 1928 she had been honorary chair of the National Committee on Household Employment, which represented a field containing a large proportion of black and immigrant workers. In her third article in the *Woman's Home Companion* series, she had admonished her readers: "One has no more right to expect sweat-shop hours and wages in one's own home than in a factory." She eagerly accepted Woodward's invitation to monitor the development of the Household Workers' Training Program, which from a modest beginning under FERA had expanded under the WPA to train about twenty thousand women, ages eighteen to sixty-five, for employment in private homes or public institutions. The Household Demonstration Centers, most of them located in urban areas, were intended to elevate the status of an unskilled occupation to that of a skilled profession. Roosevelt was as disappointed as Woodward that conditions within the field of domestic service were too rooted in tradition and subject to the laws of supply and demand for a WPA work project to overcome. Nonetheless, her interest never waned and she returned to the subject many times in her writings. In 1940 she charged that the project had foundered because in many locales sponsors could not be found. Housewives, fearing that they would have to pay more than three dollars a week for trained servants, simply did not wish the project to succeed.

Neither Roosevelt nor Woodward ignored the failure of the WPA to deal fairly with minorities, both in the employment of unskilled needy women and in the appointment of supervisory personnel. When Mary McLeod Bethune asked ER to assist her in promoting a more equitable distribution of federal benefits to black women and children, the latter agreed to open the White House for a conference on the subject. She invited more than fifty leaders of constituent organizations within the National Council of Negro Women to attend a forum on April 4, 1938. The NCNW representatives were joined by more than a dozen women directors of federal bureaus and offices, who were convened by Woodward to hear the NCNW resolutions and recommendations regarding the shortcomings of WPA programs, social security benefits, public health services, and other federal welfare programs. In her remarks to the assembly, Roosevelt emphasized the effectiveness of local inquiry: "I make it a great point wherever I go to ask what is being done." She recommended that biracial women's committees should work together in each community to focus the attention of community officials and sympathetic citizens on the needs of all people regardless of race. In private conversations, she and Woodward discussed the possibility that government agencies would add prominent black women in at least an advisory capacity. The belated efforts to include more minorities in staff positions as well as on local relief rolls was thwarted when congressional economy advocates succeeded in scaling down relief appropriations in 1938. By then the entire WPA structure lay in jeopardy.

The volume of Eleanor Roosevelt's mail did not diminish with the establishment of the WPA. In the first four months of 1938 alone, her staff handed over 2,550 letters to Woodward's office. An analysis of the referrals of White House mail made by the Women's Division in the spring of 1936 shows an increase not only in the volume of letters but also in the number of problems raised. Women wrote of delays in their assignment to WPA work, of their ineligibility for work because of age or disability, and of the barriers that confronted mothers of small children when they sought work relief. Many letters clearly demonstrated that the security wage paid by the WPA was too low to support a family. Single women expressed their resentment that married women whose husbands had jobs were given work in private industry. And there were numerous complaints about the policies of other New Deal agencies. As the complaints and requests for assistance continued to arrive, the staff of the Women's Division maintained the practices established in earlier years. When a letter describing the needs of a sixteen-year-old crippled girl in Mississippi reached the White House in 1938, it was sent from Washington to the office of the Mississippi director of women's work, and then to the chief health officer of the state, and on to the state vocational rehabilitation director, who wrote the young woman, "I think everybody from the President's wife on down the line is very much interested in your welfare." The girl was given training intended to make her self-supporting.

Early in 1938, it became apparent that Congress intended to curtail the operations of the Works Progress Administration and that the women's and professional projects were especially vulnerable. Roosevelt and Woodward concentrated their efforts to save the programs they both thought most valuable: handicrafts, arts, and institutional services. A private citizen, ER could not appear before congressional committees as director Woodward could, and did, in January 1938, to press eloquently for continued appropriations, or as she did in August when she defended the Federal Theater before the House Un-American Activities Committee. But the first lady could publicize the work of the women and professionals, as she did in January when she took a party of White House guests to a large exhibit at the Smithsonian that featured the work of more than 400,000 WPA workers. She insisted, too, that the president attend. Impressed particularly by the craft exhibits, she told the press, "We are just beginning to think of hand craftsmanship as a means of livelihood." In July, Woodward spent a day at Hyde Park discussing with her friend the institutional service projects, which provided unskilled, clerical, research, and professional workers for hospitals, county homes, and similar community social services. Woodward followed up the visit with an extensive memorandum justifying the projects, for Roosevelt's use in pleading their case with her husband. A month later the Hyde Park hostess received the regional directors and sat them down to lunch with the president.

Although the budget-cutters prevailed and the women's activities were scaled down, they survived. In 1940, after Woodward had left the WPA

for the Social Security Board, the new women's and professional work
director, Florence Kerr, received the same support from Eleanor
Roosevelt that her predecessor had enjoyed. When the division conducted
a nationwide celebration of its endeavors with the theme "This Work Pays
Your Community," ER helped initiate the week-long open house that
showcased the projects. She spoke by radio to the more than 600,000
project workers who attended twenty-five cent dinners in their own communities on May 20, 1940. The work that she had observed was an "object
lesson in democracy. . . . You've made [American communities] better
places in which we may all live and work together. And at the same time
you've been winning the bread and butter for the loved ones in your
homes." She described her visits to the clinics, the school lunchrooms, the
sewing rooms, the adult-education classes, the nursery schools, and the
homes assisted by housekeeping aides. Convinced that such work was as
socially rewarding as it was economically essential to the individuals it
sustained, ER remained a champion of the women's work-relief projects,
until the final units were liquidated after World War II began and the
WPA was at an end.

The work-relief inequities for women that troubled Roosevelt and
Woodward took on new dimensions after the Social Security Act was
passed in August 1935. Both women welcomed the commitment to economic security and general welfare that the measure reflected. The first
lady's mail soon revealed inequities, however, in the sections concerning
mothers' pensions (i.e., aid to dependent children), unemployment compensation, and public assistance for the aged and handicapped. She asked
Woodward for advice on handling the complaints and queries from
mothers who were struck off work-relief rolls because benefits were now
available to them under Social Security. The new WPA certification rules
required that work relief was to be limited to persons who could not
qualify for assistance under other federal programs, including Social Security. But the monthly checks under Social Security depended on match-
ing contributions from the states, and the size of contributions varied
widely by state. In many states the Social Security payments were actually lower than the WPA wages that women had been earning. Women,
quite reasonably, wondered why they were expected to give up their
WPA jobs to accept mothers' pensions.

These inequities, Woodward pointed out in her memoranda to
Roosevelt, resulted from the premise of the Social Security Act that,

through the enactment of supportive legislation and the appropriation of sufficient funds, the individual state should provide the primary assistance given to mothers. There were other aspects of the new law that affected women adversely. The new WPA rulings meant that, in order to draw mothers' aid, working mothers had to stop working until their youngest child reached the age of sixteen. But it was likely that by the time they reentered the work force they would have lost their skills or would be denied an opportunity, in the first place, to learn a skill through placement on one of the work-relief training programs. Both Roosevelt and Woodward argued forcefully that public policy should not discourage mothers from working in either private or government jobs, including work relief.

In December 1938, Woodward left the Women's and Professional Division to succeed Molly Dewson as one of the three members of the Social Security Board. During the six years of Woodward's tenure on the board, she and Roosevelt put forth the same kind of effort for expanded Social Security benefits for women that they had for the work-relief programs. To enlighten the public about the benefits available to wives, widows, and mothers was one of their goals. Another was to educate the states to the fact that they must assume a larger financial responsibility for public assistance and unemployment compensation. In that regard they relied a great deal upon Jane Hoey, an old New York social work friend of ER, who had become the director of the Bureau of Public Assistance of the Social Security Board. In January 1940, the three women conducted a radio dialogue over the CBS network to publicize important changes in the Social Security program, becoming effective that month, that expanded protection under the insurance program to include an individual wage earner's wife and surviving minor children. The Social Security Act "is helping families to fulfill their enduring responsibilities to their own members, young and old," Roosevelt said in her concluding remarks, "and to that greater family we call the Nation." It was a theme she returned to many times in subsequent speeches and her newspaper columns.

At Woodward's suggestion, Roosevelt occasionally received the Social Security regional directors at the White House, just as she continued to discuss the WPA women's work with the regional staff brought to her by Florence Kerr. Meeting with Social Security directors would "encourage and inspire them to get Mrs. Roosevelt's reaction to their activities," the board member wrote to ER's secretary. Woodward, as well as other members of the Social Security Board, relied upon her to place their ideas before the president with a hope that he would include in his speeches and congressional contacts the subject of more liberal Social Security provisions.

After the United States entered World War II, new problems relating to women and security engaged the mutual interest of Woodward and Roosevelt. In November 1942, at the former's invitation, the first lady reported at a session of the Social Security Board on her recent trip to England. She described the day nurseries for children of women engaged in war production and the mobilization of women in hospitals, factories, and auxiliary military services. The inference was, of course, that the United States could learn from the British experience. Within a year, Roosevelt had invited Woodward to her office to discuss a new problem reflected in her mail—assistance for the children of servicemen lost in the war, for whom there were no Social Security provisions. It was a subject already under consideration within the Social Security Board and one for which recommendations were to be made to Congress. As the end of the war approached, Woodward asked Roosevelt to give attention in her daily column to the federalization of unemployment compensation, which she believed to be essential to meet the problem of postwar mass unemployment: "We think it is desperately important to create *now* a Social Security system complete and strong enough to meet the problems that will arise with the demobilization of our armed forces and the shift from a war to a peace-time industry." In 1945, when Congress appeared reluctant to broaden Social Security to include health and disability insurance and to provide coverage for domestic workers, Woodward drafted letters for Eleanor Roosevelt's signature that called for more liberal provisions. In the last exchange between the two before the Social Security Board was abolished under executive reorganization in July 1946, they turned to the matter of Social Security coverage for farm workers and a strategy for the passage of a revised Wagner-Murray-Dingell bill, which would provide many of the Social Security reforms they had long discussed.

After 1946, when Eleanor Roosevelt was no longer first lady and Ellen Woodward had moved into the Office of International Relations within the new Federal Security Agency, the two long-time advocates of greater economic security for women had less occasion to consult each other. Their exchanges were less frequent and were concerned mainly with their separate activities and travels on behalf of international welfare programs. When Woodward finally retired from government service at the end of

December 1953, at age sixty-six, she wrote her partner in reform, "Whatever I have been able to accomplish for the welfare of people, *you* deserve the major credit."

SOURCES

The most valuable source on the association of Eleanor Roosevelt and Ellen Woodward is Record Group 69 in the National Archives, which contains the official records of the FERA, CWA, and WPA, of which the "White House Correspondence" files are the richest. Other rewarding manuscripts are in the extensive Eleanor Roosevelt Papers in the Roosevelt Library at Hyde Park, New York, and the Ellen Woodward Papers at the Mississippi Department of Archives and History in Jackson. Useful material is also at the Roosevelt Library in the Mary (Molly) W. Dewson Papers and the Harry L. Hopkins Papers. Some Roosevelt-Woodward letters and memoranda are in Record Group 47 (the records of the Social Security Administration), others are in the National Archives, and still others in the Washington National Records Center at Suitland, Maryland. Tamara K. Hareven's biography *Eleanor Roosevelt: An American Conscience* (Chicago, 1968) is a moving account that contains much valuable information; it reveals ER's deep compassion for women and minorities. Ruby Black's contemporary tribute *Eleanor Roosevelt: A Biography* (New York, 1940) tells of her concern about needy women. Susan Ware, in *Beyond Suffrage: Women in the New Deal* (Cambridge, Massachusetts, 1981), describes Ellen Woodward as one of the effective women administrators of the era, as does Elsie L. George in her doctoral dissertation "The Women Appointees of the Roosevelt and Truman Administrations (American University, 1972). My own previous work on Ellen Woodward or on women's work relief appears in two articles, "Ellen S. Woodward: The Gentlewoman as Federal Administrator" (*Furman Studies*, December, 1980) and "The 'Forgotten Woman': Ellen Woodward and Women's Work Relief During the New Deal" (*Prologue*, Winter, 1984). "Mrs. Roosevelt's Page," which ran from August 1933 to July 1935, in the *Woman's Home Companion*, and her "My Day" newspaper column touch upon the subjects of work relief and social security.

Ingrid Winther Scobie

Helen Gahagan Douglas and the Roosevelt Connection

N 1939, HELEN GAHAGAN, a glamorous and dynamic woman with an incisive mind, enjoyed a reputation as one of the nation's prominent actresses, as an opera singer of some distinction, and as the wife of one of Hollywood's popular and highly paid romantic stars, Melvyn Douglas. Like many members of the film community, she had become absorbed in the fight against European fascism and the pressing national problem of migrant labor, particularly critical in California. But no astute observer of the state's political scene would have predicted that within five years Helen Gahagan Douglas would win the first of three successive terms to Congress and, in 1950, become California's Democratic candidate for the United States Senate. The story of her unanticipated and rapid move into a full-time political career, relinquishing her earlier commitment to the theater and opera, is a story whose major theme is friendship with Eleanor and Franklin Roosevelt. That friendship began over dinner at the White House in November 1939. A close look suggests that Helen Gahagan Douglas belongs near the top of that select and talented group of women, including Frances Perkins, Molly Dewson, Ellen Woodward, and Florence C. Allen, who were launched into prominence during the New Deal. She was the only woman elected to national office during the New Deal who enjoyed both the strong, effective political support and the personal friendship of the Roosevelts.

Helen Gahagan was born and raised in Brooklyn, the older daughter of a prosperous and locally prominent family of three boys and two girls.

[153]

Her father Walter, owner of a large and successful dredging and construction firm, provided his family a comfortable life in a large duplex on Prospect Place, where they were sheltered from sights of poverty and social and racial injustice. Mother Lillian Mussen Gahagan, reared in a musical home and possessing a fine voice, invited musicians into the Gahagan home for visits and entertainment. These articts complemented the politically conservative social and civic leaders whom Walter Gahagan brought home. The children all attended private schools, and their parents demanded as much excellence from the girls as the boys. Helen, the middle child, early showed dramatic talent, an imaginative mind, a love for the spotlight, and a strong distaste for her parents' emphasis on traditional academics, although she did love to read. At her father's insistence, she entered Barnard College in 1920. But in May of her sophomore year, instead of studying for final exams, she made the rounds of theatrical agents. Through connections with friends of her high-school drama teacher, she landed a small part in an off-Broadway play; three weeks later, producer William Brady offered her a part in "Dreams for Sale" by Owen Davis. In her first Broadway performance this tall, slender, dark-haired beauty from Brooklyn's elite "conquered the dramatic world of Manhattan overnight," to use one critic's words. In the variety of star roles that followed, she joined that small group of actresses—including Ethel Barrymore, Jane Cowl, Katharine Cornell, and Helen Hayes—who dominated Broadway in the 1920s.

Despite her success and maturing talent, Helen showed signs of restlessness. She remained dissatisfied with the roles she played. Also, her mother pushed her constantly to take voice lessons. Beginning in 1928, she closeted herself with a recently immigrated Russian voice coach; in 1929 she made her operatic debut in Czechoslovakia. Further European engagements followed, but in the summer of 1930 she returned to New York, partly because of her father's serious illness, to take the lead role of a temperamental opera star in David Belasco's production of a new Hungarian comic romance, "Tonight or Never." Belasco, noted for his astute casting of male and female leads, selected a newcomer to Broadway, Melvyn Douglas, as Helen's leading man. The two fell in love, undoubtedly enhancing the reality of the on-stage affair, and toward the end of an enormously popular eight-month run, they married. During that time Melvyn signed a contract with Hollywood producer Samuel Goldwyn, who had bought the movie rights of "Tonight or Never" for Gloria Swanson. In September 1931, after a delayed honeymoon in Europe and Helen's American operatic debut in Cleveland, the couple trekked across the country to create a new life for themselves in Hollywood.

Once established on the West Coast, Helen kept busy with singing, radio, and theatrical contracts, and one movie. She provided encouraging support to Melvyn in his fast-moving screen career. In 1934 and 1938 she gave birth, respectively, to Peter and Mary Helen. The first hint of a new professional direction for her came following a trip to Europe in 1937. Helen embarked on an extensive tour of various European opera houses, climaxed by an engagement at the Salzburg Festival. Melvyn joined her for a portion of the trip. Both became aware that the Europe they loved was disintegrating, and they were devastated by the changes brought on by the fascist regimes. An attempt in Munich to recruit Helen as a Nazi sympathizer awakened her to the stark realities of the times. "[I felt] just as if I'd been hit in the solar plexus. . . . I [wondered] why I didn't know more about what was going on. . . . I was isolated in a world that was going to collapse around me."

The episode had enough impact that Helen Douglas reneged on a fall singing engagement with the Vienna Opera. She returned to the United States and continued an active program of concert engagements. But for the first time ever, she felt concern for the world outside her personal life. She and Melvyn, who already had a highly developed social conscience, joined the Hollywood Anti-Fascist League, an active group reflecting the intensely anti-Nazi climate in Hollywood. Melvyn Douglas took the lead in moving into the political arena. Through the Motion Picture Democratic Committee, which he helped form, Melvyn led the Democratic efforts in Southern California for Culbert Olson's campaign for California governor in 1938, earning considerable recognition both at state and national party headquarters.

Helen remained marginally involved in politics until late 1938, when at Melvyn's invitation a newly created Hollywood group, the John Steinbeck Committee to Aid Migratory Workers, used the Douglases' spacious home for a meeting. Helen's cousin, who lived with the Douglases and served as their secretary, beckoned Helen to the terrace to listen to the animated discussion about the conditions of the California migrants. As Douglas recalled, she went out the door and stood at the back of the meeting, listening to "tales of personally witnessed horror and the indifference of the state authorities. I could not know it then [but] that afternoon I took my first step into politics." She later accompanied Melvyn to another Steinbeck Committee meeting, "with no intention of getting involved," where the group discussed the possibility of raising money to host a Christmas party for migrant children. At one point, however, Helen interrupted the discussion, suggesting how simple it would be to solicit donations from merchants. Before she quite realized what had happened, she ended up in charge of the party.

Her curiosity led her to find out more about migrants, and throughout 1939 she moved increasingly into the circle of those who were demanding more state and federal government assistance for the migrant camps administered by the Farm Security Administration (FSA) under the Department of Agriculture. Although this work increasingly involved her with New Deal activities in California, she hardly considered herself anything other than an actress and a singer. Nevertheless, without a clear sense of direction, she suddenly found herself so wrapped up in talks about migrants that she committed herself to few singing and acting engagements.

When Governor Olson appointed to the Steinbeck Committee chair, Carey McWilliams, chief of his Division of Immigration and Housing in early 1939, the organization asked Douglas to replace McWilliams. Organized primarily to arouse public awareness of the migrants' plight in housing, food, and labor conditions, the committee had little political power. Together with another, more influential, private organization, the Simon Lubin Society, the Steinbeck Committee solicited money to help improve migrant conditions and to educate the public. Under Helen Douglas, asserted one specialist on the migrant problem, the group became "more paternalistic," concentrating primarily on the Okies. But in terms of legislative goals, Douglas fought to protect the civil liberties of all agricultural workers, supported inclusion of workers under existing labor and social security legislation, and argued for additional housing, health services, and food distribution centers. Douglas spoke wherever she could get a chance, to state and federal investigating committees, political organizations, women's clubs, civic and church groups, academic gatherings, and student clubs. She and Melvyn, who also took an interest in the migrants' plight, visited the camps as often as possible.

Like most California liberal organizations in the late 1930s, the committee did not escape red-baiting. The organizations worked together in a loose confederation referred to as the United Front, but to conservatives they were all the same—"Communist-infiltrated" at the least, and often charged with consisting entirely of "fellow-travelers" if not Communists. Rumors circulated that Communists belonged to the Steinbeck Committee. It did not help any that the group had donated funds to the Cannery, Agricultural, Packing, and Allied Workers of America, organized in mid-1938, branded a Communist-front organization by the powerful right-wing growers' association, the Associated Farmers.

Within a few months, those who dealt with the migrant problems in the state were beginning to realize that Helen Douglas spoke very effectively and had considerable political potential. One FSA camp director urged the Douglases to assist in the weekly camp shows as well as to get Hollywood people to "portray a true picture of the conditions as they actually exist [which] would do more to arouse public opinion than anything else yet accomplished." The president of the San Francisco Center of the California League of Women Voters, also an active member of the Democratic party's Women's Division, complimented Helen Douglas in June 1939 for the "comprehensive and moving picture" of the migrants she presented in a speech to the organization. During the year, she was appointed to the State Advisory Committee of the National Youth Authority.

Douglas, of course, never approached the level of expertise of McWilliams or of Paul Taylor, professor of economics at the University of California, Berkeley, two leading experts on migrants. But her knowledge about migrants' condition and, perhaps more importantly, her ability to articulate this information in an exceptionally effective way, eventually brought her to the attention of officials in Washington. Arthur Goldschmidt, a life-long friend who worked for the Interior Department under Harold Ickes in the late 1930s and early 1940s, recalls talking with Douglas after she gave a speech. "I found myself subjected to an intense cross-examination—grilling might not be too strong a word. She accepted no vague generalities. . . . Her questions were not naive . . . I came away . . . enchanted with a sense of wonder at Helen's display of energy—at the physical, emotional and mental drive of this beautiful and glamorous person." Helen herself described her approach in a newspaper interview in the summer of 1939. She gushed, "The loads and loads of statistics I read! . . . But every bit of it is necessary. You must be armed with facts and figures. The time has passed when one can just go out and be emotional and expect to get anything done!" The interviewer closed with an apt description of Douglas:

Helen Gahagan presented a picture that movie magazines have taught you to expect of the beauties of the film world. While she talked with me she reclined on a chaise longue, wrapped in a heavenly pink velvet negligee. Blue chiffon bound her lovely head. But there ended the similarity of the movie magazine hollywoodites.

Thirty minutes with Helen Gahagan leaves you with the impression that here's a woman who thinks straight, who'll keep at a problem until it is solved, no matter how big that problem is, [and who will] work unceasingly to help preserve and maintain democracy and all that it stands for in America.

In addition to this intense curiosity, Douglas brought to her new-found avocation several unusual qualities that made her successful in active politics. In the first place, her theatrical training and experience, her ability to absorb and synthesize information, and her dynamic method of communicating in a convincing and disarming way resulted in real political strength. Second, Helen was beautiful. Her striking glamor, coupled with the aura of Hollywood, took people aback, particularly in the male political world. A college friend, Alis de Sola, wrote in 1937:

I always feel a little baffled when I think of Helen Gahagan. You sense that curious quickening quality the moment she comes into a room, a tall radiant woman with a quite unreasonable beauty and an air of going somewhere very fast.

Her effect on other people is something like that of a very potent cocktail. She makes them feel excited and rather brilliant and as though they, too, were on their way to some astonishing goal. After she leaves, they may wonder just where they did think they were going and what in hell they would have done when they got there but, while it lasts, it's a very pleasant feeling, indeed.

Third, the Douglases enjoyed both social credentials and economic resources that permitted them to travel without restraint and to seek out and cultivate whomever they might choose. The lack of financial restraint had particular significance for Helen's political career for it allowed her the means to play the political game in ways most women could not. She could fly to Washington to consult, travel throughout the state for meetings, speak nationally, and hire adequate household, childcare, and secretarial help.

In addition, the Douglases felt second-class to few people, and many within the liberal community in Los Angeles delighted in contact and friendship with the popular Hollywood couple. With some of these new acquaintances, they encouraged discussion of issues by holding a Sunday forum in their home. They also met a wide variety of people by traveling all over California. A few of those whom the Douglases met, as they plunged headlong into politics, became close friends. These included Remsen Bird, president of Occidental College, who relished involvement in liberal causes and Hollywood connections; Alexander Meiklejohn, the famed civil libertarian, and his wife, economist Helen Everett Meiklejohn, who together established the School for Social Research in Berkeley; Charles Hogan, later the first United States ambassador to the United Nations; and Aubrey Williams, head of the New Deal's National Youth Authority.

It was Williams who first called the Douglases and their California political activities to the attention of the Roosevelts. By 1939, the country finally took the migrant situation seriously as a result of unrelenting pressure from individuals and organizations. FDR recognized the urgency of the problem, and once Olson defeated the ultraconservative governor, Frank E. Merriam, President Roosevelt could work more effectively with California government officials. He ordered a federal investigation in early 1939. The sudden public preoccupation, buttressed with support from Washington, received a tremendous boost from Steinbeck's *Grapes of Wrath*, a book that also stimulated furious controversy. Two other books furnished additional persuasive documentation—McWilliams's *Factories in the Field*, and the moving pictorial study *An American Exodus*, by Paul Taylor and his wife Dorothea Lange, a widely acclaimed photographer noted for her stunning FSA photographs of rural conditions during the New Deal. In addition, the findings of the La Follette Committee, investigating how migrants were often deprived of their civil rights, added to the swell of public outrage. Williams realized that the Roosevelts would be keenly interested in Helen Douglas's firsthand knowledge of the migrant camps. Both had read Steinbeck's moving account. Williams also recognized that Melvyn could help the president in mobilizing Hollywood's talent and financial resources behind the waning New Deal and the coming 1940 election. "When I was on the West Coast," he wrote FDR on July 18, 1939, "I had a long talk with Melvyn Douglas, who you will remember is one of the top flight motion picture people. Mr. Douglas discussed at length the part that he felt motion picture and radio people could play in the fight for our program. He . . . expects to come East sometime . . . and he is anxious to see you."

The invitation to the White House soon followed. When Mrs. Roosevelt learned the Douglases planned a trip to Washington in November, she wrote Helen: "Mr. Aubrey Williams tells me you will be in this part of the world. . . . The president and I would so much like to see you. Would you be able to dine with us on November 29th and spend the night?" A week later, the Douglases arrived, a bit in awe of their forthcoming experience. Said Helen, many years later in her book *The Eleanor Roosevelt We Remember*, "I remember well my first visit to the White House and the emotional impact it had on me. . . . I had to swallow hard and blink my eyes to keep back the tears." At dinner that night, the Douglases joined Assistant Attorney General Norman Littell and his wife; Aubrey Williams; Colonel Francis Harrington, head of the Works Progress Administration; and several members, including Joseph P. Lash, of the controversial Youth Congress, currently under investigation by the Dies Committee. The president had his mind more on the recent Russian invasion of Finland, but he also asked about the hearings that day on the Youth Congress. After dinner, he withdrew while the others discussed a topic of strong mutual interest—the organization of liberals in the West.

The Roosevelt dinner highlighted the Douglas visit to Washington, but numerous high-ranking New Dealers entertained the visitors. Williams arranged a luncheon for Melvyn. The twenty guests included Attorney General Frank Murphy (soon to be appointed to the Supreme Court); Littell; Secretary of Interior Harold L. Ickes and his assistant Oscar Chapman; Judge Francis Biddle, who became attorney general in 1941; Representative Jerry Voorhis, an effective young New Dealer absorbed with the migrant issue; and others who clustered around the president, including Ben Cohen, Isador Lubin, and Tom Corcoran. As Ickes recorded in his published diary, Douglas told the group that the Motion Picture Democratic Committee would "do what it could for the New Deal and I agreed with his statement that this group could be very influential," although "two or three Communists, rather prominent in the organization . . . will have to be sidetracked since they continue to be apologists for Stalin." Other engagements included lunch with Harold and Anna Ickes, a visit with Secretary of Labor Frances Perkins, dinner with the Littells, and another dinner with United States Court of Appeals Justice Justin Miller and his wife. Dorothy McAllister, the sparkling and talented head of the

Democratic National Committee, also gave a magnificent party in honor of Helen, to which a number of cabinet members were invited.

The Douglases left Washington having established firm links with the sources of New Deal power. Williams had correctly guessed that they and the Roosevelts would take a liking to each other. That dinner proved to be the beginning of a close personal and political relationship that in time took on many ramifications and that had a major impact on Helen Douglas's life. Almost immediately the pattern of that friendship, from which both couples stood to benefit, took shape. Both Douglases found themselves involved more and more with New Deal concerns. ER delighted in Helen's energies, which continued, for a time, to concentrate on migrants. Melvyn plunged into the challenges of the coming primary battles; the already factionalized Democrats had divided bitterly over the issue of FDR's third term. The Douglases enjoyed open access to the intimate atmosphere of the White House, including its use as a base of operations whenever in Washington. ER began a practice of visiting and often staying with the Douglases on her trips west. Neither Douglas felt shy in contacting the Roosevelts or any of the cabinet members they had met concerning their political concerns or interests. The president appointed both Douglases to various White House boards and kept abreast of what the Douglases were doing.

When the Douglases returned home following their exhilarating week in Washington, Helen became engrossed in the final arrangements for the Steinbeck Committee's second Christmas party for migrants. She hastened to communicate the success to Eleanor Roosevelt through a detailed letter to her secretary Malvina Thompson. Her main efforts, Douglas wrote, had centered on the conservative forces—Chambers of Commerce, police, ranchers, mayors, church groups, journalists—in the Imperial Valley who "were convinced . . . that we were coming down with a red flag in one hand, a bomb in the other, with the film 'Grapes of Wrath' under our arms, for the express purpose of stirring up discontent." Her letter went on to mention the existence of "a large group of . . . liberals [whom we must] contact and morally support." At the end of the missive in a postscript reminiscent of the social charm and grace that she had exhibited while in Washington, she added that Melvyn and she had sent the president and the first lady some wine, which they hoped had been "aged long enough to please them."

Despite Douglas's delight at the response of the more than eight thousand migrants who came to the Christmas party, she had a problematic relationship with certain Steinbeck Committee members whom she believed to be Communists. Later in the month she resigned and joined with Melvyn, who had left the Motion Picture Democratic Committee for similar reasons, to organize a group of like-minded liberals as the California Citizens Council. She wrote Voorhis, with whom she had begun to correspond regularly about their mutual interest in migrant labor: "We find ourselves in [the] absurd position of most liberals today. The Communists call us reactionaries and the reactionaries call us Communists!" Despite her departure from the Steinbeck Committee, she went on, "I shall continue to try and spread light on the agricultural question—viewing it from a national as well as a local point of view."

Late in January 1940, Helen Douglas became involved with the upcoming annual convention of the Democratic Study Clubs in California. She had a spot on the program to talk about migrants, and she also planned to entertain Frances Perkins, the keynote speaker. The study clubs originally met to investigate and discuss political issues, playing a less active role than the Democratic party's more recently formed Women's Division, an official arm of the party. Although many women belonged to both organizations, the Women's Division gained a more liberal reputation. Both groups, however, served as a training ground for women who later moved into elected or appointed political positions. The president of the California Study Clubs in 1940, Nettie Jones (Mrs. Mattison Boyd Jones), also held the position of head of the Women's Division for Southern California, although she felt more comfortable politically with the study club women. A prickly Democrat, active in California politics since the days of Woodrow Wilson, Jones took charge of the convention arrangements, including the efforts to persuade Perkins to speak. Jones had learned in October that Perkins was "seriously considering" the engagement. Not until November, however, after Perkins had talked with Helen Douglas, did she decide to accept the invitation. Jones ecstatically pledged the cooperation of all the women's political groups in the state, but soon many women doubted her intentions because she did not include all groups in the planning. Toward the end of January, open hostility erupted among Democratic women leaders, both in the Bay area and in southern California. Actually, the negotiations over Perkins merely served as a pretext for political feuding that had much deeper roots. The clashes were linked to the battles in Sacramento between the Olson liberals and "economy bloc"

Democrats who opposed the high cost of the governor's program to bring the New Deal to California. Red-baiting charges of corruption in the state's relief administration, which provided financial aid to migrant workers, plus three recall movements against the governor further complicated the issues.

The women's fight revealed deep schisms among the various women's groups that went beyond these more general issues—long-term divisions between women in the north and south, between the Women's Division and the independently organized Democratic Study Clubs, between political and nonpartisan groups including the League of Women Voters, and between politically conservative and liberal women.

Helen Douglas kept out of the fighting over Perkins. In the long run, her neutrality significantly enhanced her political status. She busied herself with her own plans for Perkins—a reception and an intimate dinner for leading Los Angeles people, including some conservatives she felt ought to meet Perkins, in the hope it would decrease their hostility to President Roosevelt. None of the women involved in the tussle were invited. Douglas also knew that, because of her prior contact with Perkins in Washington and because of Melvyn's stature in the party, she would have easy access to the secretary of labor during the convention.

Despite all the disagreements among the women, the response to the Perkins visit was excellent both in the north and the south. In addition, the Douglases' party for Perkins helped to establish a connection between Helen and Perkins totally independent of the women's groups. Shortly after returning to Washington, Perkins wrote Helen an unusually warm note:

> The evening at your house was of great importance and help to me . . . in comprehending the fears, the hopes, the doubts . . . of influential Californians, who are conservative but not irresponsible. . . . I am very grateful to you for the effort, the discrimination, the warmth, and the taste with which you gathered together that particular group. . . . I hope that our friendship has only just begun. . . . Please always look me up when you are east.

Also in February, the national office of the Women's Division, in its widely read monthly magazine *Democratic Digest*, published an article by Douglas on migrants. In it Douglas spelled out the history of migrant problems, detailing migrant life in the FSA camps, and concluded by urging the FSA to be broadened by "cooperation of city, county, and state governments." Help for migrants must evolve into a desire on the part of individual communities to assimilate the migratory worker and recognize him for his true worth—a vital and necessary element of the agricultural structure [and] as a human being whose mental, physical and spiritual welfare affects the community and the country at large.

Shortly after Perkins returned to Washington, Douglas received a letter from McAllister thanking her for her "splendid article . . . one of the finest we have ever printed in our magazine. . . . Already I have received many letters of interest from . . . readers." McAllister closed by inviting Douglas to the Women's Division's National Institute of Government, scheduled to meet in Washington during early May to focus on campaign issues and effective party organization: "You have so much to contribute to such a meeting." Many wrote Douglas directly about her piece, including Supreme Court Justice William O. Douglas, who jotted on a note, "Dear Mrs. Douglas. . . . I found your recent article on migrant workers . . . *most* interesting."

Helen's attention turned next to ER's April visit to California. President Roosevelt had urged members of his cabinet and other important advisers, including his wife, to investigate personally the migrant situation, in order to demonstrate administrative support and gather firsthand information. Early in the year, Douglas wrote her new friend: "I [just] received word . . . that you would like to see some of the Farm Security Administration camps when you come to California. May I offer my services to you . . . in arranging as comprehensive a tour as possible?" Eleanor Roosevelt accepted, barring any complications, and Douglas asked Paul Taylor, the leading academic expert on agricultural labor, for his advice as to the best camps to tour. Careful planning for the trip paid off. ER and the Douglases took a four-seater private plane into the lush San Joaquin Valley where they spent an unforgettable day, accompanied by FHA regional head Larry Hewes, visiting several sites. After the trip, Douglas sent her a copy of Taylor and Lange's book, *An American Exodus*, with the hope that she would publicize it by mentioning it in "My Day." Lange wrote Douglas after the visit, "You are a valiant champion, and did a great job for Mrs. Roosevelt. We [Californians] have a lot to thank you for."

Eleanor Roosevelt found the visit very informative, particularly as it reassured her about conditions in the FSA camps and convinced her that Steinbeck's *Grapes of Wrath* did not exaggerate the migrant crisis. For three days, she filled her column with enthusiastic comments about the trip.

She wrote Helen, "I know the President will be enormously interested in what I have to tell him." She continued, "I am counting on having you stay at the White House when you come to Washington for the National Institute of Government." Douglas was on her way up.

While Douglas's visibility in California and her credibility in Washington were increasing rapidly, Jones's position as the leading Democratic woman in southern California steadily eroded. Despite the success of the Perkins visit, many women remained angry that Jones had left them out of the planning of the event. Some decided that "they would leave no stones unturned in their attempt to defeat Mrs. Jones' chances for being National Committeewoman" in June, when convention delegates would elect a new person for the position. Jones herself acknowledged that she faced factionalism in the Women's Division. She wrote McAllister that the Perkins affair had been wonderful but that had it not been "for the federated clubs the whole thing might have been a complete fizzle" owing to the factions in the Women's Division. But "on the surface, everything was beautiful."

At this juncture, few people spoke openly of Douglas undermining Jones's authority, although Jones undoubtedly perceived Douglas as a threat. Jones had been very cordial to Douglas while planning the Perkins affair and urged Douglas to speak at the banquet. Nevertheless, in March, only a few weeks after the luncheon, Mattison Jones, a prominent Los Angeles lawyer and active conservative Democrat, wrote Governor Olson a letter containing charges typical of those other liberals in the late 1930s experienced. "I have read with extreme regret your appointment of Miss Gahagan on one of your commissions." He charged, offering no evidence, that at a recent speech, Douglas had "revealed unquestionably to an audience of over 700 people that she was a Communist. . . . I hope you will not consider this a letter written with any motive other than in the interest of our Party and our country."

In addition to the increasing challenges to Jones's authority following the Perkins visit, tensions mounted among active Democrats as political battles in Sacramento spilled over into the selection, qualification, and campaigning for convention delegates in preparation for the May presidential preference elections. Concerned with the California situation, in mid-March the president sent Ickes out for a meeting of key Roosevelt-slate Democrats, which included the principal organizer, Governor Olson, and Melvyn Douglas. The *Los Angeles Times* wrote: "California's Democratic party has become the New Deal's problem child [and it is about to get a] good, old fashioned spanking [from] the capable hands of Secretary of Interior Ickes." Although Nettie Jones was selected as one of the slate delegates, her political standing diminished even further during this fight. She complained to McAllister that "the men have been so stupid, and some of them are acting like a lot of old fishwives, each wanting to be a prima donna. . . . It just makes me sick. No woman was ever consulted about the setup on the delegation, and they have only four women [out of 48 delegates] on it." Four days later she sounded off again. "The men make a terrible mistake by holding this conference in San Francisco with Mr. Ickes with no women present, or none having been consulted." Ickes detailed his meeting with the various factions within the pro-Roosevelt group in his diary. "I felt that I had done a good job, but I was thoroughly tired. . . . I didn't find Democratic politics in a very healthy condition in California, although everyone seemed to think Roosevelt would carry the state if he were nominated."

In addition to being left out of the Ickes meeting, Jones discovered in mid-April that she had not been included on the executive committee of the Roosevelt delegation campaign committee, "which truly was a peculiar thing, since Melvyn Douglas, one of the delegates, was made chairman. One would naturally expect that the head of the women's activities in the south . . . would be on the Executive Committee by virtue of recognizing organization work rather than personalities." As a finishing blow, she wrote McAllister, she had not seen Mrs. Roosevelt when she came to visit the migrant camps. "We were all disappointed," she wrote McAllister, "but none of us knew where she would be stopping." Helen Douglas undoubtedly did not feel any need to include Jones or anyone else in her special trip with the first lady.

As the scene shifted to Washington in May with the National Institute of Government, Douglas acquired still more prestige within Democratic circles. The three-day conference was the highlight of her trip, which stretched into six weeks, taking her to Grand Rapids, Chicago, and Oklahoma for speeches on migrants before several national conferences of social welfare professionals. The Women's Division of the Democratic National Committee, which sponsored the Washington convention, predicted that between four hundred and five hundred women from all over the United States would attend this important conference, the first of its kind, designed to prepare these party leaders for their critical role in the coming election. McAllister had prepared a superb program, including seminars with cabinet members and other top administrative officials, and a tea hosted by the president and the first lady on the White House lawn. McAllister's office had individually contacted every Democratic congressman and senator to encourage them to invite their state's best women and also to arrange appropriate entertainment for the delegates in Washington. Extensive publicity preceded the conference, highlighting the key women who would attend. Douglas figured prominently in advanced press releases from the Women's Division headquarters. All the planning disintegrated, however, when instead of five hundred women, five thousand poured into the capital. No one was prepared for the ensuing crush; everything had to be rescheduled. James A. Farley, Democratic National Committee Chairman and a presidential aspirant, appeared "embarrassed" and "bewildered," as well he must have been given his tendency to discount and ignore women.

Since Perkins had planned a dinner honoring Douglas on May 1, Helen arrived a day ahead of the California delegation. "I loved every minute of [the party]," she told Perkins, and it undoubtedly got Douglas off to a running start. She also faced no problem with hotel space; she and Molly Dewson—much revered and loved by the Roosevelts and Democratic women leaders—stayed at the White House. Douglas's talk on "The Problem of Migratory Labor and How It is Being Met" formed part of the session "The National Conservation Program for People, Soil, and Water." Originally set up as a roundtable discussion, it had to be moved to the Department of Commerce Auditorium to accommodate the crowds. McAllister, of course, was euphoric over the response to the institute and resulting press, for it offered concrete evidence that women had the ability and the interest to play a significant role in the fall election, and demonstrated that many in the Washington power structure and within the party took the women seriously. The success also hinted of the bigger triumph yet to come at the national convention when women played the most significant role in the history of the party. After the institute, McAllister wrote Jones, who had not attended because her husband was seriously ill, with details of the triumph. The institute was excellent, she wrote, and California was well represented. Helen Gahagan Douglas was just marvelous; she "gave one of the most brilliant talks of the Institute" and closed the conference by singing the "Star Spangled Banner." Jones, who consoled herself about missing the conference with the May 7 victory of the Roosevelt slate, undoubtedly received little comfort from McAllister's news.

Douglas, meanwhile, stayed on at the White House and enjoyed a round of parties in her honor. Perkins's assistant, Mary LaDame, gave her a tea; the Justin Millers, William O. Douglases, the Voorhises and Lubins all had dinners for her. Mrs. Roosevelt entertained Douglas for lunch as did Mr. and Mrs. Ickes. Douglas also enjoyed a good visit with Secretary of Agriculture Henry A. Wallace. In subsequent months and years, Douglas would enjoy easy access to these and other New Dealers, which greatly furthered her political objectives. Douglas took a week off to visit her mother in Brooklyn, and then returned to Washington on May 20 for a meeting of the White House Advisory Committee on Community Services, to which ER had appointed her. The events of May left no doubt that Douglas clearly had established herself as a very attractive political newcomer; she enjoyed national respect for her insights on the agricultural labor crisis and had considerably expanded her professional and personal contacts in Washington.

Douglas returned to a tense political situation in California, exaggerated by the national panic over Hitler's successes in Europe and FDR's shift in attitude toward neutrality. A long, reflective letter to ER revealed Helen's distress over recent red-baiting attacks against Melvyn from the American Legion and on the floor of the State Assembly. Simply by association, the charges implicated Helen. That she had some cause for concern is suggested in a letter from Margaret Workman—a well-respected liberal, a convention delegate, and a close friend of the Douglases—to McAllister:

> Helen and Melvyn have been perfectly wonderful in the contribution they have made [here.] The recent episode has unfortunately lessened their influence with public opinion to a marked degree. It will take some time to overcome the fear that has been produced by all the publicity. They are vulnerable in only one way—the fact that they have not been identified with the people or with the Democratic Party for a longer period. I feel but cannot prove that this whole situation was planned and executed by reactionary forces within our own party.

Mrs. Roosevelt hastened to reassure Douglas that the publicity would not harm her in the long run. After all, Mrs. Roosevelt had experienced many similar attacks. In the letter written on June 6, she addressed her as Helen for the first time, indicating a new level of closeness. "I loved your letter and I wanted to send you a wire at once to tell you not to be worried when they accuse you and Mr. Douglas of being Communists." She had heard that Helen did a "marvelous piece of work" when she testified before a congressional committee at the end of May. "Everyone said you were exactly right and that you touched everybody there and yet were very restrained. . . . [I also heard] you were excellent at the Social Workers meeting. . . . So you can feel that you are doing very good work. . . . The President sends you both his kindest regards. . . . Do not [overdo] and kill yourself, because we need good people alive."

The unsettling publicity, which even made *Time* magazine, did not affect McAllister's opinion of Douglas either. In preparation for the July nominating convention, McAllister asked eighteen top Democratic women to serve on an advisory committee to the platform committee. Although such a committee had existed for each convention since 1924, in 1940 its formation took on considerably more significance. In February, the Democratic National Committee had passed a resolution to be presented to the convention delegates requiring that the platform committee include one man and one woman from each state and territory. The 1940 advisory committee, therefore, was to draft plank proposals on the assumption that they would be taken up by a platform committee composed equally of men and women. McAllister wanted veteran congresswoman Mary Norton as chair; others included former congresswoman Nan Wood Honeyman from Oregon; Utah's national committeewoman Carolyn Wolfe, formerly head of the Women's Division following Dewson; and Virginia Gildersleeve, dean of Barnard College. The only nominee from California was Douglas. McAllister did not release the committee membership to the press until shortly before the convention, but she provided advance notice to the heads of the Women's Division in the states where she had appointed members. When Jones learned that Douglas had been selected "because of her interest and knowledge in one of the most serious economic and social problems we face," her distrust of and distaste for Douglas increased.

Meanwhile, tensions in California mounted as the convention date drew closer. Not only was FDR's nomination for a third term at stake, but the delegates would elect a new national committeeman and committeewoman. The outgoing holders of those positions, former senator William McAdoo and San Franciscan Lucretia Grady, wife of Assistant Secretary of State Henry Grady, held the respect of their colleagues. But many felt that Governor Olson, who badly wanted the nomination, should be named. As Grady lived in Washington, some of the delegates felt they should name a California-based person, and that the positions should be rotated between the north and south. McAllister kept in touch with the women. She received information that some members were circulating a petition for Grady. In addition, she learned that the California delegates had received a letter signed by hundreds of southern California women. "She has done so much . . . in point of service [that] she is the only one to be considered. . . . We feel it is justly due her after these long years of unselfish, constructive service to our party." Just before the convention, another Jones supporter hastened to write McAllister, "It has come to my attention, authoritatively, that . . . Helen Gahagan is eager for this appointment and that efforts are being made by a few of her friends in the South to secure it for her." The problem with Douglas, she continued, was that she would be directing a play in New York in the fall and thus could not participate in the fall campaign. After Lucretia Grady, the Women's Division could not withstand another absentee national committeewoman. Since the future of Democratic women in the state "rests upon leadership which has proven itself in loyalty and performance," Jones clearly deserved this honor.

The California delegation left San Francisco for Chicago by train. Melvyn, a delegate, planned to fly, but Helen, his alternate, took the train. The *San Francisco Chronicle* reported after the train left Denver with Colorado delegates aboard that the California delegation was having an "acrimonious row over the selection of a new national committeeman and national committeewoman." The delegation planned to settle the matter, which centered around Olson's desire to succeed former senator McAdoo. If the delegation elected Olson from southern California, then many felt the national committeewoman should be from the north. But most delegates seemed initially to favor Nettie Jones. Some felt Douglas fell "too far left." After much haggling, the final ballot gave Olson the position with thirty-three votes; the two other candidates received eight and five votes each. Helen Gahagan won a surprising victory, garnering twenty-nine votes over Jones who received fifteen (a third candidate got one). The *Chronicle* predicted her election would be sure "to attract national attention."

A popular explanation of her victory, offered by males on the scene, was that she was elected simply as a trade-off to Melvyn, who really deserved to be selected committeeman but had deferred to Olson. Douglas, the argument ran, had little political standing in July 1940; only in the fall did she begin to build her credibility independently of her husband. This theory fails to take into account Helen's activities during the first six months of that year. Consciously or unconsciously, she had acquired the necessary stature, minus the traditional long apprenticeship generally required of political women, for the position of national committeewoman. Her political standing, closely linked to her ties with the Roosevelts, combined with her personal assets, made Douglas an attractive alternative to Nettie Jones. Most of the California delegates decided Douglas was the only logical choice.

Winning this office thrust Douglas into the center of activity at the convention, an exciting one for women. McAllister became the first woman to address a convention; for the first time, women participated on the resolutions committee. The convention also adopted the fifty–fifty resolution for the Platform Committee, thus ensuring women half the seats. These innovations, although they did not signal more power for women immediately, opened new doors and had a symbolic significance.

After the convention ended, Helen Douglas moved quickly to prepare for the fall campaign. She canceled her acting commitment for the fall, declaring she would not do another play until after the election. She worked to unite the various factions, although Jones complained in October: "I have not been consulted about any of the set-up as to the Women's activities. . . . I honestly thought that when Miss Gahagan assured me that I would have full charge of the Women's campaign that she meant what she said." On August 12, Douglas inaugurated the election efforts in California with a kickoff luncheon in the Hollywood Bowl, a gathering that "served to indicate restoration of harmony in the ranks of the Democratic women that were badly shattered by the election of [Douglas instead of] Jones." Both Eleanor Roosevelt and Frances Perkins sent telegrams that were read to the large gathering. ER's message sent "Greetings and good wishes to the Democratic women of Southern California and to Mrs. Douglas. I know Mrs. Douglas will do an excellent job." Perkins added, Douglas's selection as national committeewoman "is of great importance not only to the women of your state but to all others in the country . . . because of [her] understanding of public affairs." McAllister, who supervised the individual states' activities very closely, did not restrain her relief over the success of Douglas's efforts in organizing the California women. McAllister wrote her September 23:

> I receive letters almost every day telling me what a wonderful job you are doing in California. The women are enthusiastic over your leadership and appreciate your intelligent grasp of the issues and devotion to the New Deal cause. You have accomplished more in the short time since you have been National Committeewoman than anyone else has in the state in years.

In addition to her important work with women in California, Douglas also gave a number of speeches nationally at the request of both the Women's Division and the main office of the Democratic National Committee which coordinated all election efforts. She gave the kickoff speech for Oregon Democrats at the end of August and several speeches in September. During the critical week of October 19–25, the National Committee sent her to five pivotal states for major addresses, including Ohio, Illinois, and Wisconsin. Although Eleanor Roosevelt had an extraordinarily busy schedule for the fall, she found the time in mid-October to come to southern California at Douglas's invitation for a "gala tea" and campaign speech for the Democratic women; and Douglas introduced ER to the gathering, clearly establishing her own closeness to the first lady. Also during the fall, she assumed two more official titles. The party's state chair, William Malone, appointed her vice-chair of the California party structure and head of the Women's Division—Douglas now held the top three women's positions in Democratic state politics. Malone assumed that by appointing one woman to all three, he would diminish what little influence women had in California politics. Douglas not only organized Democratic women into a bloc possessing considerable power, she eventually made inroads into the male power structure through her own rise in political stature.

Both Helen and Melvyn, whose campaign efforts had concentrated on large rallies using Hollywood personalities to attract audiences, felt euphoric over FDR's third-term victory. They received invitations to the inauguration and enjoyed considerable publicity while in Washington as part of the "influx of film stars" who came to help celebrate. During the festivities, the Douglases stayed with Harold and Anna Ickes. Afterward, Melvyn returned to California and Helen stayed on, moving into the White House for a few days at the end of January. She wrote ER on February 12: "Thank you for my beautiful visit at the White House [and] for all your kindness to me. My visits with the President and you are something that you must know I prize very dearly." She continued with some political business and closed the letter on a personal note: "Peter [who had been quite ill] was very happy with the presents you sent him. He sends you his love and says that he will write you as soon as he is able to sit up. We are all looking forward to having you with us in California in April."

Over the next decade, Douglas's political stature grew rapidly. In 1942 the Democratic party in Los Angeles briefly considered her as a possible congressional candidate but eventually chose Will Rogers, Jr. She then turned her energies to organizing successful campaigns to defeat three Republican congressional candidates, in a year when Republicans gained seats nationally. She helped Rogers defeat Leland M. Ford, who had viciously attacked Melvyn Douglas in a speech in Congress earlier that year; and she helped George E. Outland defeat A. J. Dingeman in the Eleventh District of Santa Barbara and Ed V. Izac defeat James B. Abbey in San Diego's Twenty-Third District.

In 1944, at the urging of retiring New Dealer Thomas F. Ford from Los Angeles, and with the enthusiastic support of President Roosevelt, she ran for Ford's congressional seat in the Fourteenth District and won. She was the first Democrat and only the second congresswoman elected from California, and one of the twenty-nine women in the country elected to a full congressional term up to that time. Perhaps even more important, she was the first Hollywood figure ever elected to national political office. She won reelection by a larger margin in 1946; in 1948 she defeated her opponent by a substantial majority. She could easily have retained her seat, but late in 1949 she decided to challenge Senator Sheridan Downey, up for reelection in 1950. Downey withdrew from the campaign in the spring of 1950, and Helen Douglas emerged victorious in a rugged Democratic primary battle against Manchester Boddy, a conservative Los Angeles newspaper publisher. Douglas then faced what was to be the culminating event of her political climb, the acrimonious fall campaign against Richard Nixon.

Over these years, the Douglas-Roosevelt friendship continued to grow. During the war, both Helen and Melvyn spent considerable time in Washington, Melvyn up until 1942 when he entered the Army, but Helen all during the third Roosevelt term, until her election to Congress. She continued to enjoy access to the White House, staying there, for example, while looking for an apartment in early January 1945. The president's death did not alter the closeness of the two women. They served together in the 1946 United Nations Assembly, ER as a delegate and Douglas as the alternate for Adlai Stevenson. In 1950, ER spearheaded the fundraising, among her national women's network, for Douglas's Senate campaign. After the campaign the Douglases moved to New York, where ER also lived, and they saw each other frequently. Shortly after ER died in 1962, Helen Douglas published *The Eleanor Roosevelt We Remember*, a moving and personal tribute to the distinguished woman Helen Douglas had so loved.

The relationship of Helen Gahagan Douglas and the first lady catapulted Douglas into politics and gave her significant political benefits. The achievements of Douglas during her years of prominence—and the qualities that stirred admiration during the long political twilight that fell over her career after 1950—testify to a considerable capacity for political leadership. But she needed the right opportunity and the proper backing to propel her, and the Roosevelts, especially ER, deserve the credit for offering a helping hand and for shaping her approach to politics at the beginning of her career.

The impact of Eleanor Roosevelt on Douglas was more far-reaching than merely political prestige and personal friendship. Douglas looked to the first lady as her political role model. She mobilized the rank-and-file California women astutely and successfully, following the pattern that ER had established with the Women's Division. In Congress, one of Douglas's primary contributions was to emphasize the education of the voter as a method to influence legislation. Here too she emulated the techniques ER had used to reach out and touch the ordinary American. During the Truman years, Douglas was the politician who most reflected the legacy and style of Eleanor Roosevelt. A long-time activist in California's Democratic politics recalled his first personal contact with Douglas. Although he had worked for her 1950 Senate campaign, he did not meet her until the 1956 presidential race when she came through Fresno County to campaign for Adlai Stevenson. His words sum up the comparison simply and succinctly.

One was inclined to think of Eleanor Roosevelt when one met [Douglas]. She was a great lady. . . . There was a graciousness about her, a maturity, a willingness to take us young people seriously, no tendency to talk down at all, a willingness to listen. Both of them struck me the same way—of being the same sort of person. I don't think I've heard the word statesperson—but 'statespersonlike' if you will.

Both women, he concluded, were extremely impressive people.

SOURCES

This article is drawn from extensive research on the relationship of Helen Gahagan Douglas to significant themes in twentieth-century America. Over one hundred manuscript collections have been examined for this study. The most relevant to Douglas's relationship to Eleanor Roosevelt in the early years include the following: Anna Eleanor Roosevelt Papers, Democratic National Committee Papers, Women's Division of the Democratic National Committee Papers and various presidential files at the Franklin D. Roosevelt Library at Hyde Park, New York; Helen Gahagan Douglas Papers in the Carl Albert Center, Western History Collection, University of Oklahoma; personal papers of Helen Gahagan Douglas, New York City; Melvyn Douglas Papers, Wisconsin State Historical Society; personal papers of Melvyn Douglas, New York City; Harold Ickes Papers at the Library of Congress; and various collections at the Bancroft Library, University of California, Berkeley, and Special Collections, University of California, Los Angeles.

Published works used in preparing this essay include: Robert E. Burke, *Olson's New Deal for California* (Berkeley, California, 1953); Larry Ceplair and Steven Englund, *The Inquisition in Hollywood: Politics in the Film Community, 1930–1960* (Garden City, New York, 1980); Walter J. Stein, *California and the Dust Bowl Migration* (Westport, Connecticut, 1973); Helen Gahagan Douglas, *A Full Life* (Garden City, New York, 1982); and Harold L. Ickes, *The Secret Diary of Harold L. Ickes*, vol. 3, *The Lowering Clouds*, 1939–41 (New York, 1954). Also useful is Thomas H. Arthur, "The Political Career of An Actor: Melvyn Douglas and the New Deal," a doctoral dissertation (Indiana University, 1973). In addition, newspapers and general works on the New Deal, on and by Eleanor Roosevelt, and on California politics and women in politics provided essential background material.

The research upon which this article is based was funded in part by the National Endowment for the Humanities, the American Philosophical Society, and the Eleanor Roosevelt Institute at the Franklin D. Roosevelt Library.

Richard S. Kirkendall

ER and the Issue
of FDR's Successor

"IS THERE ANYTHING I can do for you?" a stunned Harry S. Truman asked Eleanor Roosevelt upon learning of the death of the president. "Is there anything *we* can do for *you?*" she replied. "For you are the one in trouble now." Several days later, employing a quite different tone, the new widow wrote to Henry A. Wallace: "Though I hope to see you today and perhaps to talk with you more about my hopes for America and the future, I do want you to know that I feel that you are peculiarly fitted to carry on the ideals which were close to my husband's heart and which I know you understood."

As these exchanges suggest, to Eleanor, Wallace, not Truman, seemed to be the appropriate successor to FDR. She had not always felt such enthusiasm for Wallace, although she had helped him obtain the Democratic nomination for the vice-presidency in 1940, but they had become close allies during the war. Yet, in 1944, her influence with her husband now very weak, she had failed to save Wallace from his enemies, and Truman had displaced him as the person in line to succeed Franklin Roosevelt. The story of Eleanor Roosevelt and the issue of her husband's successor testifies to her importance in the politics of the period and suggests that unhappiness in the marriage of Eleanor and Franklin had political consequences.

During New Deal days, Eleanor and Henry had rather negative opinions of each another. She disliked his major farm program, which was designed to raise prices paid to commercial farmers. Like many other urban liberals, she complained about Triple-A's destruction of pigs and cotton and cuts in farm production. She preferred the agencies—the Resettlement Administration and the Farm Security Administration—designed to help the rural poor, and she pressed him to do more for such people. On one occasion, troubled by a report on the sharecroppers of southeast Missouri, she suggested that FSA should "look a little farther" into what Missouri was doing. In response, he labeled the picture of suffering and privation "fairly accurate" but denied that Triple-A should be blamed and stressed the relevance of "basic population facts." Thanking him for his letter, she asked: "Should we be developing more industries and services? Should we practice birth control or drown the surplus population?"

Eleanor also regarded Wallace as too cautious on racial matters. She had become one of the most outspoken champions of change in this area of American life, and she urged him to do more for rural blacks. He appeared to her, she later confided to historian Sidney Baldwin, neither fully to understand nor adequately to sympathize with the problems of black farmers and to resent her efforts to prod his Department of Agriculture toward a more positive approach to their needs. He did suggest to one of his aides, Will Alexander, that the New Deal might be "undertaking to do too much for the Negroes."

Wallace, an Iowan serving as the New Deal's secretary of agriculture, also had misgivings about the first lady. He did invite her to address groups in the department, such as a conference of rural and urban women designed to enlarge their understanding of "the problems of bringing about an increased, balanced abundance for us all" and a gathering of agricultural and home economists aimed at guiding "production plans . . . and ways of using family resources for better living conditions in the farm home." It seems likely he was influenced by a desire to show her that the interests of the department had expanded under his leadership and that he did not believe in an "economics of scarcity." He also advised her on farm matters, assured her that he shared her interest in preventing the demise of the family farm, and thanked her for her efforts in 1940 to prevent people from "becoming hysterical about possible food shortages."

Yet, Wallace did not trust Eleanor Roosevelt's judgment and feared her influence. He warned Alexander, FSA's head from 1937 to 1940, against associating with her. To Wallace, one sign of her unreliability had been her enthusiasm in 1933 for another Iowan he distrusted, Milo Reno, the president of the Iowa Farmers' Union and the leader of the Farmers' Holiday Association. "I'd seen him at close range and knew that he was a man of no fundamental intellectual substance, although he was a very dramatic leader," Wallace recalled in his oral history memoir. ER pressed her husband vigorously to swing things in Reno's direction, but the president resisted her strongly and backed Wallace.

The president's wife was a person of influence in New Deal Washington, and she used it to help Henry Wallace in 1940, but she did so to serve the interests of the president, not the Iowan. In fact, she had not favored him for the presidency when it had been assumed that, as she hoped, FDR would not run for a third term, and she did not personally advocate Wallace for the vice-presidency during the preconvention debate over that issue. Later, she commented in her memoirs that she did not know him well at the time.

Wallace worked cautiously to gain a place on the Democratic ticket. He had no wish to challenge Franklin Roosevelt and, soon after war began in Europe, publicly called for a third term. While not discouraging talk of his own nomination for higher office, Wallace assured the president of his loyalty. In May 1940, when Iowa Democratic leaders proposed to Roosevelt that the state's national convention votes should be pledged to Wallace, the latter wrote to FDR to say "most emphatically that I am ready to do anything possible in this connection that you may wish me to do." Whenever his admirers and others spoke to him about the presidency or the vice-presidency, he responded that "the question was whether or not the powers that be thought that the party stood a chance of winning in November with me on the ticket." Prior to the convention, FDR did encourage Wallace's hopes for the vice-presidency but did not say clearly that he was his choice.

The Democratic National Convention, held in Chicago that year, featured a struggle between New Dealers and conservatives for control of the party, and was complicated by debate over the tradition against third terms for presidents. Many delegates grew angry after Roosevelt's followers made it clear they were eager to break with the tradition and maintained that FDR was willing to do so. Alarmed by the mood, Secretary of Labor Frances Perkins, a long-time associate of the Roosevelts and an active advocate of Wallace for the vice-presidency, called the White House from Chicago to urge the president to come out and address the gathering, but he refused, hoping to avoid pressure to make promises. It was agreed that his wife should come instead. "You know Eleanor always makes people feel right," he said. "She has a fine way with her."

Before ER could make the trip, her husband added to the turmoil by announcing his choice for the second spot. He may have decided before the convention but delayed so as not to lose the support of the many hopefuls and to make certain that the politically influential secretary of state, Cordell Hull, did not wish to run. Now firmly settled on Wallace, FDR informed Mayor Kelly of Chicago, Perkins, and Harry Hopkins of his decision; they in turn, along with others, such as Wallace's aide Paul Appleby, spread the word and sought to build support. Senator James F. Byrnes, though unhappy with the selection, worked with special effectiveness on Wallace's behalf. Henry, of course, accepted the president's decision without hesitation and prepared an acceptance speech that stressed the importance of the administration's leadership and of national unity.

From FDR's point of view, Wallace had major assets. He had admirable intellectual and moral qualities and seemed to be growing as a politician; he agreed with the president on both foreign and domestic issues; he had built strength among liberals and labor in the cities to complement his support in the farm areas, and he would be a worthy successor, should fate remove FDR from office. "[I]t was assumed that politically he would help in the farm states," recalled Samuel Rosenman, one of Franklin Roosevelt's closest associates at the time, "[b]ut what appealed to the President more was that Wallace was then an out-and-out New Dealer, in whose hands the program of the New Deal—domestic and international— would be safe." As Roosevelt wrote to Senator George Norris right after the convention, "Wallace is a true liberal—far more so than any of the others suggested for Vice-President—with the possible exception of Bill Douglas. . . ."

When the delegates learned that FDR wanted Wallace and then that he would decline the nomination for the presidency if the convention rejected his wishes, grumbling grew louder. Many other men wanted the nomination and had their supporters. The discontented protested against dictation and insisted that Wallace was a poor choice. They complained that he had been a Republican until only a few years before, that he did not have a wide following, even in the Corn Belt, that he was too idealistic, even a mystic, and not a good politician, and that he would not "balance" the ticket. His nomination would put two New Dealers, two internationalists, on the ticket. As such arguments were made, FDR carried his threat to the point of preparing a statement declining the nomination. The party, the statement explained, had not made "overwhelmingly clear its stand in favor of social progress and liberalism" and had not shaken off "all the shackles of control fastened upon it by the forces of conservatism, reaction and appeasement. . . ."

As discontent mounted, Eleanor Roosevelt flew to Chicago to do what she could to calm the storm. She came at the request of Frances Perkins, seconded by Jim Farley, the chair of the Democratic National Committee. When she arrived, her husband had been nominated, but the debate over Wallace was raging, very painfully for Henry and his wife. Speaking calmly but firmly, the first lady urged the delegates to support the president, and they did, although not unanimously. Wallace received only 627 out of 1,100 votes and his leading opponent, Congressman William Bankhead of Alabama, picked up a substantial number. The mood remained so dark that Wallace reluctantly accepted advice from Byrnes and Hopkins not to give his acceptance speech at the convention.

In her speech, Mrs. Roosevelt had not stressed Wallace and his virtues. Instead, she had spoken of the need in critical times to back the president. She believed, as she later explained, that "if Franklin felt that the strain of a third term might be too much for any man and that Mr. Wallace was the man who could carry on best in times such as we were facing, he was entitled to his help," and she tried "to persuade the delegations . . . to sink all personal interests in the interests of the country and to make them realize the potential dangers in the situation we were facing." She was in Chicago as Franklin's helper, and Henry was Franklin's choice.

Had Eleanor Roosevelt not spoken, Wallace might have been rejected. Both Hopkins and her husband thought highly of her performance. Farley, though not happy with the outcome, believed she had "saved the day for the President." Many others, including Frances Perkins, Senator Norris, and numerous editorial writers, expressed similar views at the time. "That victory was finally realized is due, in my opinion, more to you than to any other one thing," Norris wrote to her. "That one act makes you heroic." She was effective, biographer James R. Kearney has suggested, not only because she was a woman and the president's wife but also because she "was looked up to; her 'sense of politics' and keen political perceptiveness were valued."

After the convention, Eleanor Roosevelt did express more enthusiasm for the candidate, although mainly, it appears, in hopes of winning over the discontented members of her party. "Secretary Wallace is a very fine person and I am sure will strengthen the ticket," she wrote in her newspaper column. "I have always felt in him a certain shyness and that has kept him aloof from some Democrats, but now that he will be in close touch with so many of them, I am sure they will soon find in him much to admire and love."

If she had not yet become a Wallace enthusiast, Eleanor soon came to look upon him as the person who would eventually take her husband's place. Franklin laughed at a rumor that early in the third term he would resign so that Henry could move up, but she noted that he took seriously predictions that the election winner would not live out his term and thus talked often of Wallace as his successor. She assumed that the third term, given the severity of the world crisis and the state of her husband's health, might be too tough for him and assumed further that he would surely not go beyond that term and thus would be replaced no later than 1945. "Father," she wrote to her daughter Anna shortly after the election, "must build Wallace up if he is to succeed in 1944."

After he became vice-president, Wallace gained Eleanor Roosevelt's enthusiastic support. She came to admire him for the speeches he made and the battles he fought. She applauded him frequently, doing so in letters to him and conversations with him. Their meetings became frequent and were often social as well as official and, by 1943, were sometimes small affairs with the Wallaces as her only guests for dinner at the White House, or she the sole dinner guest at their home. They were eager to get together and become well acquainted, and as Wallace lost his wariness about associating with her, she discarded her doubts about his liberalism.

Speaking for "The Century of the Common Man," Wallace established himself as the leading champion in the administration of a liberal interpretation of the war and its purposes. It should, he insisted, lead to a resumption of reform at home, the weakening and eventual destruction of the imperial systems abroad, the granting of independence and self-rule to all peoples, the elevation of standards of living throughout the world, and the establishment of an international organization with its own military force to govern relations among nations. To push his ideas forward, he made use of the prestige that the vice-presidency gave him as a public speaker and the power conferred upon him by the Board of Economic Warfare, an agency that FDR created in 1941 and that Wallace chaired. He became an unusually prominent and active vice-president.

An exchange on housing in the summer of 1941 testified to the growing regard that Henry and Eleanor had for each another. She urged him to work for a bill that would include a small appropriation for public housing so as to keep alive the local housing authorities which "must be the ones to carry on when we start the real building after the defense work is over." And she added: "I know you are probably thinking about these things, and I simply want to add my interest in this whole question." Happy to know of the depth of her interest in the housing situation, he urged her to get together with Alvin Hansen, who had "been thinking generally about the magnitude of the housing job which must be done if the most serious kind of depression is to be prevented when peace comes" and was "thinking in larger terms than most of the people who have been dealing with the housing problem." The correspondence indicated that Wallace had developed an urban dimension to his liberalism and that she recognized that and no longer saw him as merely the champion of the commercial farmer.

Wallace's clash with Martin Dies further strengthened the developing ties. A Texas congressman who chaired a notorious congressional committee that investigated "un-American" groups and individuals in the United States, Dies publicly charged in March 1942 that the Board of Economic Warfare employed people who had communist ideas and affiliations and rejected the "American way of life in favor of this or that scheme for revolution." Angry that the congressman had not discussed the matter privately with him, Wallace charged that Dies was "seeking to inflame the public mind by malicious distortion of facts" and that "the effect on our morale would be less damaging if Mr. Dies were on the Hitler payroll." The first lady was delighted with the letter to Dies, "cheered" when she read it, and congratulated Wallace on his "courage and good judgment." And the vice-president responded: "Among the many letters that I received with regard to the Dies incident, yours pleased me most."

Her admiration for him growing, ER urged Wallace to address groups and meet with people who were important to her. Early in 1942, she appealed to him to speak at a large convocation in New York City of "free universities" on the subject "Our responsibility in shaping the post-war world," and she assured him that she could "think of no one who would carry more conviction and whose work fitted him better to give a ringing challenge to a great university audience. . . ." A short time later, she

encouraged him to accept an invitation to address the Southern Conference for Human Welfare, pointing out that she was "very much interested" in its work. And later in the year, she called upon him to meet with
Hilda Smith of the WPA, who was trying to work with unions and whose
agency was suffering from a severe cut in appropriations: "I really think
what she is trying to do is important and your advice would be of great
assistance to her."

Wallace's "Century of Common Man" speech, delivered on May 8,
1942, contributed in an especially large way to the development of an
alliance between the two liberals. In it, Wallace proclaimed that the "people's revolution" was on the march and would prevail, "for on the side of
the people is the Lord." Rejecting Henry Luce's proposed "American
Century," the vice-president insisted that "the century in which we are
entering—the century which will come out of this war—can be and must
be the century of the common man." Six days later, he sat next to Eleanor
Roosevelt at a White House luncheon; she was "exceedingly complimentary" about the speech, and they went on to talk about "political democracy, economic democracy and genetic democracy." Two days later, the
president began a meeting with congressional leaders by saying what a
"swell" speech the vice-president had delivered, how many good reports
he had had on it, and how much Mrs. Roosevelt liked it. Soon, she
incorporated his theory of the century of the common man into her own
statements. "I do not think this is an American century," she wrote, "I like
Vice-President Wallace's 'people's century' better."

According to ER, Wallace had achieved great stature in the eyes of a
group of special importance to her: young people. He had "appealed so
greatly to the youth of this country, and. . . . to the youth of South
America and Europe," she wrote to him in July 1942, "that I find them
counting on you as one of their leaders for the future." What happened
after the war "greatly depends on what you and people like you, give them
as objectives." A short time later, she reported to him how impressed she
was "by the effect that your speech on The People's Century has had on
young people." At recent meetings of one student group she had found
that the "speech was the basis for more real stirring of thought than
anything else which has happened and, in a way, for more conscious
desire to act, on the part of both boys and girls." Speaking to student
groups in September 1943, she commented enthusiastically on Wallace's
address: it had "created a picture in our minds and awakened our common

desire to wipe out forever the causes which bring about insecurity and war among the nations of the world."

By the summer of 1943, ER's admiration for Henry had reached a high level. "I cannot tell you how much your speeches and your interest in these questions of the future mean to me," she wrote to him in late July, "and I hope before long we can meet and talk over certain things that are on my mind." The next day, she wrote again: "I liked your speech in Detroit very much. I was sorry I could not listen to it but someone who did told me it came over the air extremely well." Thinking often about the liberal cause, its importance for the nation's future, and ways of making the liberal movement strong and aggressive again, she was pleased with the way Wallace had moved to the front. He was "showing signs of definite leadership," she remarked to another liberal.

As another election year drew close, Eleanor Roosevelt went beyond applause and endorsed Wallace for a place on the Democratic ticket in 1944. After a private White House dinner on October 17, she informed him that she and her sons and daughter were strongly against a fourth term and said that if Wallace were nominated for the presidency, he would win. Getting the nomination seemed to be the chief difficulty, largely because southerners were "dead set" against him. Yet, she assured him that she and Franklin would be for him "as the logical one to carry out the policies of the President." In a follow-up discussion the next month, Henry assured her of his loyalty to the president, and she again spoke against his running a fourth time. Her opposition to that soon weakened, and she eventually concluded that Franklin, in spite of health problems that worried her and some of their friends and in spite of her personal desire to live a different kind of life, could not avoid another race, but she did not change her mind about a place for Wallace on the ticket. Such talk and similar expressions by FDR encouraged Wallace to think that he would be renominated for the vice-presidency.

Eleanor Roosevelt and Wallace, had, it appears, only one disagreement and that concerned tactics. While agreeing that the Democratic party should become solidly liberal, they did not see eye-to-eye on one occasion as to how to reach that goal. Neither believed that Wallace should call a meeting of liberals to discuss the political situation in late 1943, and both preferred merely to encourage some of the liberal senators to speak out strongly on behalf of the cause. They did analyze the problems of the Democratic party somewhat differently, as ER stressed the southerners

while he saw the "big interests," the "bigoted Catholics," and the "venom-
ous Roosevelt haters" as the major "distracting forces." But their most
serious disagreement came early in 1944 when he gave an "all-out New
Deal speech" at a Jackson Day dinner that was not well received. One of
his hearers, ER seemed annoyed, perhaps because the speech did not fit
with the president's efforts at the time to woo southern Democrats and
might, consequently, weaken Wallace with FDR. Henry, on his part,
feared that the president's approach would result in control of the upcoming convention by "reactionaries."

Wallace had generated hostility toward himself at the same time that he
had gained Eleanor Roosevelt's backing. In fact, he had clashed furiously
with two of his colleagues in the administration: Jesse Jones of Texas, the
conservative secretary of commerce and head of the Restruction Finance
Corporation, and Cordell Hull of Tennessee, the cautious secretary of
state. The battles revolved around turf as well as ideology, for Wallace
seemed to these associates to be an ambitious man who intruded into and
sought to take over some of their territory in his speeches and his management of BEW. He also seemed to them to be an impractical man who
would upset long-established relations among peoples and classes.

Wallace's speeches especially troubled Cordell Hull. The secretary
listed the vice-president among the "radical boys" and "the post-war
spreaders of peace, plenty and pulchritude," one of his aides, Breckinridge
Long, noted. As Long wrote in his diary, Wallace's speeches did "not
exactly conform to Hull's ideas of present and post-war aims" and did "a
lot to startle people and to bolster the opposition in Congress." He
thought the president paid too much attention to Wallace, gave him too
much latitude, and relied too much on him, considering his "lack of
political experience and judgment," and the secretary instructed Long "to
try and straighten out the Senatorial mind so it will realize that the sober
philosophy of Hull will eventually guide the President and all the bally-
hoo from Wallace and his clique will not be seriously adopted as Government policy. . . ."

Seeing Wallace in similar terms, Jones complained chiefly about his
management of BEW. According to the Commerce and RFC chief, Wallace demanded that "we interfere not only with the sovereignty" of Latin
American republics "but also with the eating, housing, hygienic and
working habits of their people."

The clash between Wallace and Jones became especially heated. Late in

June 1943, Wallace publicly criticized Jones for obstructing BEW efforts to build stockpiles of critical and strategic materials, and Jones, charging that Wallace's statement was full of malice and errors, called for a congressional investigation.

As Wallace clashed with his colleagues, Franklin Roosevelt's enthusiam for him cooled somewhat. White House insiders thought they saw signs of cooling even before the end of 1942. The clash with Hull contributed, in part because the secretary of state had political strength, in part because Roosevelt thought Wallace's discussions of such matters as the mechanism of world peace were premature. The matter came to a head in June 1943 when the president met with the two men and Wallace learned that the secretary was "very allergic to my saying anything in public on matters concerning foreign affairs." Thus, the vice-president felt compelled to turn down a suggestion from Mrs. Roosevelt that he address a student group.

The clash with the Texan inflicted more damage. ER had applauded Wallace for taking on Jones for she had come to dislike him, but the fight embarrassed and angered her husband and persuaded him to shift powers away from the two men and abolish the BEW so as to end "the unfortunate controversy and acrimonious public debate. . . ." FDR ordered all agency heads who believed they must make public their disagreements with other heads to send him letters of resignation at the same time that they released critical statements for publication. Labeled by Robert Sherwood the "worst of all the public brawls that marred the record of the Roosevelt Administration," the Wallace-Jones affair persuaded the White House staff that FDR would not support Wallace at the Democratic National Convention in 1944. The affair undoubtedly did affect Roosevelt's thinking, but he continued to favor Wallace for many months thereafter, though he also encouraged others, above all Jimmy Byrnes, to hope for the job. More important, the affair provided ammunition for Wallace's foes.

Beginning in 1943, those foes inside the Democratic party campaigned strenuously against Wallace's renomination. Convinced that FDR still regarded Wallace as "heir apparent," they were determined to change the president's sentiments from pro- to anti-Wallace. The top officials in the Democratic National Committee, chair Bob Hannegan, and treasurer Ed Pauley, played leading roles in the effort, and many Democrats in and out of the administration joined. Worried about Roosevelt's health and fearful that he would die in office, they had a more-than-normal interest in the selection of the vice-presidential candidate. Fearing Wallace's ideas and his personality, they regarded him as both radical and impractical. "My own intensive activities . . .," Pauley recalled, "were occasioned by my conviction that Henry Wallace was not a fit man to be President . . . and my belief, on the basis of continuing observation, that President Roosevelt could not live much longer." Pauley's slogan was, "You are not nominating a Vice-President but a President." In their presentations to Roosevelt, the anti-Wallace Democrats insisted that Wallace would weaken the ticket, possibly dragging it to defeat, and could not assist the president effectively when the time arrived to persuade the Senate to go along with his plans for the post-war world. They also insisted that he must not impose Wallace on the convention as he had in 1940. They made such arguments even though the public opinion polls indicated, as Wallace himself pointed out to FDR, that the vice-president had much more support than any of the other people being talked of for the office.

The constant and heavy barrage from the anti-Wallace forces had a great impact on FDR. He concluded that to obtain Wallace's renomination he would need to fight as he had in 1940, but he was now unwilling to make such a fight. Perhaps Wallace no longer seemed worthy of it. But Rosenman recalled: "The President liked Wallace—he liked him as a person and as an outstanding liberal and internationalist." As FDR remarked a few weeks before the convention to several aides, all of whom opposed Wallace's renomination: "Everybody knows I am for Henry Wallace." (This was, of course, long after the fights with Hull and Jones.) But he went on the speak of the hostility toward Wallace among politicians and voters, indicating that he had been influenced by the campaign. And his son James, who visited with his father while the convention was under way, recalled that "he was resigned to the dumping of . . . Wallace; he felt that Wallace had become a political liability." It appears that Roosevelt feared an adverse impact on the party and on his own chances in November if he persisted in forcing Wallace's renomination. He had no fear about obtaining his own renomination, which he gained without a struggle. His desire to win in November so as to finish the war and influence the postwar world was very strong. He did not wish to weaken his chances by alienating members of his party.

In the end, FDR gave Wallace only a restrained endorsement and indicated a willingness to run with others. He wrote a letter to the delegates saying, as Wallace requested, that if he were a delegate he would vote for

Wallace but that he did "not wish to appear in any way to be dictating to the convention," and he wrote another letter for Hannegan's use saying that he would be "glad" to run with Senator Truman or Justice William O. Douglas and believed that either "would bring real strength to the ticket." Finally, he pressed Truman to run, sticking to an agreement he had made with Hannegan and several others shortly before the convention. Wallace brushed aside suggestions that he withdraw, battled for renomination, and demonstrated considerable strength, much more than he personally had in 1940. He even addressed the delegates in a militantly liberal speech. They, however, selected Truman.

To Henry it seemed that Franklin had been the key to the outcome, as he had been in 1940. "If Roosevelt had kept hands off I could have been named," Wallace asserted in his oral history memoir. What he resented was the Truman-Douglas letter, which he believed violated the president's promise to him not to introduce a second name. This and Roosevelt's other efforts on Truman's behalf seemed to the vice-president impossible to reconcile with FDR's remark at the end of their last preconvention conversation: "I cannot say it publicly but I do hope it will be the same old team." Meeting with the president five weeks after the convention, Wallace told him that he knew exactly what had happened in Chicago, but, in spite of that, he was supporting him because he was the symbol of liberalism throughout the world.

Franklin gave Henry no more support than he did despite the efforts of Eleanor. Prior to the convention, she had pressed her husband to back Wallace as he had in 1940, but he resisted. Faced with powerful arguments against the vice-president, he resented his wife's efforts. Franklin's visit to Hyde Park for the Fourth of July had given her an opportunity to press her case, and after he returned to the White House, Henry Morgenthau, the veteran secretary of the treasury and long-time friend and neighbor of the Roosevelts, learned that she had. "When I saw the President this morning," Morgenthau recorded in his diary on July 6, "he brought up the question of Vice President Wallace. He said that Mrs. Roosevelt is trying to force him to insist on Wallace for Vice President. . . ." It seemed to the cabinet officer that Franklin "was trying to find a way of not having Wallace." And at the end of the conversation, which did not dodge the possibility that Franklin might die during his fourth term and considered several alternatives for the vice-presidency, the two men agreed that the president must not insist upon Wallace as he had in 1940 and as Mrs.

Roosevelt advocated now. "I think it is terribly important to let the Convention pick their own man," FDR concluded. "I think it would put them in a good humor."

Whatever may have been true in the past, by the summer of 1944 Eleanor did not have great influence with Franklin. She had been pressing him on many matters, domestic as well as foreign, throughout the war, expressing her concerns and urging him not to compromise with conservatives, not to ignore domestic issues and not to think only of the war; but he had wearied of her pressures, resisted her with defenses supplied by the war, and saw her less often than he had earlier. An entry in Wallace's diary for late 1943 is representative of his responses to her: "The President had told her that so far as he personally had been concerned, it had been necessary for him to refrain from furnishing liberal leadership until the Democratic primaries were over in the southern states. He did not want a third party put in the field in the South." Years later, she summarized things in an interview with Sidney Baldwin: "My husband repeatedly emphasized that he could not afford to alienate crucial political support needed for the vital wartime programs that meant our country's very survival, by promoting issues that would have provoked unnecessary political conflict. . . . From time to time, I tried to impress on him the need for his personal intervention on behalf of some program or agency in trouble, but as time went on he became more inaccessible." Although occasionally she could accept the argument that the pressures of war "forced" him to devote his attention to it and to think of everything from the standpoint of winning it, she complained about him in some private conversations, she suggested in mid-1943 that he was "no longer guided by warm human emotion," and she expressed a wish somewhat later in the year that he would carry some of the burden of rebuilding the strength of the liberal movement and not let it get bogged down. "Just now," she complained, "he doesn't know exactly where he is going."

Rosenman noted this conflict between husband and wife. "It was hard for her to compromise, and she frequently disagreed with the President when he was willing to. She advocated the direct, unrelenting approach," the presidential adviser recalled.

Another person close to the Roosevelts, Frances Perkins, noted tension between them during the war and a decline in Eleanor's influence. "I really think you ought to be here in the White House more. I think it would be better for the President," Perkins advised. "Oh, no, Frances, he doesn't need me any more," Eleanor responded. "He has Harry [Hopkins]. . . . He doesn't need my advice any more. He doesn't ask it. Harry tells him everything he needs to know." Perkins believed that her friend "was jealous for the first time in her life. Her attachment to the President was not the usual wifely attachment. It was the maternal attachment. She wanted to advise him and he was getting his advice from Harry." The labor secretary added: "Things moved very rapidly from then on to the end and she was out of it, except that he would ask her to go and do certain very difficult chores. . . ."

Eleanor made at least veiled references to her relations with Franklin in conversations with people she did not know as well as she knew Frances Perkins. Visiting with Hyde Park guests on the Fourth of July 1943, she told a story about Franklin's sleepwalking, something, of course, that he had been unable to do for years. In the story, Franklin said to her angrily: "Why is it, when there is something I want to do, you always tell me that I can do it another time?" And Franklin seemed to hint at his feelings of resentment a short time later. After inquiring about Mrs. Roosevelt's trip to the Southwest Pacific, a White House visitor predicted: "She will be very tired." But the president replied: "No, but she will tire everybody else." (Actually, it was an exhausting trip that she had taken reluctantly.)

Their daughter Anna was especially sensitive to the relations between her parents. She recalled from her White House days (1944–1945) that although her mother knew the doctors had said her father "should have half an hour of relaxation, no business, just sitting around, maybe a drink, she would come in more and more frequently with an enormous bundle of letters which she wanted to discuss with him immediately and have a decision." On one occasion, "Father blew his top. He took the bundle of letters and pushed it over to me. 'Sis, you handle this.' "

Given the strained relations between Eleanor and Franklin, she had few opportunities to press the case for Wallace. The husband and wife were together only infrequently during the preconvention period. He spent a month during the spring at Bernard Baruch's South Carolina estate, which she visited only briefly. She moved to Hyde Park for much of the summer—to look after the grandchildren, she explained—and he came there only for the Fourth. She did travel by train across country with him during the convention period, but by then her battle was lost.

More than Franklin's exasperation over Eleanor's liberal demands contributed to her failure as Henry's champion. The unhappy condition of the Roosevelt marriage also contributed. "I don't know if she ever came to the realization that the President needed her for things other than advice," Perkins recalled in her oral history memoir. The marriage had been largely a formal arrangement for a quarter of a century. Sexual relations between husband and wife had been ended by Eleanor's decree in 1916 after the birth of their last child, and they had come close to divorce in 1918 after she had obtained proof of his affair with Lucy Mercer, a young and attractive woman who had come into the Roosevelt circle as Eleanor's secretary several years before. Only concern about the children, his political career, and the continuation of financial assistance from his mother had held the marriage together during that crisis. "Apparently . . . father and mother . . . agreed to go on for the sake of appearances, the children and the future—but as business partners, not as husband and wife, provided he ended the affair with Lucy at once, which he did," James Roosevelt reported. "After that, father and mother had an armed truce which endured to the day he died, despite several occasions I was to observe in which he in one way or another held out his arms to mother and she flatly refused to enter his embrace." At another point in his book on his parents, James wrote: "For the most part, mother just did the dutiful things." And his brother Elliott agreed, describing the ways his mother chose to give herself "the separateness from Father that she found essential."

Lucy Mercer became Mrs. Winthrop Rutherfurd II in 1920, but she and Franklin saw one another from time to time, and their visits at Baruch's estate, in the White House, and at Warm Springs, Georgia, became more frequent after Mrs. Rutherfurd became a widow early in 1944. Insisting that the relationship in its late period did not have a sexual dimension, James defined it as a "very real friendship." He was sure his father "needed a friend and felt she needed one," and he assumed "they could talk to one another as they could not talk to others." Father, Elliott maintained, set Lucy "above all other women. . . ." And Franklin's daughter, Anna, who moved into the White House in 1944 and served, in Elliott's words, as "chatelaine, confidante, and jealous protector of Father," accepted and even welcomed these White House visits, persuaded that Lucy gave her father companionship that he needed. The visits "were light-hearted and gay, affording a few hours of much needed relaxation for a loved father and a world leader in a time of crisis." Eleanor knew nothing of them.

In a significant way, Lucy and Anna were alike. They listened while Franklin talked; they did not make demands upon him. "What he missed more and more . . . was a woman's warm, enspiriting companionship, which Mother by her very nature could not provide," Elliott recalled. "She was . . . respected by Father for her singlemindedness in pursuing her causes, but [was] no kind of company when he wanted to relax without listening to her voice of conscience." At another place, Elliott suggested: "He wanted to be comforted, not coaxed and criticized by Mother as he had been all too often." Lucy was, as Bernard Asbell described her, a woman who strove to "please a man, never to challenge him." Franklin's talk, which ranged from world problems to nonpolitical things he had done, fascinated her. Anna realized that Eleanor "was not capable of giving him this—just listening," and that she, Anna, was able to serve her father for an extended period because she too "could just listen." Anna was conscious, her son recalled, "that she helped fill for her father an important emotional need, yet she also knew, and did not wish to exacerbate, her mother's distress at Franklin's easier companionship with less serious and demanding women."

Eleanor Roosevelt's failure to prevent the dumping of Wallace was another failure in her relationship with Franklin, and it greatly disappointed her. She concealed her disappointment in her memoirs but they were written after her break with Wallace in 1947. In them, she presented Wallace as having failed a test and herself as quite accepting of the results:

> The men who went out through the country to get the feeling of the people reported back that there was a strong belief that Wallace was too impractical and wouldn't help the ticket. Franklin's faith in Wallace was shaken by that time anyway; he said that Wallace had had his chance to make his mark, and since he had not been able to convince the party leaders that he was the right person for the job, it was not possible to dictate again who was to be the candidate.

In the summer of 1944, however, ER's tone was very different. She prepared a "My Day" column that proclaimed Wallace's virtues, but she complied with her husband's request not to publish it until after the convention. "I wish I were free," she commented privately, expressing her frustration and indicating that she wished she could say publicly what she truly believed when she wished to say it. At some point, apparently on the trip to the West Coast, she voiced her displeasure over the treatment of Wallace directly to her husband, showing him an article which accused him of behaving like a dictator in the episode and saying that this expressed her own views. He responded that the columnist "left out the entire point that he, F., didn't want to be a dictator," she wrote to a friend, Lorena Hickok. "Hard position when you don't want to be a dictator but want your own way."

As quickly as she could, Roosevelt wrote to Wallace to tell him "how distressed I was to have you loss [sic] out in the Convention." Ignoring on this occasion her husband's contribution, she offered an explanation of the outcome: "I had hoped that by some miracle you could win out, but it looks to me as though the bosses had functioned pretty smoothly." Asking that he "tell Mrs. Wallace I thought of her all through the balloting, remembering four years ago," she obviously recalled her own role in Henry's rise in 1940 when she had functioned more effectively. A few days later, she invited the Wallaces to spend a night with her at Hyde Park on their way back to Washington.

ER could not mount great enthusiasm for Truman as a possible White House successor to her husband. "I am told that Senator Truman is a good man, and I hope so for the sake of the country," she wrote to Wallace. "I am much more satisfied with Senator Truman than I would have been with some of the others who were considered," she informed a friend. Jimmy Byrnes headed the list of the others given serious consideration, and she did not trust him, in part because he was a southern Democrat with a position on the race issues that she despised.

Although Truman semed superior to Byrnes, Wallace ranked far above both. Answering the charges that had been made by his enemies in their conversations with her husband, Roosevelt expressed her views in the "My Day" column released right after the convention and in a review of Henry's latest book, *Democracy Reborn*, which appeared two weeks later in *The New Republic*. "It is known everywhere," she wrote in her column, "that he has consistently proved himself a friend of the average man and woman in his own country." She recalled his distinguished father and grandfather when she wrote that he had "inherited both idealism and the ability to fight for the things in which he believes." Reflecting the influence of his vice-presidency on her own appraisal of him, she suggested that he had "made far more of the office . . . than most men have been able to make in the past." She admitted that not everyone shared her opinion of his services in that office: "When he has thought things were worth doing, he has done them, no matter how much it cost him personally." And perhaps with her own husband as the implied comparison, she maintained that "Wallace would rather be defeated in a fight which he had undertaken than trim his sails or disavow a belief which he held."

In a challenge to the view that he was "a dreamer, an impractical person, a mystic," she insisted instead that he was "a realist." "He is an economist and he has a practical mind," she wrote in "My Day." Praising him as a man of "curiosity, and of deep religious feeling, not bound by any particular doctrine," she advised readers of *The New Republic* that his speeches revealed "he has to be practical because his scientific training was too intense to allow loose thinking." Readers of the speeches would also learn that "out of his background, nothing which was not truly American could possibly grow."

By now, Eleanor had even accepted Henry's initial farm program as an indication of his practicality. "In 1933 he recognized that he could not embark on the realization of his own theory of abundance until he had cleared away the wreckage left by the past, and changed the political and economic philosophy which had preceded him," she wrote in the review. "That is the attitude of a practical, straight-thinking person."

She did concede some ground to his critics, including her husband. "Mr. Wallace never was a politician and is not a very good one now, but he had long been a thinker and a writer," she observed. "That is why his speeches, until very recently, read much better than they sound. He has had to become a speaker." Narrowing this concession still more, she pointed out in her column: "At times, to meet existing circumstances, he has had to accept certain modifications of his own objectives, but never has he changed his goal."

In one important way, Wallace seemed to ER to be the greatest man of his time. He had become a statesman, "driving into the minds of the American people certain truths made clear as no other statesman in this period has done." Those truths were the truths of liberalism. "He believes in the rights of people—all people, not just a few," she maintained in "My Day." Evidently, her earlier reservations about him on racial issues had disappeared. "If one were to pick out the one outstanding and continuing theme of all that Wallace says, it is his belief that whatever is done, must be done for the general welfare of the majority of the people," she wrote in

The New Republic. "This belief colors his attitude on domestic as well as international problems."

Although these public expressions of admiration for him pleased Wallace, he soon came to believe, it appears, that Eleanor Roosevelt may have hurt him more than she had helped him. During the fall, he learned of "a rather strong feeling," as he expressed it in his oral history memoir, ". . . that Harry Hopkins had replaced Mrs. Roosevelt as an effective influence on Roosevelt. . . ." Looking back some years later, Wallace had doubts about the theory and the related one that the president had in the past "leaned on Mrs. R for advice" and was "very much guided" by her, but he suggested that if a change had taken place "fatigue from Mrs. Roosevelt was the cause" and that she and Franklin had long had "a very abnormal relationship." At the time, however, he took the theory about change more seriously and noted in his diary in December that "Morgenthau attributes everything that is going on now to Hopkins." From "other sources" he, Wallace, had learned that Hopkins "furnished the President a list of the people who see Mrs. Roosevelt," and that "the Hopkins who once felt that the way to White House power was through Mrs. Roosevelt. . ., has now won out and has ousted Mrs. Roosevelt, herself." When Morgenthau learned that Wallace wanted to become secretary of commerce, he asked him if Mrs. Roosevelt knew what he wanted and said she was "very, very strong" for him. In response, Wallace noted that "this would make me weaker for I have the feeling that at the present time he [FDR] fights everything she is for."

. What if the Roosevelt marriage had been a happy one? Would Eleanor have been able to persuade Franklin to insist upon Wallace's renomination in 1944? And would history have moved differently if Wallace rather than Truman had become president on April 12, 1945? Those who see history as propelled solely by great impersonal forces, such as capitalism, answer no to the last question. But some who emphasize the importance of the individual in history see the substitution of Truman for Wallace and then for Roosevelt as a series of events of large significance. Eleanor Roosevelt, who had helped Wallace rise to the vice-presidency and then came to admire him as the great champion of liberalism, tried but failed to block the switch from Wallace to Truman, and soon death made Truman Franklin's successor. To Eleanor, who has assumed that the succession issue was very important, Harry did not seem to be the right man for the job.

SOURCES

The Eleanor Roosevelt Papers are in the Franklin D. Roosevelt Library at Hyde Park, New York, while the Henry A. Wallace Papers are scattered among three institutions (the University of Iowa, the Roosevelt Library, and the Library of Congress) but also available on microfilm. ER's memoir *This I Remember* (New York, 1949) covers these years; Henry Wallace did not write one, but he did leave an extended oral history memoir at Columbia University and a large diary, most of which has been published by Richard Lowitt, "Henry A. Wallace and the 1935 Purge in the Department of Agriculture," *Agricultural History*, vol. 53 (July 1979), 607–21, and John Morton Blum, ed., *The Price of Vision: The Diary of Henry A. Wallace 1942–1946* (Boston, 1974). Other relevant manuscripts include the Harry S. Truman Papers in the Truman Library and the Henry Morgenthau Presidential Diary in the Roosevelt Library.

The oral histories by W. W. Alexander and Frances Perkins at Columbia University are helpful, as are many published memoirs, diaries, journals, and collections of letters: James F. Byrnes, *All in One Lifetime* (New York, 1958); Jonathan Daniels, *White House Witness: 1942–1945* (Garden City, New York, 1975); James A. Farley, *Jim Farley's Story: The Roosevelt Years* (New York, 1948); William D. Hassett, *Off the Record with F.D.R. 1942–1945* (New Brunswick, New Jersey, 1958); *The Memoirs of Cordell Hull* (New York, 1948); Fred L. Israel, ed., *The War Diary of Breckinridge Long: Selections from the Years 1939–1944* (Lincoln, Nebraska, 1966); Jesse Jones with Edward Angly, *Fifty Billion Dollars: My Thirteen Years with the RFC* (New York, 1951); Frances Perkins, *The Roosevelt I Knew* (New York, 1946); Elliott Roosevelt, ed., *FDR His Personal Letters: 1928–1945* (New York, 1950); James Roosevelt and Sidney Shalett, *Affectionately, F.D.R.: A Son's Story of a Lonely Man* (New York, 1959); Samuel I. Rosenman, *Working with Roosevelt* (New York, 1952); Robert E. Sherwood, *Roosevelt and Hopkins: An Intimate History* (New York, 1948). On the Roosevelt marriage consult Bernard Asbell, ed., *Mother and Daughter: The Letters of Eleanor and Anna Roosevelt* (New York, 1982); John R. Boettiger, *A Love in Shadow* (New York, 1978); Elliott Roosevelt and James Brough, *A Rendezvous with Destiny: The Roosevelts of the White House* (New York, 1975); Elliott Roosevelt with James Brough, *Mother R: Eleanor Roosevelt's Untold Story* (New York, 1977); James Roosevelt with Bill Libby, *My Parents: A Differing View* (Chicago, 1976). Important and relevant secondary works include

Sidney Baldwin, *Poverty and Politics: The Rise and Decline of the Farm Security Administration* (Chapel Hill, North Carolina, 1968); Jason Berger, *A New Deal for the World: Eleanor Roosevelt and American Foreign Policy* (New York, 1981); James MacGregor Burns, *Roosevelt: The Lion and the Fox* (New York; 1956); Burns, *Roosevelt: The Soldier of Freedom* (New York, 1970); Bernard F. Donahoe, *Private Plans and Public Dangers* (Notre Dame, Indiana, 1965); Doris Faber, *The Life of Lorena Hickok: ER's Friend* (New York, 1980); Alonzo L. Hamby, *Beyond the New Deal: Harry S. Truman and American Liberalism* (New York, 1973); James R. Kearney, *Anna Eleanor Roosevelt: The Evolution of a Reformer* (Boston, 1968); Joseph P. Lash, *Eleanor and Franklin* (New York, 1971); Norman D. Markowitz, *The Rise and Fall of the People's Century: Henry A. Wallace and American Liberalism, 1940–1948* (New York, 1973); Robert L. Messer, *The End of an Alliance: James F. Byrnes, Roosevelt, Truman, and the Origins of the Cold War* (Chapel Hill, North Carolina, 1982); J. Samuel Walker, *Henry A. Wallace and American Foreign Policy* (Westport, Connecticut, 1976).

In working on this essay, I have been helped by conversations over the years with Frank Freidel, Anna Roosevelt Halsted, William R. Emerson, Robert H. Ferrell, and Patrick J. Maney; an extended interview with a long-time Wallace associate, Earl Bressman; and a grant from the Graduate College, Iowa State University. I am grateful also to Glenda Riley, Richard Lowitt, and my colleagues in a history discussion group for improvements in the manuscript.

PART 4

PARADOXES

Tamara K. Hareven

ER and Reform

S OMEWHERE BETWEEN THE two extreme images of Eleanor
Roosevelt—that of the shallow busybody first lady and that of the
humanitarian reformer and consummate politician—stands a complex figure full of contradictions and paradoxes, a social reformer who
could not be easily stereotyped. Her omnipresence and involvement in
many different causes, her paradoxical statements, and her support of
seemingly contradictory causes bewildered her contemporaries and left
even her supporters feeling that her activities had no coherent pattern.
Despite these apparent inconsistencies, however, Eleanor Roosevelt's reform activities did have an underlying coherence that began to take shape
during her apprenticeship in the social reform movements that flourished
from the Progressive Era through the New Deal. The most consistent
elements in her approach were a commitment to social justice and equality
and a conviction that the federal government and the states must take
more active roles in achieving these goals. Consistent also was her pragmatic style. Although she was an idealist—and as the New Deal's inside
critic she insisted on reform rather than stopgaps—she was ready to work
for social betterment step by step and to compromise under the pressures
of political reality.

Traditionally, historians of reform have divided the first half of the
twentieth century into three periods. In the first, the Progressive Era,
social reform peaked just before World War I and found its political
expression and support in the presidencies of Theodore Roosevelt and
Woodrow Wilson. It was a period when many identified "progress" with
social justice. Economists, sociologists, philosophers, clergymen, and so-

cial workers insisted that poverty and other social evils were not divinely ordained trials or punishments for sin, but arose from human acts and ideas; the social and physical environment, therefore, had to be improved and made wholesome by human action. Muckrakers and writers of the realistic school exposed political corruption, exploitation, poverty, and life in the slums of industrial America. It was the age of Jane Addams at Hull House in Chicago and Lillian Wald on Henry Street in New York; of voluntary associations agitating for the protection of women in industry and for the abolition of child labor and sweatshops. In an atmosphere tense with protest and the zeal of crusaders, President Theodore Roosevelt dramatized reform issues, proclaimed that the age of governmental benign neglect was over, and became the hero of the Progressives.

The second period, in the conventional view of American reform during the twentieth century, is that of the 1920s, when the crusading zeal had begun to ebb. Under the combined impacts of the return of "normalcy" and "business as usual" after the war and the basic conservatism of the country, the national coalition that had sustained Progressivism collapsed. The third period of reform is the New Deal, which represented a revival of Progressive reform energies and a departure beyond Progressivism toward the welfare state.

Recently, scholars have begun to revise this three-part analysis of the first half of the twentieth century. Increasingly, it is becoming evident that significant reform energies did survive during the 1920s, though at the local and state levels rather than the federal level. They survived in the work of such voluntary organizations as the National Consumers' League, the settlement-house movement, and the newly organized League of Women Voters. These groups drew from the renewed enthusiasm generated by the passage of women's suffrage in 1919. In a decade of surface prosperity and political conservatism, these organizations began to build diverse new networks of reform efforts. They trained a new generation of professional social workers and reformers, among them Harry Hopkins and Frances Perkins, who were to become major architects of the New Deal's relief and reform programs. They provided continuity between Progressivism and the New Deal.

Eleanor Roosevelt's own awakening to the struggle for social justice stemmed initially from the "noblesse oblige" attitude typical of her class. As a youth, her only exposure to reform activities came from volunteer work with the Junior League, especially her visit to the Rivington Street

Settlement House in New York. Although a niece of President Theodore Roosevelt, she was for many years hardly touched by the high tide of Progressivism. Preoccupied with her family, in the period before World War I she considered politics a "sinister affair," about which she professed to know so little that she could not explain to inquiring Europeans the relationship between the federal government and the states. In her autobiography she never mentioned the intellectual background of the age, nor referred to books of the period that might have influenced her. When describing Theodore Roosevelt's greatness as a leader in a history book she began writing in 1929, she ignored his role as a Progressive reformer.

During World War I, her work for the Red Cross jolted her dormant social conscience. Her real apprenticeship to reform occurred later, though, during the 1920s, following her husband's crippling illness, when efforts to maintain Franklin Roosevelt's contact with politics involved her in reform work and political training. By this time she had demonstrated a sensitivity to human suffering, an indignation over poverty, and a readiness to serve. But she still lacked intellectual commitment and mainstream political experience.

Her training during this decade began with the Women's City Club of New York and League of Women Voters, whose members taught her how to compile and analyze legislation. Through work with Louis Howe, the New York Women's Democratic Committee, and the New York State and National Democratic Committees (especially through her campaign work for Al Smith) she learned the political realities and the mechanisms by which reform could be achieved. In her work with the New York settlement houses, she developed close ties with Lillian Wald, founder of the Henry Street Settlement, and Mary Simkhovitch, head worker at the Greenwich House. The settlement work focused her attention on the complexity of urban problems and on the interrelationships among poor housing, poverty, crime, and disease. Through their example of personal devotion and service, the settlement workers convinced her that for future reform a sense of personal responsibility to one's community and social service was as important as legislation. Surprisingly, the settlement workers did not inspire in her a lasting interest in immigrants, toward whom they were directing most of their efforts.

From the National Consumers' League, Eleanor Roosevelt learned the value of social investigation and exposé as first steps toward reform. Her guide, the league's founder and president, Florence Kelley, took Roosevelt on visits to politicians and legislatures in the campaign to protect women in industry and to abolish child labor. She instilled in Roosevelt her faith in the power of the boldly stated fact and insisted that information was half the way to reform. The conception of the reformer as investigator and educator, inspired by Florence Kelley, emerged as a central feature of Eleanor Roosevelt's reform work. Through Rose Schneiderman, president of the New York branch of the Women's Trade Union League (WTUL), Roosevelt became familiar with the trade unions, formed her commitment to the rights of labor, and adopted the definition of a "living wage" that included—in addition to food, housing, and clothing—considerations such as education, recreation, and emergency needs, especially for sickness and accidents. This was the beginning of her lifelong support of the WTUL and of fair labor standards. The 1920s exposed her to idealist reformers—both survivors of the Progressive Era and a new generation of professional social workers and political activists.

Eleanor Roosevelt's apprenticeship in the 1920s was crucial for her own development as a reformer, and for the access that reformers and reform movements gained to the New Deal programs. Later, through her own experience and her presence, she would provide a channel through which the energies of the voluntary reform associations and their leaders could move into the New Deal's reform program and machinery. As a result of her own training and through her own career, Eleanor Roosevelt thus provided an important bridge between earlier Progressive ideals, the reform movements of the 1920s, and the New Deal.

Eleanor Roosevelt plunged into social reform without a clearly formulated philosophy, a plan, or a program. Driven by idealism, she embarked on social reform and political activities at a point in her life when, like some other women reformers, she was experiencing a void in her life—a need to be active beyond the domestic sphere. In her case, the plunge into reform was also an escape from the pain of discovering her husband's affair with Lucy Mercer in 1918. She was also pushed into reform and political activity by the architects of her husband's political career following his polio attack. Thus, the timing of her entry into the reform scene at the point in her personal life at which she entered, and the historic moment in American reform at which she entered, were crucial for the subsequent course of her career as a reformer.

Underlying Roosevelt's social concern was her humanitarianism, her identification with the suffering of individuals, and a commitment to social justice. She transcended the view of her class and of her generation that poverty was a manifestation of personal failure. From Progressive reformers she adopted the view that poverty was a social problem, a result of inequality and of the maldistribution of economic resources. ER had already developed these convictions at an earlier point, but the shock of the Great Depression in itself had an important transforming effect on her social ideas. It marked her transition from sporadic activity in civic affairs and politics to a commitment to social reform. She had seen misery and poverty before, but had assumed that the system was sound, that slums, crime, poverty, and labor problems were blotches that could be removed through the dedication of social workers and legislation. The depression forced her to the soul-shattering realization that something was wrong in the system itself: she began to question the very assumptions of American society and culture.

Eleanor Roosevelt felt an era was coming to an end. Often before, she had expressed apprehension about the changes that were taking place in American society: the general instability, the erosion of family autonomy, the impersonality of life in large cities, the restlessness, the endemic poverty and unemployment even during prosperity. But she had never anticipated such a crisis. Now it reverberated up and down the land.

Mainly under the impact of the depression, Eleanor Roosevelt came to look at economic security as the indispensable pillar of democracy. She defined economic security as an economic level "below which no one is permitted to fall, and keeping a fairly stable balance between that level and the cost of living." Her definition included the right of a laborer to a useful and remunerative job, of a farmer to a fair return for his produce, of a businessman to protection from unfair competition, of every family to a decent home, and of every person to adequate care, proper education, and provision for old age.

Further, the Great Depression taught her that equality of opportunity meant more than an "honest broker" government; it meant constructive aid to underprivileged groups and a social and economic system that would guarantee their individual rights. The government had to undertake the positive role of furthering social justice and guaranteeing minimum economic security. As previous essays in this book have indicated, when Eleanor Roosevelt arrived in the White House in 1933, she was already an experienced politician and a committed social reformer. But she had no clear plan. In her energetic plunge into new activities as first lady, Roosevelt dramatized and advertised the mood of the early New Deal: frantic action, readiness to experiment, concern for the "forgotten man," and a realistic recognition of the grimness of the social problems of the depression, accompanied by a faith in combating them.

Though she initially viewed her role as that of auxiliary to her husband, Roosevelt also started to work independently for the causes she deemed important. In the beginning, she did not plan her course. She picked up new causes as they came along. "Somebody asked me to 'come and let us show you what is happening here,' and, being interested, I went. Then another invitation came, and I went. And each thing I saw proved so fascinating I found myself going more and more, farther and farther." Quickly, however, she developed the mechanisms for investigating social problems on a human level, established channels of direct communication between the general public and the White House, and developed her own role as intermediary between the New Deal and the public and between New Deal administrators and the president. She developed the power inherent in the position of first lady into a unique instrument for furthering social reform.

In sustaining this role, the first lady had several advantages. Unconstrained by any official administrative position, she could speak out more freely than could the president. She had access to New Deal agencies through their heads and administrators. From the beginning of the New Deal, administrators turned to her for help and contact with the president; gradually, she took the initiative and sent them her queries, criticisms, and advice. Because of her influence, even those who felt uneasy about her interference continued to appeal to her when they needed her support. Even her enemy and public critic, Westbrook Pegler, recognized the emergence of a reform agenda in the first lady's activities: "Mrs. Roosevelt has been too busy with such trivialities as old-age pension, a ban on child labor, and the protective health of mothers and children," he wrote in his column on April 25, 1935.

Roosevelt's support of New Deal relief and reform programs reflected her concern with the welfare of individuals, as well as with larger social problems. Her efforts to build lasting social reform elements into temporary relief measures and her campaigns for the launching of far-reaching reforms, such as social security or fair labor standards, had an important effect on the shaping of the New Deal's reform agenda that went beyond emergency measures and helped lay the foundation for the welfare state.

As first lady, her attitude toward relief agencies revealed a skillful combination of reformer and politician. On the one hand, she tried to supervise the administration of the various relief agencies and to see that they had an impact at the grass-roots level. At the same time, she tried to construct elements of permanent social reform rather than view New Deal measures strictly as temporary measures.

During the "First Hundred Days" of the New Deal, Eleanor Roosevelt began to assume new responsibilities. She was concerned that, in the rush and excitement accompanying the launching of new projects, human dignity should not be sacrificed to administrative expedience. The New Deal should not defeat its purpose by overlooking the needy groups that had been habitually ignored—single women, youth, blacks, and sharecroppers. At the same time she sought a rational administration of work relief, with a view to the needs of communities and an emphasis on productive employment rather than "busywork."

In the complex administrative machinery of government relief, Eleanor Roosevelt occupied the unique role of intermediary between the average person and the government. People in trouble, encouraged by her public invitation to write about their problems, called for help. In addition, she developed the practice of forwarding the letters requesting help to the National Democratic Committeewoman in the state from which the letter came. The committeewoman took the case to the appropriate relief agencies.

In her concern for the "forgotten" in American society, Eleanor Roosevelt went beyond her Progressive predecessors and pushed the New Deal's relief programs and reform measures to encompass the groups that had been previously left out. She focused on the establishment of relief agencies for women and youth and emphasized equal treatment for blacks. The Swain essay details how she quickly and effectively helped launch special programs for unemployed women. By December 17, 1933, about 100,000 women were among the 2,610,451 workers under the FERA and the Civil Works Administration (CWA). Thirty-five states appointed women directors to head work projects for women. At ER's insistence, Hopkins issued recommendations to include women wherever possible in the reemployment program. He suggested that they be given clerical jobs, even if this meant transferring men from such positions to other jobs. In this case and others in the 1930s, Eleanor Roosevelt's advocacy of women was motivated not as much by feminism as by her quest for social justice.

Wandersee's essay describes how the National Youth Administration, more than any other agency, was Eleanor Roosevelt's direct creation. ER's involvement in the establishment of the NYA expressed her concern for combining relief with lasting reform. She visualized the project that eventually became the NYA as a community effort. It was to be geared directly for youth rather than through the regular relief channels, and was to supply not only relief work, but meaningful occupations with a training value. During its entire existence Roosevelt was constantly on the alert to see that NYA services extended to the homeless, to transients, and to black youth. From 1936 on, she worked toward making the agency permanent and toward extending it to previously overlooked groups. Of all the New Deal agencies the NYA was exemplary in its employment of blacks. It was largely due to Roosevelt's vigilance that the NYA had its remarkable record of black employment.

The breadth of Roosevelt's relief concerns, particularly her commitment to folk culture and to the popularization of the folk arts, was expressed in her support of the WPA's writers and arts projects. She supported these efforts out of sympathy for unemployed artists and writers, a lively interest in the development of a national style, and a desire to stimulate the public's receptiveness to the arts. Experimenting with government patronage of the arts was particularly appealing to her because it carried a potentially lasting impact.

The arts and writers' projects also appealed to her sense of history and tradition. She saw these projects as the cultural counterpart of soil conservation and reforestation—an effort to preserve national resources. It was an expression of the rediscovery of common people, a new interest in their welfare, lives, and culture, as an important part of American culture. Roosevelt became progressively more convinced of this parallel. ER supported the collection of information on cities and whole regions for local guides (information that might otherwise have been lost to posterity), the preservation of historical documents, and the microfilming of old newspapers. The WPA Writers' Project amassed huge collections of folklore, slave narratives, local guides, and the Index of American Design which were all part of this effort.

Roosevelt's populist view of the arts was also expressed in her support of the WPA's Theater and Arts projects. Rather than turn the White House into a bastion of high culture, she supported the traveling concerts and "Caravan Theater" projects, for people who had never had the opportunity to see the theater or the arts:

> Last year, and I imagine we will find this duplicated this year, the average weekly audience of these Caravan Theaters were over 500,000 people. These plays are given free, of course, and for this reason many people who have never been able to, see and attend.

> Somehow we must build throughout this country a background of culture. No nation grows up until that has been accomplished, and I know of no way which will reach more of our people than the great plays of the past and present authors.

Although Roosevelt rarely agreed to assign a rank to the projects she was supporting, her commitment to black equality took a high place. From the 1930s on, the rights of blacks emerged as one of her major causes. She began to advocate the urgency of fighting discrimination long before the race riots of the 1940s brutally awakened many Americans to this necessity and long before "civil rights" had become a central reform issue. She was the only one in the New Deal administration to express an active interest in blacks and to take a personal and semiofficial stand on civil rights, even when she risked antagonizing political support for the president. Detailed information about the early support she gave NAACP Secretary Walter White in 1934, to obtain federal antilynching legislation can be found in the Zangrando essay.

The development of Eleanor Roosevelt's stand on racial discrimination parallels the changing emphases within the civil rights movement itself. She began by addressing whites and blacks in different terms. To white audiences she emphasized that discrimination was primarily a moral issue, which endangered the very fiber of American society. Although ER attacked inequality in a general way, she specifically distinguished between political and legal inequality on the one hand and social inequality on the other. She admitted that progress toward a voluntary social acceptance of blacks as equals would be slow, because it was impossible for any government to dictate it; it could develop only as people progressed spiritually. The government, however, had to remove all legal barriers, ensure equality in the courts and in employment, and prevent limitations being placed on people "except such as may be imposed by their own character and intelligence."

When addressing blacks, however, Roosevelt talked in the Booker T. Washington tradition. She stressed that blacks had to be as much responsible for their fate as whites and called on them to be practical and to develop their abilities and skills within the existing social framework. She urged them to compromise and use a "certain amount of intelligence in trying to fit the person who is capable of doing, to the job he can get." In answer to the question whether the federal government had any responsibility for the existence of separate lockers and lunchrooms in federal buildings in Washington, Roosevelt said diplomatically, "I think the federal government is established in a city which is still largely a Southern city. Now, like it or not, we cannot change things in a day." However, she was less compromising on the rights of black labor. When the minimum wage was introduced, and employers decided that if they had to pay a minimum of fourteen dollars a week, they would rather pay it to white workers than to blacks, Eleanor Roosvelt stated emphatically: "It is a question of the right to work, and the right to work should know no color lines."

As on other reform issues, Roosevelt fought segregation and discrimination by setting a personal example, anticipating much of the activism of the Civil Rights movement of the 1960s. In 1938, while attending the Southern Conference for Human Welfare in Birmingham, Alabama, she saw the delegates seated in two separate rows according to color. She took a seat on the side marked "Colored" and refused to move to the "White" side. When police threatened to break up the meeting, she reluctantly took her chair to the platform facing the audience, but placed it closer to the blacks' side. On that occasion, however, she was bolder in her conduct than in her public statement. When asked later by newspapermen for her opinion of the Alabama segregation law, she controlled her indignation and said that it was "a question for Alabama to decide." Moreover, by 1940 she had not yet mentioned desegregation in educational institutions, housing, and public service as major goals of civil rights.

Eleanor Roosevelt thus used the New Deal's framework to benefit blacks by concentrating on the development of segregated employment opportunities, proper housing, education, and medical care. Soon after her arrival in Washington in 1933, she started her campaign for the liquidation of the alley dwellings in Washington, most of which were black ghettos. Following the pragmatic spirit of the New Deal, she seized upon the opportunity provided by its various agencies to try and achieve equality for blacks within those relief agencies, particularly in the NYA.

Though the New Deal did not deliberately take the initiative on legislative reforms for desegregated equality, it at least offered blacks an opportunity to benefit from the general improvement of social and economic conditions, in which they shared with other depression-stricken groups.

To her credit, after all this legislation passed in the "First Hundred Days," Eleanor Roosevelt warned that the New Deal was still far from meeting its major goals. And throughout her White House years, she remained both the New Deal's advocate and its critic. After her husband's death in 1945, she lost her unique power position and her role of protector, but remained active in the public arena and continued to defend the New Deal's reform tradition as a "private citizen." Now she idealized it and made its principle the yardstick of all government policies. She realized that new problems had to be met with new answers, as long as the New Deal's principles were maintained. As the living symbol of the New Deal, she carried political power. Reform organizations courted her approval, and candidates in the Democratic party sought her endorsement. However, she identified the Democratic party with the reform tradition, and as the New Deal's custodian she refused to allow opportunists to use the New Deal as a slogan to further their own interests.

Roosevelt's reform agenda in the postwar years remained similar to that of the 1930s, but her outlook on some causes advanced while on others it remained the same. Partly, this was a result of a change in her own ideas; partly, it was the opportunity to be more outspoken, since she was no longer bound by her position as first lady. In particular, she began to change her goals and emphasis toward civil rights. In addition to the old issues, she now unequivocally stressed desegregation in housing, education, and other public facilities as the most important goal. She hailed Freehold, New Jersey, for integrating its grammar schools, and she saw a victory for civil rights in the Supreme Court decisions against restrictive housing covenants and in the banning of racial segregation at Washington National Airport.

Eleanor Roosevelt still did not demand legislative enforcement of social equality. "No one can tell me I've got to ask someone for dinner I don't want to, and neither can they tell me not to ask people I want to ask." In addition, she came to recognize the issues concerning blacks as a race problem with foreign policy implications. Earlier she had considered discrimination against blacks mainly in the context of domestic social justice. During the war she became more sensitive to the problems of blacks, but at the same time her disillusioning encounters with the Soviets in the UN after the war made her more cautious about discussing America's race problem in international arenas.

In the last decades of her life, Eleanor Roosevelt increasingly viewed American society from a world perspective. Like idealist Progressive reformers, she wanted to see the victory of democracy and social justice in the world, but unlike Woodrow Wilson and other Progressive idealists, she did not believe in the imposition of American ideals abroad. In her work with the UN Human Rights Commission, she realized the potential influence of the Third World and the impact of diverse economic conditions and cultural traditions on international relations. Her world experience fostered her commitment to pluralism, both at home and abroad.

It would be impossible to place Eleanor Roosevelt's reform thought into a particular mold because it was so flexible. She had no conscious program and devised no tools. She was pragmatic, adaptable, willing to experiment, and committed to social justice rather than to dogmatic ideology. Because she was not burdened with having to make major political decisions, she was less compromising on principle than the president and New Deal politicians could afford to be. She adopted causes as they arose and was often ahead of her time. In her statements, she often appeared as an uncompromising idealist; in her work within the administration and later in political affairs and in the UN she revealed a skill in practical politics and an understanding of the subtle exercise of power and influence.

Though Eleanor Roosevelt was not a profound or systematic thinker, her ideas took shape as she applied them to new circumstances. Under the impact of the depression, she stressed social and economic security as the basis of democracy. World War II accentuated her earlier emphasis on racial equality and the U.S. role as world leader. World problems at the UN led her to see domestic issues as inseparable from world conditions. Although she had occasional utopian lapses, she constantly tested her ideas by realistic standards. Advocating gradual reform within the existing system, at no point did she fool herself into believing that equality, liberty, and world peace could be achieved in her generation.

SOURCES

The voluminous Eleanor Roosevelt Papers of the Roosevelt Library in Hyde Park, New York, contain Eleanor Roosevelt's correspondence and drafts of her writings and speeches. Eleanor Roosevelt's correspondence with government agencies is also in the files of the FERA, CWA, WPA, and NYA at the National Archives. Eleanor Roosevelt's published writings include a syndicated column, "My Day," from December 30, 1935 to September 11, 1962, and numerous articles in the popular press. In addition ER published monthly columns in magazines, where she replied to readers' questions. In some cases, New Deal administrators sent in questions when they wanted ER to explain, publicize, or advocate certain issues. The columns were: "If You Ask Me," in the *Ladies' Home Journal*, June 1941–May 1949, and in *McCall's*, April 1953 to November 1962; and "Mrs. Roosevelt's Page," in *Woman's Home Companion*, August 1933 to July 1935.

ER's autobiographical writings include: *This Is My Story* (New York, 1937); *This I Remember* (New York, 1949); *On My Own* (New York, 1958); *It's Up to the Women* (New York, 1933); *Ladies of Courage* (New York, 1954); *Tomorrow is Now* (New York, 1963); *The Moral Basis of Democracy* (New York, 1940); *This Troubled World* (New York, 1938).

An analysis of Eleanor Roosevelt's emergence and role as a reformer is in Tamara Hareven's *Eleanor Roosevelt: An American Conscience* (Chicago, 1968). Biographies of ER include Joseph Lash, *Eleanor and Franklin* (New York, 1971) and *Eleanor: The Years Alone* (New York, 1972).

Abigail Q. McCarthy

ER As First Lady

ELEANOR ROOSEVELT WAS first lady for over twelve years— longer than any other woman—and during a period crucial in our history. She was at the heart of change, and often its source. No other first lady has had her influence. No other has been so much the center of controversy. No other has so affected the lives of the women who followed her.

There is general agreement that Eleanor Roosevelt had a pivotal influence on the role of the first lady: we measure not only her successors but her predecessors by her character and achievements. In 1976 I talked about this with the wives of the twelve candidates for the presidency— women who ranged in politics from Joan Mondale to Nancy Reagan and in background from Eunice Shriver to LaDonna Harris. I spoke with Ella Udall and Cornelia Wallace; Helen Jackson and Bethine Church; Rosalynn Carter and Marvella Bayh; the then first lady, Betty Ford, and Beryl Bentsen. I also talked with former first lady Lady Bird Johnson and former vice-presidential wives Muriel Humphrey and Barbara Bush. Inevitably, when talk turned to their conception of the first lady's role, they mentioned the deep influence of Eleanor Roosevelt: "Of course, since Eleanor Roosevelt. . . ." It was a recurring phrase.

Today, we take certain aspects of the first lady's role for granted. Although she is not elected or appointed, the first lady has all the obligations of office and directs not only a household staff but an office staff provided for in the budget of the United States. From the day of her husband's election until the day she dies, she is accompanied by security agents. Her travel is carefully planned. During his tenure of office her every move is scrutinized by the press. She represents the nation both at home and abroad. Her tastes, her preferences, her sense of place in history affect ours.

Being first lady is not a casual or part-time occupation, but a full-time job. The elevation to this high status comes quickly and, obviously, without any real preparation. Betty Ford spoke of this from her own experience. Just at that time in life when "most mothers of families can look forward to a little time for themselves," she noted, "all of a sudden, I have a full-time job—a job I didn't choose or plan for." Her life, she said, was like a corporate executive's: "I'm at my desk every day and busy with staff meetings and planning of events." The first lady's role is the epitome of what sociologist Hanna Papanek calls the "two-person career"—that combination of "formal and informal institutional demands placed on a married couple" by reason of the husband's career. The contributions that wives in these careers make include "status maintenance, intellectual contributions, and public performance." In terms of public performance, the first lady functions as representative of the nation. She welcomes heads of state, presides at state dinners, makes public appearances in person and through the media, attends local and national celebrations, and becomes the patroness of selected charities. These aspects of the role can be compared to the duties assumed by royal families. Eleanor Roosevelt used the parallel with royalty in a letter to Jackie Kennedy: "To smile no matter how weary one is, to look well-dressed and interested at all times is a remarkable feat, especially when it is considered that we do not have the long training given to royalty to meet these situations."

In terms of status maintenance and intellectual contribution, the first lady is expected to be a kind of national wife—the embodiment of American womanhood (an ideal that evolved throughout the nineteenth century). The modern office of first lady differs markedly from that of the nineteenth century. Then, as historian Barbara Welter has observed, the first lady's principal duties were social, not political. Even the social obligations were regarded as onerous by some first ladies, who avoided them by claiming invalidism (then a perfectly acceptable excuse for not going out in society) or religion. Rachel Jackson and Eliza Johnson claimed the latter, and a long list of first ladies, from Elizabeth Monroe and continuing through Lucy Hayes, retreated to the upper floor of the White House as invalids. As to intellectual contribution, Welter has commented that although nearly every president talked politics to his wife, "there has been a tendency on the part of biographers to discount completely any role or influence of the wife. . . ."

The emphasis on social aspects tended to enforce a uniformity of public behavior on the various women who played the role, and this was true up to and through the presidency of Herbert Hoover. First Lady Lou Henry Hoover was, in the White House, "a far cry," notes Welter, "from the tomboy Lou Henry who majored in geology at Stanford, an extraordinary thing for a woman to do, who translated the *de re metallica* from the Latin, and bicycled through the Chinese Revolution amid spraying bullets, and single-handedly organized a committee to return 10,000 Americans from overseas. . . ." Lou Hoover's personality became submerged in the role she played as the president's wife, a role still defined by the outworn norms of the previous century. What made Lou Hoover's position especially poignant, however, was that women's position in society had changed.

In the early nineteenth century, Alexis de Tocqueville had observed the fact, puzzling to him, that American women, unlike European women, seemed to disappear from the public scene once they married. This resulted partly from the patriarchal repressiveness of the Puritan heritage in early America, but also from the overwhelming responsibilities that women bore in the home. For Charles Wilson Peale, portraitist to the elite of the young country and a typical eighteenth-century generalist, marriage was "a social bond . . . by which harmony, industry and the wealth of the nation are promoted." According to his biographer, Peale was convinced that the family circle provided the moral education of the next generation, where were taught "discipline, balance, duty and benevolence; virtues highly important to the young American republic." His thinking was typical of the times. Even Abigail Adams's famed plea to her husband to "remember the ladies" and grant them rights of citizenship was argued on the assumption that the "ladies" were responsible to society as mothers and educators of *men*.

By the 1840s, this theory of the female role was expanding to include realms beyond the home. Strong-minded women of the time felt the contradiction between the subordination of woman and the ideals of a nation that prided itself on its democratic spirit. Educator Catharine Beecher (sister of Harriet Beecher Stowe), for example, thought of women as teachers to the nation and tried to reconcile their patently inferior position by elevating the tasks they performed. In a sense, Beecher took

Peale one step further, by ascribing to women a central moral and educative role not only in the family but in a web of institutions that included the family, the school, the church. Women, she argued, should function as exemplars and teachers of a national morality both at home and in the classroom, both privately and publicly. As the century progressed, women became the civilizing and community-building force on frontier after frontier and the moving force behind the abolition and temperance movements.

By the turn of the century, a combination of education and zeal for uplift and reform blossomed into the formation of women's associations and the establishment of such organizations as settlement houses. Professionalized social work and prison work were added to the "traditional" women's occupations of nursing and teaching. The "Lady Bountiful" charitable enterprises of upper- and middle-class women were becoming quasi-professional volunteer activities in the service of organizations like the Red Cross and the Junior League.

Eleanor Roosevelt, sixteen years old when the century turned, conformed to this emerging ideal of woman. She had been prepared by her education at Allenswood to enter activities that would improve the world. As a debutante, she took up volunteer work that exposed her to social conditions demanding reform. As a young wife, she was active in the Consumers' League, the Women's Trade Union League, and the League of Women Voters.

She became a practical politician and party worker, not only in behalf of her disabled husband, but because of her own interests. As she wrote in a League of Women Voters' bulletin: "On the whole the Democratic Party seems to have been more concerned with the welfare and interests of the people at large, and less with the growth of big business interests. . . . If you believe that the people must struggle slowly to the light for themselves, then it seems to me that you are logically a Democrat."

Last of all, she had been the very active first lady of the largest state in the union. She came to the White House with a lively sense of the people, of their variety, of their needs, and of what government could do to change their lives.

Of all the first ladies, then, Eleanor Roosevelt had the most complete preparation for the role in all its aspects. In addition to being from a family established in New York society, she was also from a presidential family. Her consciousness of what a first family could be must have been affected by her closeness to the family of her uncle, President Theodore Roosevelt. Studies have shown that women of achievement are often influenced by the strong male role models in the family—if not a father (which was sadly unlikely in Eleanor Roosevelt's case), then a brother or other close relative. As a young woman, she must have seen that the White House was indeed, as Theodore Roosevelt put it, "a bully pulpit."

Theodore Roosevelt's presidency has been characterized as the first media presidency; Eleanor Roosevelt became the first media first lady. She gave women journalists a status and opportunity they had not previously enjoyed by holding her own press conferences, restricted to them, and dispensing hard news at these conferences so that newspapers and syndicates had to add women to their staffs. "But it was not just that she legitimized them as journalists," says Doris O'Donnell, daughter of Doris Fleeson, one of the columnists closest to ER,

> but that she made them part of what was going on. It was in the Roosevelt administration that the press—largely writing press then—became part of the establishment—literally the fourth estate. The age of the muckrakers was over for the moment. Just as the president legitimized the press by establishing regular press conferences, so did 'Mrs. R.' as the press women called her. But I think there was a difference.

The difference, as O'Donnell sees it, lay in the fact that, in befriending the press, FDR skillfully used journalists for his purposes (and for the best interests of the nation, as he saw those interests). Through them, through the control of information and access, he had a tool with which to confound his enemies. "Mrs. Roosevelt used them too" says O'Donnell,

> but in a very different way. *She enlisted them in her causes.* She had an extraordinary creative capacity to see how people could best use their talents. These women had fought their way to the top in their professions against great odds. Some of them were hard-bitten. They were not easily taken in. But they responded to Mrs. Roosevelt's vitality, sincerity, strength of character and her real interest in them.

O'Donnell goes on to cite the example of her mother,

> a Kansas populist brought up to be distrustful of the Eastern seaboard elite. She was cynical about most people, but she was never cynical about Mrs. Roosevelt. I think Mrs. Roosevelt represented to her the ideal of what woman

could be. She realized what Eleanor Roosevelt was or tried to be and she internalized it—made it part of her own work and life.

In much the same way as she was able to enlist journalists, Eleanor Roosevelt was to enlist labor leaders, educators, women in government, and youth leaders. By the time she reached the White House, she had long since learned to reach across all barriers to create friendships, whether with a Kansas populist like Doris Fleeson or a black leader like Mary McLeod Bethune. "No head of state was received like Mrs. Bethune," wrote J. B. West, White House usher; "Mrs. Roosevelt would run down the drive to meet her and they would walk up the drive arm in arm."

With Eleanor Roosevelt as chatelaine, the White House became the symbol of the inclusiveness of true democracy. She was prodigiously hospitable. "It seems that there were never less than twenty for lunch," says J. B. West. In her autobiography, *This is My Story*, she lists those entertained in one year: over four thousand for lunch, more than nine thousand for tea, and others for dinner almost every night when she was not traveling. Undoubtedly, she began inviting people in numbers in order to bring the world to a stricken husband, but by the time of the height of her activities as first lady her hospitality had become a means of catalysis, of bringing people together for their mutual benefit and to further the causes she believed in.

She had feared, leaving New York for Washington, that her life would narrow, her activities would be curtailed, and that, like Lou Hoover, she would become only a figurehead—a ceremonial presence. Franklin Roosevelt depended on her too much for that. Secretary of Labor Frances Perkins tells us how it was:

> They had not been in Washington a month before the President asked her to go down into the southern Appalachian region, from which he had had pathetic letters, to see what the problems were and what could be done. Then he asked her to go to a meeting of an organization interested in social progress, to represent him and say on his behalf, as well as on her own, how much they were interested in the program. He gave her many assignments after that. The hardest perhaps was to go to the Pacific front during the war.

As first lady, Eleanor Roosevelt claimed the public sphere for wives once and for all. In doing so she altered the position of the political wife and what was expected of her. She herself was unique, but her image is refracted and reflected by those who came after her. Helen Jackson, wife of the late Henry Jackson, senator and two-time presidential candidate, has summed up the nature of the change:

> Eleanor Roosevelt changed forever the role of political wives in the United States. We hold press conferences, make speeches, appear on television, assist in fundraising, and participate in all aspects of campaigning and the official life.

The change, however, was not immediate, although Roosevelt obviously entertained the hope that other first ladies would use the "office" as she had. One of her first acts after the president's death was to offer to introduce Bess Truman to "the girls" of the press corps, at what she assumed would be the latter's first press conference. According to Frances Perkins, the new first lady was filled with trepidation at the prospect. Perkins advised her that if she didn't want to have press conferences there was no need to have them—that she thought there was no precedent for doing so other than that set by Eleanor Roosevelt, who was a special case. Whether thus persuaded or not, Bess Truman never did hold a press conference and left relations with the press to her highly respected social secretary, Edith Helm.

Bess Truman and Mamie Eisenhower preferred to restrict their activities to providing companionship to their husbands and acting as White House hostesses—almost in the mold of the nineteenth-century first ladies. They were both of Roosevelt's generation but lacked her background for translating social and official position into opportunities to affect the common good. Nor, it would seem, had they a desire to do so.

Presidents Kennedy and Johnson and their staffs seem to have recognized, in the expansion of and emphasis on the first lady's office, a way of giving an added dimension to their administrations. Jacqueline Kennedy's choice of staff was at least approved in the West Wing; both President Johnson and Elizabeth "Liz" Carpenter have told of Johnson's summoning the latter to his office and telling her to "get over there and help Lady Bird." Each first lady added something to the public role. Jacqueline Kennedy became the first first lady to lead an official commission. Lady Bird Johnson's "beautification" project, despite the somewhat gimmicky tone of its title, bore real results by calling attention to the environment and improving the quality of life in towns and cities, especially Washington, D.C. The so-called Billboard Bill, abolishing commercial advertising signs along highways built with federal money, was passed with her support (and with some presidential arm-twisting in Congress).

By the time Pat Nixon entered the White House, the pattern was set. The question was not whether she would have a project but what her project would be. Her choice of using her official status to call attention to "voluntarism" was innocuous and in the good Republican tradition of deemphasising government aid. But it must be remembered that she was also the first first lady to be sent to a foreign country as personal representative of the president during peacetime. Betty Ford set out to emphasize the arts but, almost by accident, became an exponent of feminism and a sponsor of the Equal Rights Amendment, although her sponsorship was largely a public relations effort that had little practical political effect.

Rosalynn Carter quite deliberately set out to emulate Eleanor Roosevelt. She sensed, it would seem, that she had to make an overt effort to rescue the "office" of the first lady from mere celebrity-hood and the appearance of influence. Her insistence on regular office hours and on having a business lunch with the president on a weekly basis, like his other advisers, was part of this effort. But her lack of a Washington base and a limited rapport with the press—a radically different press corps in the post-Watergate era than that dealt with by First Ladies Kennedy, Johnson, and even Nixon—brought the effort little success.

Her failure points to a basic difficulty in what has come to be the establishment of a quasi-official office, that of first lady. Hanna Papanek expressed it well:

> The limits to acceptable participation by the wife in the husband's public image are illustrated by those cases where the wives become public personalities themselves and no longer operate only in the context of the husband's role. The key expression which indicates that these stereotyped limits have been exceeded is the statement 'she is a . . . in her own right'. . . .

Other difficulties inherent in the increasingly public role of the office are illustrated in the experience of Eleanor Roosevelt. First of all, the public side of her life often curtailed the private satisfactions of family life, a fact she recognized. In her autobiography she wrote that "public life . . . is fine for one's ideals but it is very high in personal sacrifice. . . . No matter what happens . . . I do not think a woman ever feels the loss in personal relations is compensated for. . . ."

Secondly, although Roosevelt was better equipped than some of her successors to deal with the fact, she depended heavily on the press, especially the women of the press. It can even be said they made use of her to call attention to conditions that interested them, and to reach the president. In some sense they "made" her, even as she "made" them. Anne Cottrell Free, who was one of the younger reporters admitted to the group close to Mrs. Roosevelt, has noted with some disapproval that they protected her. "There was a great deal of hinting and prompting at those press conferences," she told a seminar on first ladies at Hunter College in 1982. "'Are you sure you want to say that, Mrs. Roosevelt?' 'Wouldn't you like to say this, Mrs. Roosevelt?' It wasn't exactly objective journalism."

An incident related by Dorothy Roe Lewis, one of the four reporters assigned to cover Eleanor Roosevelt during the 1933 campaign, seems to bear this out. "Through the many months of the campaign, the election and the aftermath," she wrote in an article in the *New York Times* in 1981,

> it had been our job to stay with the unpredictable Eleanor Roosevelt wherever she went, whatever she did, and she set a hectic pace. Although most of us were half her age, we were exhausted just keeping up with her. We also had become fond of this unorthodox lady, and apparently she held the same feeling toward us.

Recounting an incident that shows the interdependence of press and future first lady, Lewis relates how ER had promised to return and describe to the press the postelection official call the Roosevelts were about to make on the Hoovers at the White House. When she returned, Roosevelt reported excitedly that she had overheard Mr. Hoover ask her husband to join in a proclamation to close the banks and that her husband had replied that if Hoover did not have the courage to do it alone he would do it after taking office.

> One of us said, 'Mrs. Roosevelt, you don't really want us to print that, do you?' Then everybody was trying to talk at once: 'Don't you realize what would happen if that story went out tonight? The New York Stock Exchange would close. The country would go off the gold standard. There would be a worldwide panic. Besides, it's all hearsay. We couldn't quote either President directly. . . . It's all right, Mrs. Roosevelt. If you will promise not to tell anyone else about this, we will promise not to write it.' And, so far as I know, none of us did, until now. We didn't even tell our editors.

The first lady had become an avenue to the highest levels of a political administration—but she could also put it at risk.

As we know now, the roles of Eleanor Roosevelt and President Roosevelt in the two-person career grew less complementary as his need lessened and her interests became more insistent. By the time J. B. West became chief White House usher in 1941, there were, he says, two kinds of guests—FDR's people and ER's people. Allowing for a possibly jaundiced point of view on his part, it does seem to most observers that she tested the limits of a presidential wife's involvement.

After the United States entered World War II, Eleanor Roosevelt took a government appointment in her own right as assistant director of the Office of Civilian Defense. She hoped that the volunteer participation program could be used to enhance the quality of life through projects to encourage physical fitness, improve nutrition, and reduce illiteracy. But her broad concept of the OCD and the people she appointed to staff positions evoked so much congressional hostility that she had to withdraw.

Eleanor Roosevelt's patriotism, too, often came under attack, and the absurd lengths to which some officials from military intelligence and the FBI went to discredit her have only recently come to light in Joseph Lash's last book, *Love, Eleanor*. Hanna Papanek comments:

Women who develop their own public image, starting from their base as the wives of prominent personalities, usually evoke fierce attacks and loyalties which are partly based on their having violated stereotyped standards of proper behavior in the vicarious achievement role. The complex career of Eleanor Roosevelt illustrates the development of this pattern especially well, particularly the process of rejecting the shadow role (Lash, 1971, 1972). In her case, it is perhaps possible to speculate that her husband's disabling illness made it first possible for her to develop a more activist role in the public eye and to be accepted in such a role, at least at the beginning, by those who later became detractors.

In 1982 Senator Denton of Alabama attacked wives of certain senators, in a manner reminiscent of the attacks made on Eleanor Roosevelt. Denton said that Betty Bumpers, founder of the antinuclear coalition Peace Links, and those associated with her like Teresa Heinz and Nicole Tsongas, were cooperating, wittingly or not, with the Soviets and their aims. The attack, made on the Senate floor in violation of tradition and senatorial courtesy, suggests that even today the political wife who is active in her own right is at peril when her activism is in the political sphere and when it is not seen as in the direct service of her husband's role or cause.

In many respects Eleanor Roosevelt's most enduring legacy to her successors was the life of her own she built on the foundation of her experiences as first lady. More than sixteen years after her husband's death, she was functioning as a world figure, while most of the people associated with FDR's presidency had faded from sight. She felt, rightly, that she had made a success of her professional career, and done so "on her own." Perhaps more than any other person, she was responsible for the United Nations adopting the Declaration of Human Rights. In her UN work she demonstrated unlimited patience, the ability to learn quickly, and an understanding of the world that made her a prophet about troubles yet to come from what is now called the Third World. As informal ambassador-at-large, she was greeted by cheering—and in India worshipful—crowds. She overcame the anti-American feeling of those years through her good will and the sheer force of her presence. She was called, not without reason, First Lady of the World.

SOURCES

In addition to the wives of the presidential candidates for 1976, mentioned at the beginning of my essay, I interviewed Doris O'Donnell, daughter of columnist Doris Fleeson, and Roosevelt's presidential advisers James Rowe, Jr. and the late Benjamin Cohen. The two-person career is discussed in detail by Hanna Papanek, *Changing Woman in a Changing Society* (Chicago, 1973). My comments on the nineteenth century draw heavily from Barbara Welter's unpublished paper, "First Ladies Before Eleanor Roosevelt," delivered at The First Lady: Is There an Office?, a conference sponsored by Hunter College and the Roosevelt Institute in June 1983; Lillian B. Miller and Harry N. Abrams, *Charles Wilson Peale and His World* (New York, 1982); and Katherine Kish Sklar, *Catharine Beecher, A Study in American Domesticity* (New Haven, Connecticut, 1973).

My comments on Eleanor Roosevelt herself are based on many books and articles, including: Joseph Lash's books *Eleanor and Franklin* (New York, 1971), *Eleanor: The Years Alone* (New York, 1972), and *Love, Eleanor: Eleanor Roosevelt and Her Friends* (New York, 1982); Dorothy Roe Lewis,

"What F.D.R. Told Hoover, March 3, '33," *New York Times* (March 13, 1981); Frances Perkins, *The Roosevelt I Knew* (New York, 1946); J. B. West, *Upstairs at the White House: My Life with the First Ladies* (New York, 1973); Bernard Asbell, ed., *Mother and Daughter: The Letters of Eleanor and Anna Roosevelt* (New York, 1982); and three books by Elliott Roosevelt (with James Brough)—*An Untold Story: The Roosevelts of Hyde Park* (New York, 1973), *A Rendezvous with Destiny: The Roosevelts of the White House* (New York, 1975), and *Mother R: Eleanor Roosevelt's Untold Story* (New York, 1977).

Lois Scharf

ER and Feminism

"SHE TALKS LIKE A social worker and acts like a feminist," wrote journalist Ruby Black about Eleanor Roosevelt in 1935. "Social worker" was not a complimentary term when spoken by a feminist like Black. It connoted an approach to women's welfare completely at odds with the strategy of activists like Alice Paul, head of the National Woman's Party, who had introduced an equal rights amendment in 1923. To party feminists, only a constitutional amendment that ensured equality under the law for men and women would guarantee full political participation and economic opportunity for American women. To social workers and reformers,* the proposed ERA threatened to destroy the protected position of working women that had been painstakingly constructed over the past three decades. Both reformers and feminists wanted to enhance the well-being of women, but they defined female rights, needs, and the means of addressing them differently.

To Black, Woman's Party member and ERA advocate, there was no doubt that Eleanor Roosevelt stood firmly in the company of the reformers. Yet it was not quite so simple as that. As Washington correspondent for United Press International, Black regularly attended the women-only press conferences that Roosevelt had initiated when she arrived at the White House. These sessions contributed to the professional

---

*Historian William L. O'Neill used "social feminists" to describe those women who were concerned with women's rights but who subordinated those issues to more broad-based social welfare and reform they believed were more urgent. "Hard-core" or "extreme feminists" distinguished those women whose focus was women's rights. I have used "reformer" and "feminist" to distinguish the two groups and avoid confusion resulting from the use of "feminist" and "feminism" in both contexts.

stature of women reporters and reminded them of the first lady's special
qualities—qualities that set her apart from the wives of other presidents.
By describing her as a feminist, Black seemed to imply that narrow
definitions of feminism inadequately described Eleanor Roosevelt; that
although she opposed the constitutional amendment, for example, she
would be evaluated more fairly on the basis of her sensitivity to many
issues regarding women's position in society; that she should be judged by
the degree to which she engaged in self-directed, independent action.
Black's effort to place Mrs. Roosevelt firmly in the feminist ranks was
meant, it seems, to bridge the rancorous schism that had developed in the
postsuffrage women's movement.

The split among activist women after 1920 centered on protective legislation for female workers. The efforts of social reformers to improve the
wages and working conditions of women date from the late nineteenth
century. Earlier in the century, reforming efforts had centered on attempts to improve the physical working conditions of all wage earners,
male and female. Most state legislatures were unwilling to enact such
laws, however, and the courts overruled those that were passed. Reformers therefore turned their attention to legislation that would protect
the most vulnerable segments of the laboring population, children and
women.

This approach proved more successful. Child-labor laws were passed in
most states and, when combined with laws mandating longer periods of
compulsory schooling, effectively reduced the number of workers under
the age of fourteen. Reformers also succeeded in having laws passed that
limited the maximum number of hours women could work in a week.
Their efforts seemed guaranteed for all time when, in 1908, the U.S.
Supreme Court upheld the constitutionality of the Oregon ten-hour statute. Campaigns for new legislation on behalf of working women quick-
ened. Laws for minimum wages, factory safety standards, elimination of
night work and exclusion from potentially dangerous occupations were
added to the agenda.

To the reformers it was self-evident that the best way to improve the lot
of women was through such protective laws. Their approach was colored
by the view that women, being biologically different from men, and also
being the mothers of the next generation, should not be expected to labor
in the workplace under conditions identical to those of men. This gradualist approach, which had slowly begun to regulate working conditions in

behalf of women, would be imperiled by the blanket equality amendment introduced by the National Woman's Party.

This is not to say that reformers and feminists could not agree on some common goals—suffrage, for example. As the first generation of well-educated women moved into regulatory and service spheres of government as experts, advisers, and lobbyists, the reformers assumed that women would have an added and powerful voice in shaping social legislation. Once the right to vote had been won, however, the split between reformers and feminists could no longer be avoided, because it soon became evident that the vote alone was not producing the political gains and legal equality for women that feminists demanded.

While reformers and feminists worked together for female suffrage during the first twenty years of the century, ER could not be counted in either camp. Like a number of single, wealthy young women of the Junior League, she had volunteered time at the Rivington Street Settlement House, where she taught calisthenics and dancing to slum children. She had joined the National Consumers' League, a women's organization committed to abolishing child labor and regulating working conditions of women. She had even accompanied an investigator on a survey of work patterns in garment factories and department stores. But these activities ceased when she married.

The years as a new wife and young mother of a growing household were devoted to familial concerns and social activities appropriate to the conventions of her age and class. Franklin Roosevelt's appointment as assistant secretary of the Navy and the family's move to Washington coincided with the surge in the campaign for women's enfranchisement, but the movement made little impact on his wife. When the United States entered World War I, Eleanor Roosevelt made her first venture into sustained public volunteer work through the Red Cross. She demonstrated her capacity for hard work and organization during long days at Washington's Union Station canteen as well as on Navy Department projects ranging from knitting sweaters to arranging patriotic rallies. These tentative but successful and rewarding efforts were a prelude to the flurry of political activity and education that soon followed.

With the end of the war and Franklin's abortive vice-presidential candidacy in 1920, the Roosevelt ménage returned to New York City. There Eleanor selectively chose the associations and societies to which she devoted her time, interest, and energy. After some hesitation, she chaired the legislative committee of the New York State League of Women Voters. The league, successor to the National American Woman Suffrage Association, was dedicated to the education of newly enfranchised women. While it never retained the commitment or numbers of women who had swelled the ranks of the suffrage movement in its last, successful years, the league did include among its reconstituted membership many of the most capable leaders. Two such women in New York were Elizabeth Read, a lawyer by training, and Esther Lape, who had taught at major colleges. Intimate friends themselves, they became political mentors and close friends of ER. They introduced her to the issues that had engaged their attention along with the struggle for the vote, such as the abolition of child labor and the passage of protective legislation for women workers, and new concerns that veterans of the suffrage battles in and out of the league were making their own in the early 1920s, such as the peace movement. Read and Lape undertook "the intense education of Eleanor Roosevelt," as Roosevelt herself put it.

The Women's Trade Union League (WTUL) also engaged her attention. A reform organization dating from the early twentieth century, the WTUL was unique in its conscious efforts to bridge the gap between middle-class social reformers and working-class women. The latter were encouraged to join the leadership ranks of the group, and special classes were organized to teach the skills that would enable working women to assume responsible positions both in the league and in unions, which the WTUL was committed to help form on behalf of female workers. The cross-class relationships were generally fraught with tension, but a number of committed, union-oriented, working-class women made strong, long-lasting affiliations with the league. Rose Schneiderman, European-born union organizer for the Cap Makers, and Maud Swartz, British-trained activist for the Typographical Workers Union, were among them. They quickly became Eleanor's friends and guides to the world of industrial workers and trade unions, and especially to proposed legislative remedies.

Following on the heels of her increased efforts for the two leagues was Eleanor Roosevelt's introduction into the world of Democratic party politics. It was a logical step for a woman who had acquitted herself admirably in volunteer organizations with political overtones, and whose politically ambitious husband was now crippled by polio. Aided by former journalist Louis Howe, who was as devoted to her well-being as he was to the advancement of Franklin's career, Eleanor Roosevelt entered the male bastion of party structures. Another new pair of friends and exemplary instructors, Marion Dickerman and Nancy Cook, helped her reorganize the Women's Division of the New York State Democratic party, publish its newsletter, and establish clubs throughout the state. With coaching and constant encouragement from Howe, she even accepted speaking engagements. Dickerman and Cook were party workers who added Progressive Era experience in campaigns for suffrage, child welfare, working conditions for women, and pacifism to their postwar professional and partisan activities. From them, Roosevelt learned quickly. By 1924, she had achieved statewide political recognition and stood among the leading party women who were pledged to the presidential nomination of Al Smith. She campaigned successfully for the right of women to designate female delegates and alternates to the party's convention.

At the Democratic National Convention of 1924, as chair of the committee to assist the Democratic National Committee on Platform Planks of Special Interest to Women, ER first encountered the clash over the new constitutional amendment proposed by the National Woman's Party. Immediately following a twenty-minute presentation on the subject of effective enforcement of the Volstead [Prohibition] Act, Jane Norman Smith presented the National Woman's Party plank: "The National Democratic Party pledges itself to do everything in its power to establish Equal Rights for men and women . . . and to this end, to give its active support to securing the adoption of the Equal Rights Amendment to the national Constitution, which is now before Congress." Smith explained, in what would become standard rationale for proponents, that the amendment would not abrogate existing labor legislation; that if workers needed protection, then protection should be applied to men and women alike, because otherwise it restricted rather than protected women. In response, a speaker from the Women Representatives of Labor testified that her group was opposed to a blanket amendment and believed that allowing "any woman to work any number of hours was not a privilege but an abuse." Working women had supported suffrage in the hope that women's votes would be cast for legislation that regulated their work day. Women, she continued, were constituted differently from men, and needed some protective laws—an eight-hour day and abolition of night work for a start. Representatives of the National and New York Trade Union Leagues, even the indomitable Florence Kelley of the National Consumers' League, stressed the primary necessity to ratify the Child Labor Amendment, as well as to support eight-hour-day, forty-eight-hour-week work laws in all states in behalf of women workers, an explicit rebuke to the National Woman's Party.

The following day, the Woman's Party plank was unanimously defeated. The major recommendations made by Josephine Goldmark of the Consumers' League on behalf of women in industry were adopted, including establishment of the eight-hour day for women and their right to a living wage (the contemporary phraseology for then controversial minimum-wage laws). The confrontation over the amendment, neither long nor acrimonious, was an important opening salvo in the battle that would engage these women for decades to come.

Once the women had reached agreement, the chair presented the planks to the platform committee. The planks were rejected, which was, perhaps, no surprise given the bitter fights among factions at the convention—over prohibition and the Ku Klux Klan—and the need to cast 103 ballots before breaking a deadlock that threatened to nominate a Catholic for president. So much wrangling crowded off the platform the planks to ratify the Child Labor Amendment (Al Smith opposed it), increase appropriations to the Children's and Women's Bureaus, expand services to mothers and babies under the Shepard-Towner Act, and affirm the rights of workers to organize and bargain collectively. Given the political and atmospheric heat (100° in Madison Square Garden for days on end), a straightforward plank pledging the Democratic party to stand "opposed to the attempts of organizations or individuals to create prejudice against groups of citizens because of race, color or religion as detrimental to American institutions and national progress," was not going to attract general support among the delegates. In other ways, the treatment accorded Eleanor Roosevelt's committee presaged the diminished attention newly enfranchised women would command from party leaders. While the Resolution Committee deliberated, Eleanor Roosevelt sat outside the door of the committee room and waited. "Whatever consideration the proposals received was veiled in mystery behind closed doors," she wrote later. It was her first lesson on where women stood at a political convention.

The male leaders of the Democratic party and the egalitarian feminists of the National Woman's Party had effectively clarified the issues and mapped the boundaries by which Eleanor Roosevelt's feminism would be described and evaluated for the rest of her life. The need to cool her heels at the door of the Resolution Committee only reinforced her determination and that of her colleagues in the Women's Division to make women a factor in the party and in politics generally. After the national defeat of the party in 1924, she returned to her work at the women's division of the New York state committee. Almost single-handedly, she edited and published *The Democratic News*, raised money for the women's groups, lobbied for social legislation in Albany, and continually encouraged women to get into the trenches and become politicians, not just behind-the-scenes activists. The unremitting efforts of the militant feminists to promote a constitutional amendment threatened the social legislation she supported and met with her opposition and that of her friends.

With Franklin Roosevelt's election as governor of New York in 1928, Eleanor Roosevelt resigned from the organizations—including the state committee—with which she had been so actively associated from the beginning of the decade. Her support and involvement continued, but more circuitously. The same could be said for her efforts in behalf of women in government. By the mid-1920s she was already friendly with Mary (Molly) W. Dewson, former Massachusetts parole superintendent and Consumers' League advocate of minimum-wage legislation. At Eleanor's insistence, Molly had worked hard on the national presidential campaign of Al Smith in 1928. As a reward, Dewson wanted her reform colleague, New York factory inspector Frances Perkins, appointed state commissioner of labor. Eleanor directed Molly to her husband, and Perkins got the post—a pattern that would be repeated often at the national level four years later.

Eleanor Roosevelt minimized in public the extent of her influence on her husband's policies, even on his political appointments. But she admitted that, at times, official appointments would be discussed, and she might "go to my husband and say that I was very weary of reminding him to remind the members of his cabinet and his advisers that women were in existence. . . . As a result, I was sometimes asked for suggestions and then would mention two or three names." No doubt Molly Dewson would also suggest names. Head of the Women's Division of the national party after Roosevelt's election as president, Dewson made increased participation by women in politics a personal crusade.

With a strategically placed ally in the White House, women made significant gains as political appointees during the New Deal. Still, at the same time she encouraged women to become politically sophisticated and involved, Eleanor Roosevelt held a discouraging view of women's potential impact. In her compendium of advice, *It's Up to the Women*, she enthused over the emergence of women from invisible positions as experts and technicians into the limelight of elective and appointive posts, and she encouraged young women to begin in their communities to learn the basics of political organization and activities. But then, she admitted, doors would not open easily, if at all, into the chambers where true power lay. The outlook for women was dismal, she wrote, at the "main circle where the really important decisions in city, county and state politics are made!" Assuming her husband's administration would modify the pattern, she suggested that perhaps the effect of women would be greater at the national level.

She was right, in the sense that the New Deal engaged more women than had ever worked in Washington before. Their impact, however, is more difficult to judge. Many of the women shared common backgrounds in social welfare and reform activities; they composed a network that transplanted itself in the nation's capital. They brought the unfinished agenda of Progressive reform with them, and in the midst of the social and economic chaos of the Great Depression found powerful legislative allies and a receptive public. Work relief, social security, abolition of child labor, wage and hour standards for men and women were all incorporated into legislation and became institutionalized features on the national scene. Even the National Labor Relations Act, which was one major piece of legislation that originated in Congress rather than in the executive branch, enacted the most advanced plank of the proposals put forth by Democratic women in 1924: the right of workers to organize and bargain collectively. In fact, the high tide of New Deal successes in legislation and implementation coincided with the peak of women's participation in both the federal government and the Democratic party. It was made possible by the creation of relief and reform offices and agencies that required the expertise of social activists and welfare workers combined with the efforts of Eleanor Roosevelt and Molly Dewson in behalf of opportunities for women. But was Eleanor Roosevelt a feminist? Did she view social problems through the unique lens of gender, discover and define the discriminatory features of society, examine the underlying causes for female inferiority, and concentrate on their alleviation? Defined in these terms, the answer is a qualified no.

Female reformers did not ignore the numerous legal inequities that remained after the ratification of the Nineteenth Amendment. The League of Women Voters organized a Status of Women Committee, which worked as hard as Woman's Party members to remove disabilities in legal and political spheres, such as officeholding, jury service, and property laws. With the onset of the New Deal, egalitarian feminists and social reformers together discovered, and protested, differential wage features in the codes of the National Recovery Act (NRA); lack of relief work designed and allocated for women, and the federal government's policy of employing only one spouse, which often meant the dismissal of or refusal to hire married women. The National Woman's Party was highly vocal on these issues, but so was the League of Women Voters.

Ruby Black singled out Eleanor Roosevelt for special praise because she added her prestigious voice to the protests of women in behalf of women, and opposed, unavailingly, wage differentials based on sex. Both Rose Schneiderman on the NRA labor advisory board and Mary Anderson, head of the Women's Bureau, joined the criticism voiced by women's organizations outside government circles. But the administration's determination to certify and implement the codes as expeditiously as possible undercut opportunities to rewrite specific features. Even these women hoped that the ratification of codes would standardize rapidly deteriorating working conditions, and NRA officials ignored their unenthusiastic protests against wage differentials.

Eleanor Roosevelt was personally involved in establishing work camps for unemployed young women comparable to the Civilian Conservation Corps for young men. Without her efforts and those of Hilda Smith, eight thousand women in eighty camps would not have had the opportunity to earn fifty cents a week. The accomplishment diminishes in significance, however, in relation to the two and a half million men employed in CCC camps at one dollar per day. High hopes and lesser results characterized other work-relief efforts. In response to the absence of programs for unemployed women early in the New Deal, ER called a White House conference. With the able assistance of Ellen Woodward, work relief for women did increase, especially under WPA, but discrepancies between men and women remained in qualification, certification, project assignments, and compensation.

Women in government cared, and the first lady articulated and publicized their concerns which she shared, but the special difficulties of unemployed and underemployed women during the depression were never fully viewed apart from the overall economic dislocations, or outside the framework of general relief and reform policies. The meager impact of the collective assault by administration women on discriminatory New Deal policies reflected the priorities of Eleanor Roosevelt and her female colleagues and of their feminist self-perceptions. When they had to choose between passage and implementation of social welfare programs on the one hand, and specific attention to the position and treatment of women within them on the other, the sisterhood in the administration chose the former.

Eleanor Roosevelt and New Deal women remained reformers first, who viewed their positions as possible role models for capable, educated women to emulate. While assisting each other, they remained individuals in their accomplishments. They cared about the welfare of women as one part of a broader concern for liberal reform. Even their concerns for social welfare were coopted by their personal careers. In a speech at Wells College early in her husband's first term, the first lady pointed with pride to the accomplishments of women in his administration. Katherine Lenroot of the Children's Bureau, Josephine Roche of the Treasury Department, even Secretary of Labor Frances Perkins herself "started out to improve living conditions for every one [sic] and ended up becoming successful and interesting themselves." Concern for and work in social reform—with or without a strong feminist component—was a fertile training ground for productive careers in government. Personal achievement characterized the women active in the formation and implementation of New Deal policies.

If a single issue demanded their collective attention, it remained the threat of the Equal Rights Amendment and the persistence of the National Woman's Party's efforts to gain support. Through the 1920s and early 1930s, the militants remained few and isolated from most organized women. Yet what they lacked in numbers they compensated for in dedication, intensive educational and lobbying efforts, and an uncanny ability to garner publicity. Then, during the Roosevelt administration, two trends turned the National Woman's Party from a thorn in the side of social reformers into a perceived threat to be taken seriously.

The first significant development stemmed from the nature of specific New Deal policies which indicated that protective legislation for women alone might no longer be the only court-sanctioned approach to legislating work standards. The provisions for labor guidelines in NRA industrial codes established minimum wages and maximum hours for both men and women, and although the federal statute was declared unconstitutional in 1935, certain labor features were reincorporated into new legislation. The right of men and women to unionize was enacted even more forcefully in the National Labor Relations Act (NLRA) of 1935. The Fair Labor Standards Act (FLSA) of 1938 legislated hours and wages guidelines for men and women as well as the abolition of child labor.

These victories for the social reformers presented them with new dilemmas. Now, National Woman's Party leaders argued, the way was clear for the kind of labor legislation they had always advocated—regulation based on occupation rather than sex. For the reformers, it was an uncomfortable period of waiting to see if the FLSA withstood Supreme Court review. In the meantime, they remained committed to the rationale that had always provided the underpinning for their support for special treatment of working women—the unique physical qualities and social roles of women.

Eleanor Roosevelt had stated as well as anyone the principal differences in ideological outlook. In *It's Up to the Women*, she affirmed her belief that "women *are* different from men, their physical functions are different, and the future of the race depends upon their ability to produce healthy children." At an early press conference, she reiterated her position. "I think the National Woman's Party ignores the fact that there is a fundamental difference between men and women." Most women needed protection for physiological and social reasons, especially in light of their difficulty in organizing unions to bargain in their behalf. By the end of the decade, the NLRA and the FLSA, which passed the Supreme Court's review, theoretically undercut these arguments. But her commitment (and those of other social reformers) died hard. Still, after the Supreme Court affirmed the FLSA in 1941, she was at least willing to reexamine some protective legislation, if not her opposition to the Equal Rights Amendment itself.

The Republicans had endorsed the ERA in 1940 in a plank that withheld approval but asked submission of the amendment to the states. At the Democratic convention, Emma Guffey Miller, one of the few women active in the Democratic party who belonged to the National Woman's Party, pleaded for a similar plank. A letter from Eleanor Roosevelt was read in opposition, although her private sentiments about the needs of working-class women were changing as she saw a growing likelihood that women could participate in unions and achieve their aims through the bargaining process and union contract. "I've sent her to Chicago the message she wanted on the Equal Rights Amendment," she wrote about her letter to Dorothy McAllister, Molly Dewson's successor as head of the women's division; "I wish Industrial Women would get organized so we didn't have to continue this fight." McAllister organized a committee that held closed hearings and then presented its plank: "We will continue our efforts to achieve equality for men and women without impairing the social legislation which promotes true equality by safeguarding the health, safety and economic welfare of women workers."

Democrats accepted this plank, but the growing appeal of the ERA represented the second development in the continuing struggle over the amendment. No longer was it the special preserve of the National Woman's Party. Beginning in the mid-1930s, small professional organizations such as the National Association of Women Lawyers, National Women's Real Estate Association, and the Medical Women's National Association joined the party in support. Professional women viewed work standards as constraints on their abilities, not as protections of their physical and emotional health. In 1937, after years of official neutrality but concerted pressure by a number of local clubs, the National Federation of Business and Professional Women's Clubs endorsed the amendment. When Mrs. Harvey Wiley, former National Woman's Party president, became an officer of the General Federation of Women's Clubs in 1944, this loosest but largest federation of women's organizations joined the growing list of amendment backers.

The social and occupational status of the growing number of women backing the ERA reveal a class-based cleavage that had long marked the pro- and anti-ERA forces. Protective legislation focused on the working conditions in industry of women whose position was particularly vulnerable during the decades when labor unions, especially those based on a craft or skill, were weak and often excluded women. If limiting hours and prohibiting women from certain occupations hampered the opportunities of a few well-educated professional and businesswomen, proponents argued, it was a small price to pay for the benefits derived by female members of the industrial labor force. Most working-class women shared this view and welcomed protection. Feminists and reformers did not differ in their own background and education—they were members of the middle and upper classes—but their common social status did not result in a common evaluation of women's position in society. Feminists never swerved from their conviction that women constituted an inferior social class in need of legal equality as a group; reformers remained concerned with broad issues, primarily economic, in which women needed protection as working-class wage earners.

Social reformers and Democratic party activists held to their positions. They could still count on ER's support. She wrote to Rose Schneiderman early in 1944, when both the Democrats and the Republicans seemed on the verge of endorsing the ERA, that opponents of the amendment must adopt new tactics. She suggested that the Department of Labor make a detailed survey of all sex-based legislation, to determine which was truly necessary and which unnecessarily restrictive. Discriminatory laws should be eliminated, even though they were once needed to protect women. Economic equality had not been achieved, but disparities in the marketplace had narrowed. "Women are more highly organized, they are becoming more active as citizens, and better able to protect themselves, and they should, in all but certain very specific cases which are justified by their physical and functional differences, have the same rights as men," she wrote her friend.

These words counseled a tactical retreat to preserve the anti-ERA army intact, but they also indicate a shift in Eleanor Roosevelt's views on protective legislation. As early as 1939, she had signaled the possibility that, unlike her reformist cohort, her position was not engraved in stone. "I think we are getting nearer to the time when the stand of the National Woman's Party, which I agree is ideal, may become a practical position," she stated at a news conference. "But I do not think that the time as yet has come." Four years later, during the war, she reiterated this position: "I have always been opposed to this amendment until women in industry are more generally organized. . . . Later, as conditions improve, I may not oppose it." Then the Democratic party endorsed the ERA in its 1944 platform. Leaders of the National Woman's Party sent enthusiastic letters of appreciation to candidates Roosevelt and Wallace for their support. ER's attitude was reflected in a cursory note to Emma Guffey Miller stating that she was making no statements, since in wartime all "restrictions seem to be off. The party will do what they think is right."

Appreciation of women's contributions and support for women's rights during the war gave the ERA a boost. The proposed amendment finally reached the Senate floor for its first congressional test in July 1946. It was defeated. The newly formed National Committee to Defeat the Un-Equal

Rights Amendment boasted in its victory bulletin that, despite party endorsements, the amendment had gained only thirty-eight votes—"After 23 years, all the votes our opponents could muster." The reformers, led by chairman Dorothy McAllister, secretary Elizabeth Magee (head of the much-weakened National Consumers' League), and treasurer Mary Anderson (recently retired head of the Women's Bureau) felt vindicated. In spite of what can be interpreted as growing ambiguity on the issue, Eleanor Roosevelt joined other long-time ERA opponents in issuing a joint statement reiterating warnings on the dire consequences of an amendment.

The possibility of change in Eleanor Roosevelt's attitudes toward ERA during this period coincided with a dramatic change in her public and private status. In April 1945, Franklin Delano Roosevelt died and Mrs. Roosevelt, suddenly thrust into widowhood, became America's former first lady. Soon after her rapid packing and departure from the White House, President Truman personally requested that she accept an appointment as delegate to the infant United Nations Organization. In that capacity, she encountered the dispute over equal rights for women at the international level.

The debate over women's rights in the United States had a counterpart on the international scene, with the crucial divergence springing from the issue of industrial equality. Alice Paul and the National Woman's Party began in 1923 to build and influence a worldwide women's movement. Initial activity involved the call for positive action on equal rights at the International Women's Suffrage Alliance meeting at Rome in 1923. The alliance was an umbrella group of women's suffrage and reform organizations including the American member, the League of Women Voters. Carrie Chapman Catt orchestrated the defeat of the National Woman's Party's application for membership in the alliance and its attempt to gain approval for equal rights. The split mirrored the American break between egalitarian feminists and social reformers.

National Woman's Party members were not deterred, but shifted their attention to Latin America. The 1923 Pan-American Congress had passed a resolution to discuss women's rights at future conferences. No women were included in the delegation to attend the 1928 congress in Havana, so the National Woman's Party unilaterally appointed Doris Stevens and Jane Norman Smith and paid their expenses. The two women persuaded six nations to sponsor an equal rights treaty—an international counterpart to the ERA—and had an Inter-American Commission on Women (IACW) established for the purpose of studying the status of women throughout the hemisphere. Stevens chaired the commission.

For most of the following decade, National Woman's Party activists tried also to maneuver their equality treaty through the convoluted structure of the League of Nations. Simultaneously, they lobbied for the right of women to have nationality status independent of their spouse's nationality. The Hague Convention, which touched on the matter of nationality status, did so in a manner so discriminatory that even the League Conference repudiated it and created a Women's Consultative Committee on Nationality (1931). Both militant feminists and social reformers sat on the committee, and their divergent recommendations replicated the split between the feminists' call for a blanket ruling on the one hand, and the reformers' preference for gradualism on the other.

After the futile efforts of the National Woman's Party at the Hague, efforts were redirected toward the 1933 Pan-American Conference at Montevideo. By this time, Franklin Roosevelt sat in the White House. At Montevideo, Doris Stevens and the Inter-American Commission of Women gained support for a treaty removing discriminatory nationality and naturalization definitions and procedures. The U.S. government had not been happy at the discriminatory nature of the Hague Convention on nationality status, so National Woman's Party members were stunned when the U.S. delegation regused to sign the Montevideo treaty. Eventually, Secretary of State Cordell Hull capitulated to pressure from Alice Paul and her colleagues, and President Roosevelt signed the treaty, but not before the confused situation exacerbated the schism between women's groups.

The *New York Times* reported that the initial failure to sign the treaty could be attributed to the rift between the League of Women Voters on one side and the National Woman's Party on the other. The report also pointed out that opponents of the treaty were organizations "in both of which Mrs. Roosevelt is interested." ER denied any role in the controversy. League of Women Voters' representative Dorothy Straus reiterated the league's opposition to all comprehensive resolutions that lacked enforcement procedures and were mere statements of principle: "We are not feminists primarily; we are citizens." Whether they called themselves citizens, reformers, or humanitarians, women committed to protective legislation felt threatened by any blanket equality law or treaty—even if the focus was the nationality of women. As she claimed, Eleanor Roosevelt had "had absolutely no participation whatever in the equal rights issue at the Montevideo conference," although she was informed of the implications of the treaty as perceived by social worker and friend Grace Abbott. This treaty, Abbott wrote her, "would go directly counter to beneficent provisions of recent codes in favor of women in industry, and would be opposed to our own national interest."

In 1938 the League of Nations agreed to appoint a committee to conduct a comprehensive, worldwide survey on the status of women and even to discuss an equal rights treaty upon completion of the report. Although Dorothy Kenyon, long-time legal adviser to the League of Women Voters and ardent opponent of the ERA, was named American appointee, the hopes of National Woman's Party members revived. During the same year, Alice Paul led the formation of a World Woman's Party (WWP) to counter the specific threats to women's status posed by fascist regimes, as well as to broaden the movement for complete equality. The outbreak of World War II ended the League of Nations with its women's survey, and left the WWP to concentrate on the sheltering of feminist refugees from Europe. But first the party suffered a humiliating defeat at the hands of American social reformers.

At the Pan-American Conference scheduled to take place in Lima in 1938, the reformers planned to do away with the Inter-American Commission on Women and depose Doris Stevens as chair. Strategy was devised by Mary Winslow, former assistant to Mary Anderson of the Women's Bureau and then an officer with the Women's Trade Union League. Original proposals were made surreptitiously, and organizations like the League of Women Voters, YWCA, Consumers' League, and Councils of Jewish and of Catholic Women "did not have copies of the plan and gave their endorsements quite informally." Mary Anderson passed the proposed strategy on to a friend at the State Department, who then delivered the material to Secretary Hull and Undersecretary Sumner Welles. After a few technical changes were made, the president approved the delegates' instructions (hand-delivered and explained to him by Molly Dewson): in addition to getting "rid of the Inter-American Commission on Women, politely but definitively," delegates should provide some alternative means for considering women's interests, preferably a group composed of government appointees (not appointees of the Pan-American Union, like Stevens). Finally, the negative aspects of the Equal Rights

Treaty must be explained, and "a program for specific civil and legal rights and special industrial legislation substituted in its place."

Suspecting collusion and complicity among social feminists, their organizations, and government officials, the National Woman's Party denounced "the hand of Perkins, Roosevelt and Co. and all that Consumers' League crowd." The "crowd" achieved a complete victory, which ended NWP dominance at the Pan-American Conferences and successful advocacy of an equal-rights treaty. One month after the conference, Mary Winslow was appointed to replace Doris Stevens on a reconstituted and now "official" Inter-American Commission on Women. The *New York Times*, in two feature articles describing the Winslow selection, credited Eleanor Roosevelt for Winslow's appointment and decried the change in direction of the IACW from watchdog of women's status to clearinghouse for educational and welfare work. The articles, which read like National Woman's Party press releases, were especially strident when Eleanor Roosevelt invited Mary Anderson and Mary Winslow to her press conference following the appointment. Prominent Democrat Emma Guffey Miller and other National Woman's Party members expressed "resentment over the part played by Mrs. Roosevelt, Secretary Perkins and Miss Mary Dewson."

Eleanor Roosevelt denied any role in the appointment of Winslow, whom she claimed she barely knew. Roosevelt also denied personally cabling U.S. delegates to add support for protective legislation for women to positive statements on civil and political rights. Still, she admitted it was a stance she supported: "I happen always to have been connected with the group that does not believe in the position taken by the National Woman's Party." Her denials were disingenuous, for her "connections" to participants and knowledge of events were far closer than she admitted. Prior to the opening of the conference, Mary Winslow had sent Eleanor Roosevelt a three-page memorandum outlining the history and proposed "Plan of the American delegation to the Conference at Lima regarding the civil and political rights of women." Moreover, on January 27, 1939, Molly Dewson had written a long letter to her discussing the importance of eliminating NWP representation on the IACW. Dewson specifically asked the first lady to intercede directly with Sumner Welles on Winslow's behalf.

The onset of war did little to defuse the ill feelings between the two groups. Social reformers worked diligently to ensure that special work standards for women and children were not compromised by the labor-force needs and production quotas of a nation at war. Leaders of the World Woman's Party took their persistent demands for equality to the 1942 meeting called to lay the foundation of a postvictory United Nations Organization. At the official inauguration of the UNO in April 1945, egalitarians lobbied on behalf of equal-rights provisions in the United Nations Charter and consultant status at all meetings concerned with human rights. While gaining permission to participate in some consultant meetings, they did not achieve official standing. With the aid of female delegates from the Dominican Republic and Brazil, however, they succeeded in inserting a statement on women's equality in the charter. The next step involved lobbying for the creation of a separate committee on the status of women to implement the stated principles.

At this point Eleanor Roosevelt assumed a prominent position in the struggle. She had accepted President Truman's request that she join the American delegation to the first session of the United States General Assembly in London. She sailed fully aware of the reluctant acceptance women met in political and diplomatic affairs and the perennial need that they prove their abilities. In her final volume of memoirs she recalled: "I knew that as the only woman on the delegation, I was not very welcome. Moreover, if I failed to be a useful member, it would not be considered merely that I as an individual had failed, but that all women had failed, and there would be little chance for others to serve in the near future." In spite of her misgivings, she quickly gained the respect of dubious Republican members of the American delegation and the rest of the diplomatic community.

At her London hotel she was met by Lady Patrick Lawrence of the World Woman's Party and Betty Gram Swing, who tried to persuade her to "back a woman's group in UNO with special privileges." She politely declined support for the feminists' proposal. Several days later she recounted in a "My Day" column that "a difference of opinion is developing among the various groups of women, as to the exact representation or affiliation they desire to have with the UNO." Restating the charter's affirmation of "the equal rights of men and women and of nations large and small," Eleanor Roosevelt argued that this meant that women should participate in all UNO functions "on an equal basis—not even as specialized groups, unless they are representing some particular objective." As delegates, alternates, and advisers, women would achieve "what they want, which is to have on all important subjects the point of view of both men and women who are working together to frame the policies of the organization."

Still, the feminists prevailed and the UNO Economic and Social Council created a subcommission on women's rights. As National Woman's Party and World Woman's Party leaders began efforts to raise the status of the subcommission to a full one, Eleanor Roosevelt became head of the Human Rights Commission. She opposed the move to upgrade the subcommission to full commission status. Its chairman then appealed directly to the Economic and Social Council. Again the militant activists succeeded. The UNO met in New York in 1946, and the General Assembly adopted a resolution requesting that all member nations establish political equality for women. In effect, Alice Paul saw the equal rights treaty she had originally proposed almost twenty years earlier adopted by the international community. Paul gloated; Roosevelt was publicly noncommittal. Emma Guffey Miller, then congressional chair of the National Woman's Party, wrote to congratulate ER on the success of the equality planks and to inform her that the new secretary of labor favored the ERA at home. Roosevelt replied tersely: "I have your wire and if you will study the report you will see it recognized the need for the protection of women. I am sorry [the secretary] is in favor of the Equal Rights Amendment."

The commission, headed by Roosevelt, then began work on the Universal Declaration of Human Rights. As originally drafted, the first article stated, "All men are created equal." Members of the Commission on the Status of Women and Hansa Metha of India insisted that the phrase "all people" be substituted to avoid a literal interpretation in their respective nations. Althought ER originally argued against the revised wording, she finally agreed to it. Adopted in December, 1948, the declaration was not legally binding and so she continued to work on a Human Rights Covenant which nations would be obligated to implement. In the process she altered her stance on women's rights. In May 1951, when the convenant was submitted for ratification, she wrote an article syndicated in Scripps-Howard newspapers describing the "draft convention on political rights for women." The status of women varied from country to country, and written principles would not necessarily affect government policy or personal attitudes. Still, she continued, "[i]t is well to get started, and I am happy that this consideration is being given to the conditions and opportunities of women throughout the world."

In the same article she also gave new and dramatic consideration to the position of women at home. She had long thought an equal rights amendment was foolish because working women were unorganized and needed special laws for their benefit, she wrote. Now "women can be as well organized as men and are certainly able to fight for their rights." While insisting that state laws continued to hamper women more than a federal amendment would help them, "I can see that perhaps it does add a little to the position of women to be declared equal before law and equal politically and in whatever work a woman chooses to undertake."

Her new position set her apart from both her reformist friends and from feminists. Her old allies remained adamant in their insistence on the need for protective legislation for women. After the Supreme Court upheld the Fair Labor Standards Act, in 1941, feminists felt vindicated and demanded legislation at state and federal levels in behalf of men and women, not extensive union organizing of female workers. In effect, the educated, articulate, upper-middle-class women on both sides of the struggle continued their patronizing advocacy positions in relation to other groups of women. Eleanor Roosevelt moved beyond that posture by insisting that the American labor movement had come of age and that within its new structures, working women could define their own priorities and "fight for their rights" without special treatment.

Eleanor Roosevelt's new position was unique but fraught with irony. The ranks of the social reformers were thinning as this generation gradually retired from public life. Their organizations, such as the Women's Trade Union League and the National Consumers' League, either disbanded or were severely reduced in strength and visibility. Their programs had entered legislation through the New Deal, but implementation was coopted by government bureaucrats. In their place, by the 1950s organized labor became the leading foe of the ERA and a proponent of special laws for women. Men within the labor movement fully understood that legislated protection for women—limiting their hours, prohibiting employment in certain occupations, and regulating specific kinds of work functions—provided a noncompetitive shield for men in many jobs. Union leadership and decision making remained male preserves even in industries with large proportions of women workers.

Eleanor Roosevelt was sensitive to those women's issues that reached the inner sanctums of the political parties, but she could not extrapolate this awareness to women's positions in labor unions. With her friend

Lorena Hickok, in 1954, she wrote a tribute to political women, *Ladies of Courage*. Dedicated to Molly Dewson, the book was a laudatory compendium of Democratic and Republican women in elective and appointed office at all levels of government. They behaved like "ladies," the authors observed, and achieved distinction through commitment and perseverance. But women's accomplishments, despite the courage invested therein, often proved transitory. Hickok and Roosevelt traced the gradual downgrading and final dissolution of the Women's Division of the Democratic party, the halcyon days of the New Deal notwithstanding. Neither their advice to women on how to become political activists nor the rewards they could anticipate read much differently from *It's Up to the Women*, published two decades earlier. The meager gains of political women stemmed from an inferior status rooted in cultural ideology and social institutions. An analysis of these factors and an agenda for their virtually revolutionary change were beyond the reach of even militant feminists between the 1920s and the 1950s. It was little wonder that Eleanor Roosevelt neither understood nor examined the bases for women's inability to gain a political foothold in political parties or to achieve economic prominence and substantive gains in labor unions.

What feminist activists did do during that time was focus on legal equality for women and campaign for its constitutional guarantee. Eleanor Roosevelt finally dropped her objections to that goal. But she still refused to lend the weight of her reputation to its accomplishment. After she published her change of position in 1951, she received a request from the newly elected president of the National Woman's Party to write a letter of endorsement. Eleanor Roosevelt responded with just one succinct sentence: "While I am not going to fight the Equal Rights Amendment, I really do not feel enthusiastic enough about it to write you a letter in its favor." After several decades of translating personal conviction into public activity, taking a number of controversial positions on public issues and braving the resulting furor, Eleanor Roosevelt opted for ambiguous support and public inaction on behalf of female equality.

From the time her work ended at the United Nations until her death a decade later, the prestigious and formidable voice of Mrs. Roosevelt was heard from the ward-heeling headquarters of Tammany Hall to the convention halls and back rooms of the National Democratic party. Her concern with women's issues focused narrowly on political participation, not on broader matters of status.

A loyal Democrat, she preferred Adlai Stevenson for the presidency in 1960, but reluctantly supported John Kennedy when he was nominated. She doubted his commitment to women's rights and welfare. During his administration she chided him for appointing so few women to top positions—fewer than at any time in thirty years. Why, she wanted to know in a televised interview, in other nations can "Women . . . be found in higher positions, policy-making positions or legislative positions, than they are in this country[?]" "But I know, Mrs. Roosevelt," Kennedy replied, "I am always getting letters from you about getting women in these policy-making jobs, and we are very conscious of that responsibility."

Actually, the Kennedy administration had been decidedly conscious of women and women's issues but in unexpected ways. After four consecutive endorsements of the Equal Rights Amendment, the Democratic party platform committee changed course in 1960. Bowing to pressure from organized labor, whose support was essential for a Democratic victory, the platform committee yielded to the testimony of Esther Peterson, legislative representative of the CIO Industrial Labor Department: "We, who want equal opportunities and responsibilities for women, know that it is frequently necessary to obtain real equality through a difference in treatment rather than an identity in treatment." The arguments sounded familiar, but the faces of the opposition had changed. In addition to labor unions, the American Civil Liberties Union joined the fray, proposing constitutional arguments that the Ninth and Fourteenth Amendments gave women full guarantees without creating a special class of citizens. Along with the Council of Jewish Women and the Council of Catholic Women, these were the major forces arrayed against the ERA. The League of Women Voters still officially opposed it, but no longer played the leading role among women's organizations. The National Woman's Party was still in the forefront, led by president Emma Guffey Miller. Thirty business- and professional-women's groups joined the National Woman's Party in collective disappointment as the Democrats, bowing to union pressure, supported the extension of protective legislation rather than the ERA. After victory, organized labor was rewarded with labor lawyer Arthur Goldberg's nomination as secretary of labor and Esther Peterson's appointment as assistant secretary and director of the Women's Bureau; she was one of only nine women included among the first 240 Kennedy appointees.

Peterson quickly reversed the pro-ERA position of her Republican predecessor, although she was also aware of growing concern over the status of women in American society. The concern grew out of the social changes wrought by the great increase of women in the labor force, the economic potential of untapped female resources in Cold War competition with the Soviet Union, and the growing appeal of the Equal Rights Amendment. And there were Eleanor Roosevelt's letters and reporter May Craig's questions at Kennedy's news conferences about what the administration was doing for women. Craig's persistence met with derision, but this veteran of Eleanor Roosevelt's press briefings during the 1930s brought a special perspective to her queries that annoyed administration officials.

Both to counteract the pressure for a constitutional amendment and to demonstrate to the world the positive features of American women's status, Esther Peterson proposed a study commission. With support enlisted from other administration officials, she oversaw the creation of the President's Commission on the Status of Women and carefully selected its members from government, organized labor, the academic community, and women's organizations. As chair, she enlisted Eleanor Roosevelt, the appropriate invitation being channeled through the Oval Office. When all arrangements were in place, the president issued an executive order in December 1961 that put the stamp of approval on an undertaking initiated and orchestrated by his administrative aides.

Roosevelt brought her usual organizational skills and commitments to the commission, but they were not really necessary. From limited space in Peterson's Labor Department base and with no appropriation until the following fiscal year, she directed all functions. The commission divided its proposed survey into seven areas: federal employment, government contracts and private employment, federal taxes and social security, services for home and community, education, protective labor legislation, and civil and political rights. The last area—civil and political rights—was the one directly concerned with the Equal Rights Amendment, although the issue lay at the core of the entire undertaking.

At the first sessions of the commission in February 1962, which Roosevelt hosted at Hyde Park, she proved a safe choice as Peterson's carefully selected honorary chair. A member who represented the Council of Jewish Women voiced the feeling of her constituents that the commission was organized in order to promote the constitutional amendment. Eleanor replied simply, "It is odd, because for many years I opposed the equal rights of women." By refusing to make it clear that she had ceased to challenge the amendment, she perpetuated the notion that her opposition remained unchanged.

Following the February meetings, Eleanor Roosevelt became ill. Except for a late-fall TV appearance on "Issues and Answers" with Esther Peterson, her first and only chairing of those sessions marked her last public role. After ER's death in November 1962, Peterson wrote to member Margaret Hickey that everyone involved should "carry out the policies Mrs. Roosevelt initiated, and . . . strive to make the work of this Commission not only a memorial to its late chairman, but a fitting and appropriate reflection of the incomparable service she performed in a lifetime of devotion to the public good." Peterson assumed real as well as apparent control. In 1963 the commission's final report, *American Women*, downgraded discriminatory practices that still hampered women and presented an optimistic picture of women fulfilling their traditional, primary roles in the home and, increasingly, new roles in the workplace, where they represented a potential resource for strengthening the nation. The longer reports of the Committees on Protective Legislation and on Political and Civil Rights concluded that protective legislation was still needed, and "a constitutional amendment need not now be sought in order to establish this principle [of equality of rights for men and women.]" The report not only reiterated the views that Peterson articulated in 1960 to the Democratic platform committee, but only slightly went beyond perspectives on female status then forty years old.

Although Eleanor Roosevelt did not live to complete her task of chairing the commission, the reports provide a vantage point from which to assess her feminism. As early as 1935, Ruby Black had excused ER from the ultimate litmus test of the National Woman's Party: she did not have to back the ERA to qualify as a feminist, as long as she was conscious of the liabilities in the paths of women, articulated women's concerns over those discriminations clearly, and promoted the status of qualified women in government and the professions. But Black added personal autonomy and self-definition to more conventional concepts of public positions and actions. Roosevelt qualified as a feminist, according to Black, because she lived like a feminist—working and earning her own income, achieving a measure of economic independence, and believing that women should be recognized in their own right and not as reflections of husbands and fathers.

Black was more accurate in her evaluation than was the public, whose assessments of Roosevelt's actions were more traditional. Except for the inveterate Franklin and Eleanor haters, ER generally won widespread approval for the unique posture she brought to the role of first lady. Much of the approval and admiration derived from the belief that her frenetic activities served her husband. Lectures and radio broadcasts, newspaper columns and magazine articles, and on-site visits around the country made her the eyes, ears, and articulate exponent of New Deal policies.

Her activities fed this perception because the view was not altogether inaccurate, simply less complex than the reality. The pace of her life happily coincided with many of her husband's needs, but the prime motivation was the personal need to build an emotional life and create physical space of her own. The heartbreak and bitterness over Franklin's affair with Lucy Mercer marked the beginning of Eleanor Roosevelt's quest for autonomy. She became involved with women's voluntary associations and with substantive issues in 1920. The timing is important because her New York activities of the early 1920s have often been interpreted in a similar vein to those as first lady—as a stand-in political surrogate for her polio-stricken and recovering husband. They served that purpose, but they actually began before the crippling illness struck.

Her new public stance brought her the friends who functioned both as her educators and as her emotional supporters. Nancy Cook and Marion Dickerman even became housemates after they built their own cottage at Hyde Park, where Eleanor resided whenever she could. The living arrangement, along with political activity and part-time teaching at Dickerman's Todhunter School, was crucial in the reconstruction of Eleanor Roosevelt's life. Other friends played analogous roles, although none seems to have offered the affection and support of Lorena Hickok when Eleanor reluctantly and painfully prepared to become first lady. The emotional intensity of the relationship as revealed in letters quoted in the essay by Chafe has produced a debate about a possible sexual involvement, but whatever the outcome of that debate the Roosevelt-Hickok relationship highlights two distinct aspects of Roosevelt's female friendships. On the one hand, at critical moments in her life they furnished public direction and personal comfort. Second, the friendships were longstanding but not at constant levels of emotional intensity. While there is no evidence that Eleanor Roosevelt was manipulative in her relationship with Lape and Read, Dickerman and Cook, Schneiderman and Dewson or Hickok, there is little doubt that with time she moved above and beyond psychological dependence. Invariably, these women demanded more—often in rivalry with each other—or would have liked greater emotional returns than Eleanor Roosevelt was willing to give. Her personal relationships moved on a parallel course with her public undertakings—serially, always changing and expanding according to new needs and interests. These women provided a bridge from the inner needs of a psychologically bereft wife and mother, to a world of indefatigable activity and public adulation.

About the time of Black's article, Eleanor Roosevelt began work on her first volume of memoirs. At one point she labels herself. Her first contact with the women's suffrage movement came in 1919 (while the Nineteenth Amendment was going through the ratification process), at a lunch with Alice Wadworth, wife of one of the Senate's strongest antisuffragists. ER had no opinion on suffrage, but "soon after I undertook work which proved to me the value of the vote," she wrote, "I became a much more ardent citizen and feminist than anyone . . . would have dreamed possible." And what was feminism? She gave a definition at a 1935 press conference, in answer to a question probably asked by Ruby Black herself. Feminism, Roosevelt replied, meant a "woman should have an equal opportunity and equal rights with any other citizen of the country."

It is intriguing that she defined a noun that conventionally invoked ideology and collective efforts on behalf of a cause as individual aspirations and rights. Intentionally or not, Eleanor Roosevelt accurately described the essence of female, if not feminist, experience in the years between the surging women's movement of the Progressive Era and its rebirth in the 1960s, years that corresponded precisely with her own public career. Feminism lay dormant for almost forty years, from the time politicians discovered the impact of the "woman vote" was inconsequential in the early 1920s until, in the 1960s, Betty Friedan critiqued social prescriptions for women, and young women confronted discrimination directly in activist protest movements. But these same decades witnessed remarkable achievements by women as individuals. Often against great obstacles, women scored personal triumphs in the arts, science, popular culture, and radical and reform politics. The same cultural environment that made specific female accomplishments possible, however, mitigated against collective action in behalf of women generally.

The New Deal women were sterling examples of this development. Capable career women whose roots lay in earlier social welfare and reform, they viewed themselves as individuals whose commitments to women and to women's rights they would prove by adhering to the liberal reform agenda and by working individually in its behalf. The same can be said of Eleanor Roosevelt. Her concerns by the end of the 1930s extended beyond earlier-twentieth-century social welfare to embrace homesteads for the rural poor, programs for youth, civil rights for blacks and, later, humanitarian principles for an entire world. Within this expanding universe her interest in female opportunities remained, though expressed in an increasingly narrow concern to get competent women into politics. Her feminist vision waned as her social outlook became international. And the efforts in behalf of all issues remained individual—the most prominent example of the accomplished women who excelled without ideological and institutional feminist moorings.

She could have done worse. By the time of her death, on the brink of a reborn women's movement, a significant number of people all over the world believed that they were better because she had followed the course she chose. Today's feminists, however, are left to wonder what legacy they would have inherited if the most prominent, respected female voice of her generation had successfully bridged humanitarian reform and feminism, and had translated her belated respect for legal equality into articulate advocacy.

SOURCES

The Roosevelt Library at Hyde Park, New York, houses the voluminous Eleanor Roosevelt Papers along with collections of many of her colleagues' papers. The Mary (Molly) W. Dewson and Mary Anderson papers are at the Schlesinger Library. ER's memoirs include *This Is My Story* (New York, 1937), *This I Remember* (New York, 1949), and *On My Own* (New York, 1958). *It's Up to the Women* (New York, 1933) and *Ladies of Courage* (New York, 1954) reveal much more about her attitudes toward women than her autobiographic writings. Tamara Hareven surveyed her attitudes and public service in *Eleanor Roosevelt: An American Conscience*

(Chicago, 1968). Joseph Lash's books remain the most comprehensive biographies: *Eleanor and Franklin* (New York, 1971) and *Eleanor: The Years Alone* (New York, 1972). In response to Doris Faber's controversial biography, *The Life of Lorena Hickok: Eleanor Roosevelt's Friend* (New York, 1980), Lash recently wrote *Love, Eleanor: Eleanor Roosevelt and Her Friends* (Garden City, New York, 1982).

Equal Rights, the publication of the National Woman's Party, reveals one feminist perspective, and the National Woman's Party collection contains a number of letters and articles that define ER's position on the Equal Rights Amendment. Both are available on microfilm. Susan Becker surveys two decades of activity by the National Woman's Party in *The Origins of the Equal Rights Amendment: American Feminism between the Wars* (Westport, Connecticut, 1982). Women in the Roosevelt administration are described by Susan Ware in *Beyond Suffrage: Women in the New Deal* (Cambridge, Massachusetts, 1981). Two unpublished papers are helpful in creating context for Eleanor Roosevelt's position on women's issues: one on the international feminist struggles by Paula Pfeffer of Mundelein College, and "Kennedy's Presidential Commission on the Status of Women" by Blanche Linden-Ward of Brandeis University.

THE CONTRIBUTORS

WILLIAM H. CHAFE, Professor of History, Duke University, Codirector of the Duke Oral History Program, and Academic Director of the Duke-University of North Carolina Women's Studies Research Center, has written *Civilities and Civil Rights*, which won both the Mayflower Cup and the Robert F. Kennedy Book Award, *The American Woman*, and *Women and Equality*.

BLANCHE WIESEN COOK, Professor of History at John Jay College of Criminal Justice, City University of New York, is currently working on a biography that focuses on Eleanor Roosevelt's friendships, activities, and visions. Her publications include *The Declassified Eisenhower: A Divided Legacy of Peace and Political Warfare*, *Crystal Eastman on Women and Revolution*, and *Toward the Great Change: Crystal Eastman and Max Eastman*.

TAMARA K. HAREVEN, Professor of History at Clark University; Research Associate, Center for Population Studies, Harvard University; and Editor of *The Journal of Family History*, is author of *Eleanor Roosevelt: An American Conscience*, *Amoskeag: Life and Work in an American Factory City*, and *Family Time and Industrial Time*. She has also edited *Transitions* and *Aging and the Life Course in Interdisciplinary and Cross-cultural Perspectives*.

JOAN HOFF-WILSON, Executive Secretary of the Organization of American Historians and Professor of History at Indiana University, is author of the Bernath Prize book, *American Business and Foreign Policy, 1920–1933*; *Ideology and Economics: United States Relations with the Soviet*

Union, 1918–1933; Herbert Hoover: Forgotten Progressive; and coauthor of *Sexism and the Law: Male Beliefs and Legal Bias in Britain and the United States.*

RICHARD S. KIRKENDALL, Henry A. Wallace Professor of History at Iowa State University, has served as Executive Secretary of the Organization of American Historians. His publications include *Social Scientists and Farm Politics in the Age of Roosevelt, The New Deal: The Historical Debate, The United States 1929–1945: Years of Crisis and Change, The Truman Period as A Research Field,* and *A Global Power: America Since the Age of Roosevelt.*

MARJORIE LIGHTMAN, Executive Director of the Institute for Research in History, is Codirector of Historians, Universities, and Communities, a National Endowment for the Humanities Institute. She is coeditor of *Outside Academe: New Ways of Working in the Humanities* and author of articles in, among others, *Church History,* and *Trends in History.*

ABIGAIL Q. MCCARTHY, author and columnist for *Commonweal,* was the keynote speaker at the final seminar of the Franklin D. Roosevelt Centennial year sponsored by the Roosevelt Institute and Hunter College, New York City.

ELISABETH ISRAELS PERRY has taught European history at the University of Colorado, State University of New York at Buffalo, University of Cincinnati, and Indiana University, and is now teaching both American women's and European history at the University of Iowa. Author of *From Theology to History: French Religious Controversy and the Revocation of the Edict of Nantes,* she is completing a biography of Belle Moskowitz.

LOIS SCHARF is lecturer in American history at Case Western Reserve University. She is the Executive Director of National History Day and author of *To Work and To Wed: Female Employment, Feminism, and The Great Depression,* and coeditor of and contributor to *Decades of Discontent: The Women's Movement, 1920–1940.*

INGRID WINTHER SCOBIE, Assistant Professor of History at Texas Woman's University, has published articles in the *Pacific Historical Review, Southern California Historical Quarterly,* and *The Public Historian.* She has contributed to the *Dictionary of American Biography* and the forthcoming *Women in the American Theatre*, and is currently completing a biography of Helen Gahagan Douglas.

MARTHA H. SWAIN, Associate Professor of History at Texas Woman's University, is the author of *Pat Harrison: The New Deal Years*, and is a contributor to the *Dictionary of American Biography*, *Notable American Women: The Modern Era*, and to several encyclopedias. She has published articles in the *Journal of Mississippi History*, *Furman Studies*, *Southern Quarterly*, *Mississippi Quarterly*, and *Prologue*. She is writing a biography of Ellen Woodward.

WINIFRED D. WANDERSEE, Associate Professor of History, Hartwick College, is author of *Women, Work, and Family Values, 1920–1940* and a contributor to *Decades of Discontent: The Women's Movement, 1920–1940* and *Women, Identity, and Vocation in American History*.

SUSAN WARE, author of *Beyond Suffrage: Women in the New Deal* and *Holding Their Own: American Women in the 1930s*, has taught at Harvard University, the University of New Hampshire, and Tufts University. Visiting scholar at Radcliffe College, 1983–1984, she currently holds an American Council of Learned Societies/Ford Fellowship to complete a biography of New Deal politician Molly Dewson.

JOANNA SCHNEIDER ZANGRANDO is Associate Professor of American Studies at Skidmore College. She has contributed articles to *American Archivist*, *American Quarterly*, the *Journal of Black Studies*, and *American Studies International*. Her most recent publication is "Women's Studies in the United States: An Update on Sources," in *Sources for American Studies*. She is working on a study of women labor union organizers, 1930s–1950s, with Robert L. Zangrando.

ROBERT L. ZANGRANDO, Professor of History at the University of Akron, is author of *The NAACP Crusade Against Lynching, 1909–1950* and coeditor of *Civil Rights and the Black American: A Documentary History*. He is completing a biography of Walter White of the NAACP, and is doing research with Joanna Schneider Zangrando on the topic of women labor union organizers in the years from 1930 to 1955.

INDEX